Bicycle

John Wilcockson

Butterick Publishing . Marshall Cavendish

New York   London & Sydney

For Gai

Editor: Robin L.K. Wood
Editorial Assistant: Robert Hall
Designers: Rob Burt, Anita Ruddell
Picture Researcher: Francesca Serpell

Published and distributed by:

Marshall Cavendish Books Limited
58 Old Compton Street
London W1V 5PA

IN THE U.K., COMMONWEALTH AND REST
OF THE WORLD, EXCEPT NORTH AMERICA

ISBN 0 85685 841 2

Butterick Publishing
708 Third Avenue
New York, N.Y. 10017

IN THE UNITED STATES OF AMERICA
AND CANADA

ISBN 0-88421-156-8
Library of Congress Number: 80-12102

First printing 1980
© MARSHALL CAVENDISH LIMITED 1980
Printed in Great Britain

Introduction

One of the main attractions of bicycling is its simplicity. But it is also a complex art, the subtleties of which can take a lifetime to learn.

My research for this book has not followed the familiar pattern of perhaps a year's study of all relevant literature before setting pen to paper. The information, advice and encouragement that you will find in the following pages are the result of a lifetime's adventures with a bicycle.

These adventures have included hurtling down an Alpine pass road at night, riding a heavily loaded touring bike; toiling for hours on a difficult mechanical problem in a chilly cycle shed; racing through a storm of hailstones big enough to leave red bruises on the skin; sleeping under the stars on an Italian hillside at the end of a long day in the saddle; and cycling with a group of a thousand Americans on a 100 mile fun ride.

My teachers have been experienced tourists, chatting into the night at a remote youth hostel; Tour de France mechanics, working on a dozen bikes in a luxury hotel; Olympic coaches, discussing tactics in training camp; international officials, explaining complex regulations at a press conference; and professional racers, sharing the dinner table after a 250 kilometre race.

I hope that the result—this bike book with a difference—will appeal to both the complete novice and the more experienced cyclist. Cycling is fun: go out and enjoy it!

John Wilcockson

Editor's note:
This book was written by a British author with an international readership in mind. The spellings used are British—for example, 'tyre' for 'tire'. Where a term or word (such as 'spanner') may not be immediately recognized by American readers, we have also given the familiar term (in this case, 'wrench') in brackets. A full glossary of the most widely used cycling terms appears on pages 174–7.

Contents

On Your Bike

Know Your Machine

On The Road

On Your Bike

1

Ride A Bicycle

Future generations will look back on this second half of the twentieth century as the age of mobility. Never before has such a large proportion of the world's population had access to cheap, reliable transport. Our life-styles have been transformed by widespread use of private motor vehicles. They have given us an independence that until the late nineteenth century could be enjoyed by only a privileged minority. This freedom of movement is something that most people today take for granted – unless their means of transport is suddenly removed.

A shortage of fuel at the pumps, the confiscation of a driving licence, or costly repairs which keep the vehicle off the road for a while, can cause immense problems to a motorist. The typical

Previous pages: A lady cyclist of 1896 . . . and her modern counterpart.

motorist is probably unfamiliar with the vagaries of public transport and reluctant to attempt walking any great distance. This is one of the reasons why an energy crisis is looked upon with horror by the motor-dependent countries of the industrialized world. Yet it is clear that these oil-hungry nations cannot continue burning non-replaceable, limited-resource fuel at an ever increasing rate, and that people must use a more efficient means of private transport.

As the noisy debate on the energy crisis and on transport alternatives grows daily noisier, a quietly efficient contender – one that has been around for quite a while – comes rolling into view. It is a machine of simple beauty, born in the Victorian era, but remaining abreast of the latest in technology. It is the bicycle.

This group of Dutch cyclists can enjoy their ride all the more, knowing that traffic other than bicycles is banned from their route. The Netherlands boast perhaps the only comprehensive national network of bicycle paths in the world.

Consuming Calories

Considerable research into the mechanics of bicycling has been carried out by the London scientist F.R. Whitt, who published a paper in the journal *Ergonomics* in 1971 on the 'Energy expenditure of sporting cyclists'. Based on the power output required to overcome air resistance and rolling resistance caused by friction on the tyres and bearings, his thesis charted caloric consumption for racing and touring cyclists. The results showed that riding a touring bike at the 27 km/hour (16.7 mph) pace demanded in Dr Cooper's aerobics programme uses up about 11 calories per minute (660 calories an hour), while racing speeds of around 44 km/hour (27.3 mph) demand consumption of up to 25 calories a minute (1500 calories an hour).

These figures should be compared with results from other activities, as compiled in the May 1972 issue of the American magazine *Today's Health*, which are listed below with the cycling results added.

Bicycle racing	up to 1500
Running (16 km/hour)	900
Bicycle touring (27 km/hour)	660
Cross country skiing (16 km/hour)	600
Squash	up to 600
Tennis	up to 420
Table tennis	360
Roller skating	350
Walking (6 km/hour)	300
Slow cycling (15 km/hour)	240
Slow walking (4 km/hour)	210

The vital role that can and should be played by the bicycle was recognized in November 1978 by no less an authority than the United States Congress. A significant statement was added to the National Energy Conservation Policy Bill being promoted by the Administration of President Carter. It reads: *The Congress recognizes that bicycles are the most efficient means of transportation, represent a viable commuting alternative to many people, offer mobility at speeds as fast as that of cars in urban areas, provide health benefit through daily exercise, reduce noise and air pollution, are relatively inexpensive, and deserve consideration in a comprehensive national energy plan.*

Most of these points could equally apply to a low powered motorcycle or moped, but it is only the bicycle that can *'provide health benefits'* and is *'the most efficient means of transportation'*. These facts, proved by extensive scientific research, have been backed up by the experiences of millions of proficient cyclists. And all those cyclists can make an additional, equally telling point – bicycling is fun!

Cycling for health

The purpose of exercise is to exercise the muscles and to get your blood pumping around your body, to get it circulating. The best forms of 'circulatory' exercise are ones in which the body is working within its capabilities, with a steady intake of air into the lungs and a steady heartbeat to pump the oxygenated blood through the arteries to the muscles.

Cycling, jogging, swimming and walking are all 'steady-state', or 'aerobic', forms of exercise. The advantages of these four activities were brought to the attention of the general public by the American doctor Kenneth Cooper in his classic book *Aerobics,* first published in 1968. In this best-seller, Dr Cooper pointed out the benefits of regular exercise geared to a series of planned exercise programmes in which points are awarded for attaining specific targets in the activity of your choice. The aim is to score a given number of points each week, based on sessions of long enough duration for the exerciser to obtain a 'training effect' or, more simply, physical improvement.

For a person of average fitness, the aim is to obtain 30 points a week after a 10-week programme of gradually increasing targets. If cycling is the chosen activity, then the exerciser is expected to achieve, after 10 weeks, a ride of 13 km (8 miles) in 28 minutes – a pace of 27 km/hour (16.7 mph) – to be repeated four times a week. Each of these rides represents 8 points on Dr Cooper's empirical points chart, giving 32 points for the week. By comparison,

Cyclists formed their own local political party at Davis, a California university town. As a result, cyclist-only lanes on downtown streets have encouraged three-quarters of the population to cycle regularly. But such bicycle affluence does have its problems when it comes to finding your parked bike!

walkers would need to perform four walks of 6.4 km (4 miles) each week, each walk lasting 56 minutes.

If you are unused to regular exercise, these probably appear impossible targets and you may think that you will never be able to discipline yourself to take four bike rides a week. Such thoughts are understandable but should be quickly dispelled once you have made the initial decision to get fit. A comprehensive survey, carried out in Great Britain for the sportswear firm Le Coq Sportif, showed that cyclists were more likely to take regular exercise than participants in any other popular sport. All those people interviewed were more than 15 years old; and to the question 'Do you participate (in your particular sport) at least twice a week?', positive replies were given by 18 per cent of tennis players, 22 per cent of squash players, 51 per cent of joggers, and 67 per cent of cyclists. There are further illuminating differences in the rate of calorie consumption between different activities. These are shown in **Consuming Calories**.

One-way 'bicycles only' lanes on New York City streets have proved popular with commuting cyclists. The lanes are 1.2 m (4 ft) wide and allow cyclists to keep clear of parked vehicles.

Encouragement for regular cyclists comes from the numerous tests that show that cycling is one of the best forms of exercise for increasing your cardiovascular (heart and lung) fitness as well as for developing strong muscles and a slim body. Cardiovascular fitness is particularly important in maintaining your health in later life. Unclogged arteries and healthy heart muscle mean that your pulse rate will be slower and stronger than average. A regular cyclist probably has a heartbeat of between 50 and 60 per minute, compared with the nominal average of 72. This reduction gives the heart greater capacity and makes its work less hard – about 2,000 or more beats are saved over a 24 hour period.

It is the long, steady efforts found in cycling which are particularly beneficial in respect of cardiovascular health. This was shown by West German professor H. Herxheimer in a comparative study of 500 champion athletes, and some of the fascinating results are shown here in **Exercise and a Healthy Heart.**

With its circulatory benefits and qualities of rhythmic motion, cycling is an ideal form of exercise for any sportsmen recovering from injuries or wanting a good general standard of fitness prior to specialist training. Downhill skiers ride bicycles extensively for both these purposes, and Olympic gold medallist Jean-Claude Killy of France is as much of a bicycle fanatic as he is a ski enthusiast. Footballers recuperating from broken legs or torn leg muscles also use cycling – very gently at first – because their body weight is taken off the legs by the saddle.

Efficiency on wheels

Besides the many health benefits, cycling also scores over many other activities by being (as the US Congress put it) *'the most efficient means of transportation'.* This fact was graphically demonstrated by research done at Duke University, North Carolina, where comparisons were made between the amounts of energy consumed per gram of body weight to travel one kilometre. (The results were published in a detailed treatise by Stuart Wilson in the March 1973 issue of *Scientific American.*)

The research showed that the least efficient of the animals and machines studied was the mouse. This poor little creature consumes more than 50 calories of energy (that is 0.05 food calories) per gram of body weight to travel a kilometre. By comparison, a fly uses 15 calories of energy, a rabbit about 5 and a helicopter just under 4. The ten most efficient travellers are set out in **Energy consumed to travel 1 kilometre** which shows that the cyclist is almost three times more efficient than any other traveller tested.

The bicyclist is so highly efficient because the ergonomically evolved shape of the machine allows the body's most powerful muscles (the thigh muscles) to be used in turning the legs with a smooth rotary action at an optimum speed. A rate of 60–80 revolutions per minute – a normal pedalling speed – gives a time of leg swing of about 0.5 sec, which is a typical figure for a natural walking action.

The efficiency is, of course, further improved by the rider being as fit as possible and by the bicycle being maintained in perfect running order. Well-lubricated ball bearings are particularly important as these reduce the rolling resistance of the machine. The other bane of cycling – air resistance – can be reduced by adopting a more streamlined riding position.

One aspect of bike riding that most scientific studies seem to ignore, however, is the tremendous benefit derived from being able to rest for long periods while in motion, without losing any impetus. Freewheeling down a long hill allows your body to recuperate from the effort of climbing the hill; while the resultant energy build-up going downhill gives a positive boost to the next burst of pedalling.

These rest periods mean that a significant part of any ride is covered with little or no expenditure of energy, allowing you to ride a bike for much longer periods than you can comfortably run or walk. This fact was first made apparent to me when at college. Without any preparatory training, I was among a small group of students that set out one lunchtime to walk the 85 km (53 miles) from London to Brighton. There were just two of us left when night fell and we had covered not much more than half the distance. We walked no further because of aching muscles, blistered feet and pangs of hunger. By comparison, three years before, I had started out on a 200 km (125 mile) cycle ride in a similarly unprepared state. All five of us in the group completed the ride in about 12 hours – tired, but not unduly exhausted.

Save time . . . and money

It is these and many other similar experiences that have convinced me that the bicycle is greatly underestimated (and under-used) as that 'viable commuting alternative' mentioned by the august American legislators. Planners arbitrarily say that the bicycle is a competitive option for trips of up to 5 km (about 3 miles). My experiences (and those of others) of commuting by bicycle in America, Britain and Europe show that cycling is equally competitive (not least in journey time) for door-to-door distances of up to 25 km (15 miles).

When living in a typical industrial city of the north-east United States I could go by bike, bus or car to travel the 5 km (3 miles) to

Energy consumed to travel 1 kilometre (in calories of energy per gram)	
1. Bicyclist	0.15
2. Salmon	0.40
3. Horse	0.50–0.70
4. Jet aircraft	0.60
5. Walking man	0.75
6. Motor car	0.75–0.85
7. Cow	0.82
8. Pigeon	0.92
9. Sheep	1.00
10. Dog	1.40

Note—the weight of the bicyclist is based on the combined weight of bicycle and rider.

A bicycle can also be a beast of burden, although it is not recommended to carry as much luggage as this.

With the ever increasing price of fuel, bicycles have become a most attractive commuting alternative compared with private cars. This rider, taking part in a mass demonstration in London, gets his message home very clearly.

my office. Typical journey times were 15 minutes by bike (including carrying the bike upstairs to the office), 25 minutes by car (including a five-minute walk from the company parking lot) and about 30 minutes by bus (including a short walk at each end and waiting for the bus).

The bicycle clearly wins hands down for such a short journey – but what about the longer distances? Well, the door-to-door distance was about 25 km (15 miles) for two jobs I have had in the London area. The first was from the country into a London suburb, mostly on a fairly fast main road. I took the express bus the first few days (there was no direct train route) and found that the journey took just about one hour. After that, I regularly went by bicycle, getting the journey time down to 45 minutes. So it was still quicker, I got much fitter and I was saving a very significant amount of money.

The second job involved travelling from the suburbs to the centre of London, mostly on city streets. Again, the journey by public transport took as long as, or longer than, the ride by bike. The walk-bus-walk trip was about 90 minutes, the walk-train-walk-underground train-walk trip lasted an hour; and the bicycle ride took between 50 minutes and an hour.

Time saving is just one of the attractions of commuting by bike. It is also a good deal cheaper ('*relatively inexpensive*'), provides your daily exercise without your having to find extra time and helps towards a reduction in noise and air pollution.

Pedals don't pollute

If people take to riding bikes in such large numbers, it is easily appreciated how this helps to '*reduce noise and air pollution*'. Motor vehicles pour huge volumes of exhaust fumes into the atmosphere, and the United States, for one, has found it an uphill task trying to clean up these car emissions by stringent legislation. About 30 cities in the U.S. are now badly affected by smog, causing a definite hazard to health. Smog has also proved a problem in Australia, Japan and Western Europe.

Noise is another significant intrusion into urban life. It has been estimated that in 1980 six out of ten people living in British towns would have their sleep disturbed by motor traffic. It may be a pipe-dream to have a silent world with everyone riding bikes – although noise from bicycle bells is apparently a nuisance in Chinese cities – but a reduction in the number of motor vehicles can only be of benefit to the rapidly declining quality of urban life.

One way of encouraging greater usage of the bicycle is to provide cheap, functional bicycles at central points in towns, with citizens being able to use one of these bikes for any short trip and park it at the pick-up point nearest their destination. A number of European cities – Amsterdam (Netherlands), Berne (Switzerland) and Bremen (West Germany) – have tried this idea with some encouraging results. Another popular scheme in America and Europe is bicycle hire, the most successful schemes being those where you can rent a bike from close to a rail station. In France, the Netherlands and Switzerland the state rail companies themselves operate such facilities at hundreds of stations with great success.

The dominant sound of rush hour traffic in Peking, China is that of bicycle bells.

There are no age limits to cycling, and this French lady is obviously enjoying her ride.

A place on the planning board

Clearly, the bicycle does *'deserve consideration in a comprehensive national energy plan'*, as the US Congress agreed. As a consequence,

the US Government in 1978 pledged $45 million towards the construction of bikeway facilities in the United States. In the Netherlands, where some existing cycle paths had been ripped up to make new highways, the government reversed the policy in favour of bicycles in the mid-1970s. A substantial grant of funds was awarded for new bikeways, and this has helped the Dutch build what is perhaps the world's only comprehensive national network of purpose-built bicycle routes.

Denmark, Japan, Sweden, Switzerland and West Germany have followed the Dutch example to varying degrees; while efforts in Belgium, France, Great Britain,the US and Canada have been more haphazard. It is recognized that cyclists should not have to compete with heavy traffic for road space, but there has been international disagreement on what to provide. Among American states, Florida and Oregon have built many lengths of cyclist-only tracks, separated from ordinary roads; the city of New York has found acceptance for bicycle lanes forming part of existing streets. In Europe some towns allow pedestrians and cyclists to share paths built independently of the road network.

In Britain, central government policy since 1978 has allowed part-financing of suitable bikeway schemes, but initiative to plan such facilities has been left to local authorities, few of whom have taken up the government's offer of assistance. The only fully comprehensive scheme is at the new town of Stevenage, Hertfordshire, where more than 50 km (30 miles) of separate bikeways have been built, with cyclists being provided with underpasses to cross the busiest main roads. Similar plans have been partly executed at the new city of Milton Keynes (midway between London and Birmingham), while towns like Middlesbrough, Peterborough and Swindon started in the late 1970s to provide bikeway links between new suburbs and old city centres.

Estimates put the number of adult cyclists in Britain at about six million, representing about 11 per cent of the country's population. This compares with a proportion of 67 per cent in the Netherlands, where every encouragement is given to cyclists. An example is the campaign, launched by the Dutch government in 1978, to reach a target of two bicycles for each home – adding a modern lightweight (for leisure cycling) to the heavyweight work bike that most families already possessed.

Such efforts could increase the numbers of Dutch cyclists to around 75 per cent of the population, a level that already exists in the Californian university town of Davis. There, wide, cyclist-only lanes on downtown streets make it possible for such a high percentage of the town's population to use their bicycles every day.

Cycling in many European towns and cities is greatly encouraged by the provision of communal bicycles that can be used by anyone for trips across town. In Holland, such bikes are painted white so that they are easily recognizable, thus discouraging potential thefts. The Dutch also make things easier for cyclists by building extensive networks of bicycle paths, both alongside and independent of the national highway system.

17

It was cyclist pressure groups that made the Davis situation possible, but not until they had formed their own political party to obtain the election of their candidates to the local council!

Local participation has also been a feature of schemes in Sweden, where the cyclist is considered an essential component of the transportation jigsaw. In Västeras, a town of 110,000 people, it is planned that more than 110 km (68 miles) of special bicycle routes will be completed during the 1980s. Bikeways linking suburbs with employment centres are separated from busy highways by bridges and underpasses. The result is that in a town with one of the highest car ownership levels in Europe about 30 per cent of the population choose the bicycle to ride to their office or factory.

Facilities such as those at Davis, Stevenage or Västeras also bring many social benefits to a town. It is easier to stop and chat to a friend when you are both riding bikes, without the interference of noise and pollution from motor traffic. Greater opportunity is given to everyone – particularly the young and those who do not drive cars – to be more mobile.

Best of all – bicycling is fun

As more people take up cycling, it follows that the environment is gradually improved, which in itself is an encouragement to more people to buy bicycles. In the United States, mass rides are organized for charity, and turn-outs of more than 1,000 people are not uncommon. Cyclists of all ages, riding all types of bike, are welcomed at these social gatherings. The distances involved in these rides could be anything from 15 to 200 km (9 to 125 miles).

These mass rides give considerable publicity to bicycling and they have helped to establish a strong sporting interest in America, in both touring and racing. Cycle racing is one of the most widely practised sports in the world, with annual World Championships for professionals, amateurs, juniors and women, as well as being an Olympic sport.

Cycle racing is most strongly established in Europe (both Eastern and Western) and Japan, a nation which supports an extensive professional cycling business based on totalizator betting at track meetings. Pride of place in the sport, however, remains with the *Tour de France*, the 3-week, 4,000 km (2,500 mile) marathon that was first held in 1903 and now holds the attention of millions of Europeans each summer.

The grass roots of cycle sport are provided by individual clubs, most of which provide regular touring and racing events, social evenings, practical advice and local group rides. You may prefer the challenge of road racing, the companionship of touring rides, or the

Opposite: *Bicycling is fun – even down the cobbles of the Champs Elysees in Paris, France. This young lady is riding a small-wheel Bickerton bicycle that is sensibly light in weight and can be quickly folded and packed into a bag to allow it to be carried on the Metro or stowed in the back of a car.*

independence of your personal ride to work. But whatever your interest, the bicycle offers unlimited opportunities for sport, leisure and exercise.

To a retired couple in Florida, the bicycle could mean a daily ride along a gravel surfaced bikeway beside a canal at a gentle 10 km/hour (6.2 mph). They would probably use sturdy, traditional bikes with heavily sprung saddles. They may discover the unhurried world of nature, making their own breeze to temper the warmth of the sun on their faces. But most important to them will be the circulatory benefits of cycling that keeps the arteries clear and the heart beating regularly.

To a middle-aged business person, the bicycle could mean a daily commuting trip through city traffic at a steady 20 km/hour (12.5 mph). The bike may be a modern small-wheeler that can be folded up and stored in the home or office, or placed in the car at weekends and used for a quiet ride in the country.

To the cycle tourist of any age, the bicycle can mean a weekend away from home, perhaps with a cycling club, or a longer, inspirational tour overseas, travelling at speeds of up to 30 km/hour (18.6 mph). The special touring bike will be fitted with a wide range of gears to cover all kinds of terrain, and compact luggage.

To a cycling athlete, the bicycle could mean a weekly race of 100 km (62 miles) at 40 km/hour (24.8 mph). The machine is likely to be an ultra-lightweight bike equipped with finely engineered alloy components and tyres which, for example, weigh a mere 200 g (7 oz) each. Long hours of hard training may be rewarded by success at the end of a thrilling race, bringing inspiration to the experienced and confidence to the novice rider.

Whatever the phase of cycling that interests you, the experience can be enhanced by careful preparation and attention to detail. Remember that cycling is an indivisible combination between man and machine. There is no point in riding an expensive racing bike if your body is permanently overweight and out of condition. Equally, there should be as much emphasis on maintaining your bike in good working order as on keeping yourself in trim with regular exercise and a sensible diet.

The bicycle can be a passport to a world of health, mobility and relaxation. It has universal appeal, cutting across social barriers and national frontiers. Known by the French as *la petite reine* ('the little queen'), the bicycle can also rightly be called the 'king of the road'. If you choose your bike carefully, maintain it correctly and keep yourself fit, then that road can lead you wherever you want . . . to work, to visit a friend, to the countryside and, hopefully, to fitness and pleasure.

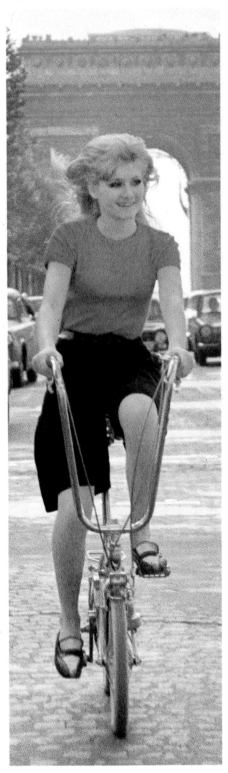

2

Bicycle History

When 19-year-old Frenchman Ernest Michaux, son of a Paris coach builder, falteringly pedalled a cart-wheeled Draisienne up the Champs Élysées in May 1861, he was no doubt amused by the astonished stares of passers-by. But it is doubtful if he envisaged the world-wide attention that would be gained by his cumbersome machine during the following decade. And he would probably have fallen from his mount in astonishment if he had been told that a century later there would be close on 40 million pedal-driven bicycles produced in the world *every year*.

The pedal was the key to the bicycle's success. It meant that the rider was fully supported by his machine when in motion, and pedalling was a rhythmic, efficient form of propulsion. This contrasts fundamentally with the jerky actions required to operate the lever and treadle system used by Scotsman Kirkpatrick Macmillan in 1839 when he built his precursor of the bicycle. Macmillan's machine used cranks fixed to the rear wheel hub and linked to two treadles operated by the rider.

Macmillan was a blacksmith in the village of Courthill near Dumfries, 115 km (71 miles) south-east of Glasgow. He used his unusual machine for frequent trips, including at least one to Glasgow: this trip was recorded as Macmillan was fined five shillings for allegedly causing a child to fall when he was riding his machine along the roadside. A copy of Macmillan's machine was made in 1845 by a friend, Gavin Dalzeel, and this model can be seen today in Glasgow's Museum of Transport. Macmillan's invention has been claimed by some as the first bicycle. The idea was not developed, however, probably because Courthill, Scotland, was not in the mainstream of the industrial revolution like Paris – where Michaux was to wheel out his pedal machine two decades later and ride the first successful bicycle.

Draisienne – *The first (1817) practical attempt to use two wheels for personal transport, it was propelled by the rider sitting astride the central seat and taking exaggerated strides along the road.*

The Draisienne which Ernest Michaux modified had a long, heavy wooden frame to support the rider, who progressed by taking alternate, exaggerated strides along the road. Such machines had been used in Paris since 1791, when the Comte de Sivrac exhibited what he called a 'Célérifère', the product of adding a second wheel to a child's hobbyhorse. But the contraption became more manageable in 1817, when a German agricultural engineer and inventor, Baron Karl von Drais (hence the Drais-ienne) patented a method of steering the front wheel by means of handlebars.

Macmillan's machine – *Invented in 1839 by a Scottish blacksmith, it was operated by the rider pushing up and down on the forward treadles, thus turning the rear wheel by means of connecting levers.*

However, the Draisienne was regarded as little more than an expensive toy and its use had not extended beyond a relatively small sector of the European aristocracy when Michaux thought of adding pedals in 1861. The old Draisienne had been brought to the Michaux workshops by a hat maker called Brunel, for repairs.

After being fixed by father Pierre Michaux, the machine was given a test ride by son Ernest. He found it an exhausting exercise and suggested to his father that he fit two footrests alongside the front wheel so that there was some support for the rider's legs on downhill sections. When contemplating the modifications, Pierre Michaux saw that the Draisienne's performance would be further improved if the legs were not only rested, but also used to help turn the front wheel – with pedals.

Velocipede – *The Draisienne was adapted by Frenchman Pierre Michaux in 1861 to produce the first pedal-driven bicycle. There was no gearing and so the machine's speed depended on the diameter of the front wheel.*

After approval from the machine's owner, the pedals were made and fitted to a pair of cranks mounted directly to the front wheel axle. Michaux based the idea on the system of handles used to turn a grindstone. So the basics of a true bicycle were born and, thanks to young Ernest Michaux being something of an acrobat, the idea worked. The Michaux machine was called a velocipede, a combination of the Latin words *velox* (swift) and *pedis* (foot).

It was more than a year before the Michaux family had satisfactorily modified the velocipede to enable it to be produced commercially. More workers were needed by 1863, when 142 velocipedes emerged from the Michaux workshops. One of the newcomers was another coach builder, Pierre Lallement, who seems to have played a considerable part in improving the basic design and helping to increase annual production to 400 by 1865.

Ordinary ('penny-farthing') – *The high bicycle evolved from the velocipede in the early 1870s.*

But Michaux senior refused to recognize his employee's part in the design modifications. These included a thinner frame that sloped to the rear wheel hub in place of the flatter, wooden beam used in the earlier Draisiennes. This allowed the weight to be reduced and the velocipede to become shorter, in turn allowing the rider to be less acrobatic.

Following further disagreements with the Michaux family, the stubborn Lallement travelled to America and took out a patent for his velocipede at New Haven, Connecticut, in 1866. But he could not sell the design commercially and hastily returned to Paris, setting up his own velocipede works in competition with Michaux. However he was too late to pose a real threat to his former employer's enterprise, that, by 1868, had moved to a new factory with 300 workers turning out 50 machines a day.

Rover Safety – *It was not until late in 1884 that John Kemp Starley produced the first Rover safety bicycle. It incorporated most of the features of a modern bicycle, notably a basic diamond-shaped frame and rear chain drive.*

This increase in business was partly due to Michaux's successful performance at the 1867 Paris International Exhibition, which had been organized as a showpiece for French industry. One of the show's visitors was a young Englishman called Rowley Turner, who was Paris agent for his father's firm, the Coventry Sewing Machine Company. He was so impressed by the Michaux velocipede that he persuaded two Frenchmen to back him in starting his own velocipede riding school, stores and workshop. The business flourished immedi-

The hobbyhorse, or Draisienne, was very much a plaything of the rich, as this print of 1818 proves. The basic machine has been adapted here to carry a lady passenger – either sitting on the front (foreground) or perched on a rather unstable-looking bench above two rear wheels (right). Such fashions did not last for long as it was difficult enough to propel one of these machines, even without a passenger.

ately as the popularity of Michaux's velocipede was now at its height.

The first bicycle race

Public enthusiasm was fuelled by velocipede racing throughout Europe. The first event, a 1200 m (1312 yd) sprint, took place in the Parc St Cloud, Paris on 31 May 1868. A similar race was held the following day in England in North London, with others being organized that summer at Padua in Italy and Ghent in Belgium.

Across the Atlantic, details of the new European craze were well documented by American journals. Coachbuilders and wheelwrights in New York and Boston began making velocipedes, and they had established a thriving industry by early 1868. One firm, Pickering & Davis of New York, was even exporting its machines to England, where the velocipede movement had been gaining momentum more slowly.

It was late 1868 when, flushed from his success in Paris, Rowley Turner travelled home to Coventry and caused something of a sensation by riding his velocipede across London to Euston railway station. His enthusiasm persuaded his father and the other two directors of the sewing machine firm to go into the velocipede business, especially as unemployment was high in the town. The works manager was James Starley, who had been engaged by Turner senior because of an aptitude for mechanical inventiveness.

Starley was quick to see the potential of the velocipede and himself became an adept rider. The firm changed its name to the Coventry Machinists Company, and production was switched to velocipedes in February 1869. It was intended to export their products to France, but the onset of the Franco-Prussian war in 1870 was to bring a halt to developments on that side of the English Channel.

In contrast velocipede riding was by this time rapidly catching on in England. *The Times* of London reported day trips by velocipede from London to Brighton (85 km, 53 miles) and a three-day ride from Liverpool to London (320 km, 200 miles). One of the longest one-day rides was from Coventry to London (150 km, 93 miles), successfully completed by James Starley and one of his workers, William Hillman.

Racing also was flourishing in England. New tracks opened at Crystal Palace in South London and at the Agricultural Hall, Islington, in North London. The first races – on gravel at Crystal Palace and on a board track in Islington – were both won by the enthusiastic Rowley Turner, who travelled back to France in November to take part in an historic event.

The world's first bicycle road race was held on 9 November 1869 from Paris to Rouen, a distance of 123 km (76 miles). There were more than 100 starters riding all types of machine – Michaux velocipedes, tricycles, quadricycles and others. Divided into two groups they set off from the Arc de Triomphe at 7.00 and 7.30 am respectively. In the second group was Turner, a 'Miss America', and a 20-year-old English-born student, James Moore.

Moore was the race favourite, having had a string of successes since he had won the previous year's first ever race in the Parc St Cloud. He was the eldest of nine children and he had moved to Paris with his mother and father, a veterinary surgeon, in 1853, when he was only four. They lived next door to the Michaux family and the boy's interest in 'bicycling' stemmed from his friendship with Ernest Michaux.

The Englishman – known as the 'Paris flyer' – was determined to win the Paris-Rouen race. There would be five check points en route, and by the first, at Epône, Moore had left behind all the riders in his group and had closed to 15 minutes behind the leader.

Cross-frame safety – *By 1888, Singer had developed this cross-frame bicycle on which the wheels were of equal size.*

Roadster – *Bicycling's popularity with women in the 1890s led to chains being fully enclosed, as in this safety bicycle of the turn of the century.*

Ten-speed – *The modern bicycle has become lighter in weight and more streamlined than its ancestors. But the basic diamond frame is retained.*

He was gaining about five minutes every hour and by Gaillon, with 34 km (21 miles) left to the finish, he had taken the overall lead.

A steady downpour had made the roads muddy, but Moore continued at his even pace and arrived in Rouen just as night was falling, 10 hours and 40 minutes after leaving Paris. His average speed was 12 km/hour (7.5 mph). He finished 15 minutes ahead of the next to arrive, the Frenchmen Castera and Bobillier, but they had started in the first group. So Moore was 45 minutes faster on actual time – a remarkable achievement worthy of the first prize of

50 golden Louis coins (themselves worth 1,000 francs; and it was reported that bookmakers took 40,000 francs in bets on the race).

Some of the credit for Moore's success was due to the special racing velocipede built for him by Parisian specialist Jean Suriray, who had fitted 9 mm (about ⅜ in) diameter steel ball bearings in both front and rear wheel hubs. Also of great benefit were the rubber strips mounted on the rims instead of the normal iron-clad wheels. Such strips had first been used three months earlier by a Monsieur Thevenon to win a series of races in the Lyon area of France.

There were 33 registered finishers in the Paris-Rouen race, the 29th and 30th positions being taken by Miss America and Rowley Turner. They had ridden together the whole distance, arriving at Rouen at dawn, exactly 12 hours after James Moore.

Turner stayed in Paris until he was forced to leave hurriedly when

Big-wheeled machines were the vogue in the 1870s and 1880s.

Far left: This sequence shows that Ordinary bicycles were not that easy to ride. The rider mounted from the rear, maintained an upright posture during the ride . . . but frequently ended up 'taking a header' over the handlebars after hitting a rock or rut in the road!

Centre: Ladies preferred the safety of a tricycle, such as the Stanley Sociable of 1885.

Below: Racing of Ordinaries was popular in both Britain and Europe.

Cycling became acceptable to all classes through the 1890s, with mass gatherings such as this in London's Hyde Park becoming the Sunday meeting place. This print was first published in the high society magazine Vanity Fair, *proving how far the bicycle had infiltrated into the upper echelons of the community.*

Prussian troops began marching on the French capital. He took back with him to Coventry several new ideas, including wire spokes for wheels, tubular frames and contracting-band brakes. On his return in 1870 there were about 50 velocipede makers in England, the majority based in London, Wolverhampton and Coventry.

While the English velocipede industry entered a period of consistent growth, all development in Europe had virtually been stopped by the Franco-Prussian war. In the United States, the picture was one of feverish activity, with manufacturers not able to produce machines quickly enough. The *Scientific American* went as far as to say that 'the art of walking is obsolete'.

Making his fortune in the midst of this boom was one of the velocipede pioneers, Calvin Whitty of New York. He had craftily looked back through the patents records, discovered the Lallement registration of 1866 and bought the rights from the Frenchman for $2,000. As a consequence he collected royalty payments of $10 for every velocipede sold by the other American manufacturers.

The American craze for the velocipede fizzled out by the end of 1871 without any form of racing having been established. Manufacturing stopped and it was another seven years before bicycles returned to the United States.

From the Ariel to the Ordinary

Technical developments were thus left to the English, with James Starley playing an important part in the bicycle's evolution. Among his inventions were a speed gear, a device for tensioning spokes, and rubber-covered pedals and footrests. So well-known was Starley that he was dubbed the 'Father of the Cycle Industry' and a monument was erected in his honour at Coventry following his death in 1881.

One of his most renowned products was the Ariel bicycle of 1871. The Ariel was a clear improvement on the velocipedes of the day, which had a front wheel of about 90 cm (35.5 in) diameter and rear wheel of 75 to 80 cm (29.5–31.5 in). To reduce weight, the Ariel's rear wheel was made smaller. To give more speed, the front wheel was made bigger. This eventually gave rise to the Ordinary bicycle with its huge front wheel of up to 1.5 m (about 5 ft) in diameter.

Starley's Ariel was a forerunner of the Ordinary, but the size of the front wheel was kept to a reasonable size by fitting a speed box to the front driving hub, which needed but one turn of the pedals for the wheel to rotate twice. The Ariel weighed about 23 kg (50 lb) and cost £8 for the basic design, and £12 for the geared model. This was cheaper than most velocipedes, which retailed at between £10 and £15.

The bigger driving wheel of the Ordinary enabled cyclists to ride at faster speeds, which made racing even more spectacular and popular. Crowds of 10,000 and 15,000 were commonplace at track meetings in London and the English Midlands, and one of the most popular performers was James Moore, the Paris-Rouen winner.

In 1872, Moore set a new unpaced record of 22.785 km (14.16 miles) in one hour. He was equally successful at racing on road and track, winning international championships at Lyon (1873), London (1874), Paris (1875) and Toulouse (1877). He retired from bike racing in 1877 when he was 28 and moved to Normandy to concentrate on the horse racing stables that he owned. He died in 1940 at the age of 91, having continued cycle touring into his eighties.

Road racing prospered on the continent, with Italy, following France's example, holding its first road race from Florence to Pistoia (35 km, 22 miles) in 1870. The winner was a 17-year-old American, Rynner Van Neste, who finished three minutes ahead of the runner-up and 30 others. Many place-to-place races were created in the

Women's lib' was first set on its way by the bicycle. This 'rational' dress of the mid-1890s would have been unthinkable attire for a woman ten years before. It is interesting to see that this lady is riding in the countryside, showing that touring was not the prerogative of men.

Erected by the British cycle industry, this memorial in Coventry is dedicated to James Starley, referred to here as 'Inventor of the bicycle, 1870'. This is a claim not made by Starley himself, but it was certainly his drive and mechanical genius that established the cycle industry in England in 1869 and led to the developments that made world leaders of British bicycles.

next five years, with the most significant being the 150 km (93 mile) Milan-Turin classic, first held on 25 May 1876. Only eight started, in pouring rain, four of them being eliminated from the race by the appalling roads. Winner Paolo Magretti finished more than one hour before the rest, averaging 15 km/hour (9.3 mph).

The French bicycle industry restarted after the war ended in 1871, getting on its feet again by 1874. Racing also re-established itself, with the two most successful riders being the brothers Charles and Jules Terront. This pair came to race at the Woverhampton track in England in 1876, the first time Frenchmen had competed abroad, and they won, returning home with £250 (then worth some US $1,000).

The Ordinary bicycle (later called the high wheeler or the 'penny-farthing') was not invented but gradually evolved. It started with Starley's Ariel and progressed with others produced by British manufacturers such as Rudge (of Wolverhampton), Humber (of Nottingham), Singer (of Coventry) and Howe (of Glasgow). The Coventry Machinists Company remained the biggest firm of all, changing its name to the Swift Cycle Company.

Bicyclists become a power

The bicycle had become the fastest mode of road transport and it was also capable of travelling longer daily distances than stage coaches or a solo horse and rider. A leader in *The Times* of London said in September 1878: 'a bicyclist can perform a journey of a hundred miles in one day with less fatigue than he could walk thirty ... Bicyclists are becoming a power'.

Bicycle riding – particularly touring – became a cult among the urban middle class, who perhaps could not afford to keep a horse, but now had the opportunity to explore the countryside under their own steam. They formed themselves into clubs, each with their own uniform of tweed riding breeches, jacket and hat, with their own enamel badge pinned to the hat.

The earliest clubs to be formed were the Pickwick Bicycle Club in London (1870), the Edinburgh Amateur Bicycle Club, and the Peterborough Cycling Club which has survived into the 1980s. There were 29 clubs in Britain by 1874, and more than 200 by 1878, the year that the Bicycle Touring Club (later given the name by which it is known today: the Cyclists' Touring Club or CTC) was established to give British cyclists a unified voice in pressing for improvements in roads and in fighting iniquitous legislation.

This was the great era for the railways and little money was available to spend on roads. There were tarmacadam surfaces in towns, but most country roads were made from chalk or sandy gravel. Without attention, these roads had become badly rutted, dusty when dry, and slippery or mud-bound in wet weather.

Vibrations caused by the deep holes and bumps forced manufacturers to add sprung frames, sprung front forks and sprung saddles to provide bicyclists with a more comfortable ride. It took great skill to master the new king of the road, which was capable of much greater speeds as components became lighter and designs more streamlined.

A large percentage of the public and the police – in America and Europe, as well as in Britain – looked upon the flashy new vehicles as a menace, upsetting horses and unsettling the quiet pace of rural life. By-laws varied from place to place and many bicyclists were stopped or arrested for offences that they had not known they were committing. There was no universal definition that a bicycle was a vehicle, and as such that it had a right even to be on the road.

Charges of 'furious riding' were commonplace and in New Jersey, US, a state law limited bicyclists' speed to 13 km/hour (8 mph). In some countries, the carrying of a lamp was compulsory after dark. But in others, cyclists were required to continuously ring their bicycle bells to warn of their approach. A particular problem was hostility from villagers, who often caused riders to crash by putting sticks through the front wheel. There was also a running battle with coach drivers, many of whom objected to being overtaken by bicyclists and having their horses frightened. There was a famous test case in August 1876 at a court in Edgware, North London, where a coach driver and his guard were fined £7 for pulling a number of bicyclists off their machines with a rope.

Police action in Britain was largely aimed at road racing, and open races contested by massed groups of riders did not return to British roads until World War II. Consequently, track racing continued to grow and the first indoor, non-stop six-day race was held in London in 1878. This form of racing became a craze, particularly in the United States.

There were six-day races in 1879 at Boston and Chicago, both won by the Frenchman Charles Terront. The high bicycle was first imported to the United States in 1877, but the disbanded cycle industry did not start to form again for another year. The first factory was set up for the Pope Manufacturing Company by Colonel Albert Pope at Hartford, Connecticut.

The first American bicycle clubs were formed in Boston, Massachusetts, and in San Francisco in 1878. Riding was difficult because of the lack of suitable roads – particularly in California – and the great distances between towns. Conditions were similar to those found in England with dusty roads in summer and quagmires in

Magazine advertising was one way of proclaiming the advantage of the early alternatives to the Ordinary bicycle. The Kangaroo was ridden to a British record of 7 hours 11 min 10 sec for 100 miles (161 km) in 1885, but this time was beaten later the same year by the Rover safety bicycle. It was the start of a new era . . .

"KANGAROO"
SAFETY BICYCLE.

Faster than any Bicycle.
Safer than any Tricycle.
100 Miles on the Road.
Time, 7 h. 11 min. 10 sec.

The Earliest 'Bicycle'?

Among a set of drawings, reputedly the work of Leonardo da Vinci, rediscovered in Italy during the early 1970s, was one depicting a chain-driven 'bicycle'. The drawing was dated 1493 and appeared on the reverse of another anatomical sketch which formed part of a book in the Ambrosiana Library in Milan. This inventive sketch clearly shows crank arms and pedals linked to a chainwheel and chain, which drive a cogged sprocket fitted to the rear wheel.

It has eight-spoked wooden cart-wheels, a sloping wooden seat and wooden handlebars connected to the front wheel.

Opposite: *Bicycle posters became an art form of their own during the boom years from 1885 to 1900. There were hundreds of bicycle manufacturers, many such as Cycles Richard of Paris going out of business as mass production saw the domination of firms such as Raleigh, which turned out 120,000 bikes a year.*

winter. To lobby for improvements, and to press the authorities for bicyclists' rights, the League of American Wheelmen was formed in 1880, modelled on the CTC in Britain.

The Ordinary was now developed to perfection, but its use was still limited to those brave enough to run the gauntlet of public opinion and to face the constant risk of falling. Manufacturers started to look for a safer bicycle design, to bring the rider nearer the ground and to lower the centre of gravity of the bike. Just as James Starley had played a large part in the bicycle's early development, a similar role was now taken by his nephew John Kemp Starley in the design of a so-called 'safety bicycle' (one which would, literally, be safer to ride).

The key to eliminating the huge front wheel of the Ordinary was the chain, which could gear a smaller wheel to the equivalent of a large one by linking a forward drive wheel to a smaller one on the rear hub. Chains had been in use for clock making purposes for more than a century. Indeed, sketches of a chain driving a toothed wheel had been sketched during the fifteenth century by Leonardo da Vinci, who has also been credited with drawing a recognizable, chain-driven bicycle during his studies.

Enthusiastic amateurs had produced versions of a chain-driven safety bicycle as early as 1876, but the first patented machine was not made until 1879. This was the Bicyclette, exhibited by Henry Lawson (manager of the Tangent and Coventry Tricycle Company) at a Paris exhibition in late 1879 and in London at the begining of 1880. Its strange shape was ridiculed in France, but the Bicyclette was better received in England.

The front wheel was still about twice the size of the rear one, but it did have the rudiments of the modern safety bike: a tubular frame with saddle positioned between the two wheels, with the pedals and chainwheel fitted to the frame directly below the saddle, and a chain driving a sprocket on the rear hub.

Lawson's machine was not a success and the first safeties to be sold in any numbers were direct modifications of the Ordinary. Both the Facile (built by Ellis & Co of London) and the Kangaroo (made by William Hillman, former associate of James Starley) utilized smaller front wheels than the Ordinary, gearing it up by means of levers and treadles (Facile) or chain and pedals (Kangaroo) mounted just below the front hub.

These machines became increasingly popular in the early 1880s, but then Lawson's chain-driven rear wheel method was taken up by other manufacturers. In 1884, Humber & Co and the Birmingham Small Arms Company (BSA) both introduced safeties that had rear wheels much bigger than the front one. These were not entirely

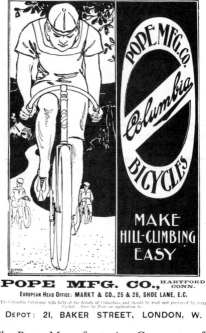

POPE MFG. CO., HARTFORD CONN.

EUROPEAN HEAD OFFICE: MARKT & CO., 25 & 26, SHOE LANE, E.C.

The Columbia Catalogue tells fully of the details of Columbias, and should be read and preserved by every Cyclist. Free by Post on application to

DEPOT: 21, BAKER STREET, LONDON, W.

The Pope Manufacturing Company of Hartford, Connecticut was America's dominant bicycle manufacturer from the time of the Ordinary through to this balloon-tyred safety of 1897. It was on a Pope Columbia bicycle that Californian Thomas Stevens cycled around the world between 1884 and 1886.

successful and it was left to John Kemp Starley to produce, in late 1884, a model – the Rover – with wheels of almost similar size.

The first design, manufactured by Starley and partner William Sutton, did not have direct steering to the front forks and it was their second version (in 1885) that finally made a breakthrough. This had a front wheel of 90 cm (35.5 in) diameter, rear wheel of 70 cm (27.5 in) and a tubular frame with two sets of forks, weighing altogether 15 kg (33 lb).

Publicity for the Rover was obtained by the usual poster and magazine advertising, but it also needed a record-breaking feat to give the new bicycle a boost. The answer was to announce a prize of a £50 gold watch for the first person riding a Rover to break the British 100 mile (161 km) road record of 7 hour 11 min 10 sec then held by the Kangaroo. On 26 September 1885, a leading amateur racer, George Smith, broke the record with a time of 7-5-16. So the Rover was speedy as well as safe.

It would be some years before the safety bicycle was finally accepted by the public, so the 1880s can be regarded as the decade of the Ordinary. This was particularly true in the United States, where the trade was flourishing, still headed by Pope Manufacturing. It was on a Pope-built Columbia bike, with a 1.27 m (50 in) front wheel, that Californian cyclist Thomas Stevens set out from San Francisco on 22 April 1884 to ride round the world. He pedalled across America to New York; across Europe from Liverpool in England to Constantinople in Turkey; and across Asia from Turkey to Japan, arriving on 12 December 1886 in Yokohama, from where he sailed back to San Francisco.

This adventurous trip was the forerunner of many more, better organized publicity stunts that the big manufacturers staged in later years. One of the best documented was by Englishman Robert Jefferson, who rode one of J. K. Starley's Imperial Rover bicycles from London to Moscow and back, a distance of 6,890 km (4,281 miles), in 49 days. The bike was equipped with Dunlop tyres, a Perry chain, a Wood's wire saddle, a Grose gearcase, and a Signal cyclometer to measure the distance covered. The year was 1895, by which time the safety had evolved into its definitive diamond frame shape.

In the ten years since the first Rover appeared, the most significant development had been the perfection of the pneumatic tyre by Scotsman John Boyd Dunlop, who was working as a veterinary surgeon in Belfast, Northern Ireland.

Dunlop's son rode a small tricycle, equipped like an Ordinary with 12 mm (0.5 in) thick solid rubber tyres. After many attempts, Dunlop finally developed (and patented on 23 July 1888) a pneumatic tyre comprising a rubber inner tube (inflated via a metal valve) surrounded by a canvas bag and protected by a rubber tread. It was fixed to the rim by cementing and binding and was about 50 mm (2 in) thick when fully inflated.

The fat, balloon tyre was at first ridiculed by many cyclists, but improvements soon made it a commercial proposition and its speed and reliability were quickly shown to be superior to the solid tyre. Dunlop tyres were first used for racing by the Irish cyclist, W. Hume, who contested and won four races at a track meeting in Belfast on 18 May 1889. Full scale production by the Dunlop factory – which moved to Coventry – then began.

Cycling into the twentieth century

It was estimated that there were 500,000 bicyclists in Britain by 1893, 200,000 in France and about 100,000 in Belgium. These numbers more than doubled by the turn of the century. Bicycling was now available to the masses, but it was also the fashionable hobby of the upper classes. It was the done thing to be seen pedalling your pneumatic-tyred safety bicycle in London's Hyde Park, in New York's Central Park or in the Bois de Boulogne outside of Paris. The comfort and safety of the latest bicycles attracted women to the sport in large numbers, an important aspect of the growing movement for female liberation.

Bicycle touring became more popular than ever, and membership of the CTC shot from 15,000 to more than 60,000 in the five years to 1899. These halcyon days occurred similarly in America and Europe, and bicycles became big business.

In Britain, bike manufacturers were the subject of major investments. The Raleigh Cycle Company was bought for £180,000 and Dunlop was taken over for £3 million (then equivalent to US $12 million). In 1896, about 800,000 bicycles were produced in Britain, many of them destined for export. There were more than 200 firms in production, but this number quickly reduced when it became cheaper to mass produce bicycles using standard parts supplied by specialist companies.

The result was over-capitalization of the industry and, in 1897, when sales dropped, there were a large number of bankruptcies. The industry became dominated by huge companies like Raleigh, which had 850 people producing 120,000 bicycles a year by the turn of the century. Raleigh's Nottingham factory also sent basic parts to Raleigh of America where 200 high quality safeties were turned out every week.

A Raleigh road racer was successfully ridden by the American sprinter Arthur Zimmerman, who won, in 1892, the British open

Bester Reifen

EXCELSIOR PNEUMATIC

HANNOV. GUMMI-KAMM-Co.
ACT.-GES.
HANNOVER-LIMMER.

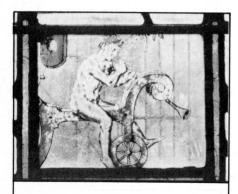

Stained-glass Bicycle

An unknown English artist, probably of the late 16th century, incorporated a bicycle-like object into a small stained-glass window in a church at Stoke Poges, Buckinghamshire, England. It is a pleasant place to visit, but it is doubtful if the window has any significance in the evolution of the bicycle. It shows two cherubs sitting on what appears to be a wooden bench with wheels, although the presence of ropes makes it more likely that the wheels were meant to be pulleys, not wheels for movement of the bench.

Right: Seen here winning the Paris-Brest-Paris race of 1901, Frenchman Maurice Garin went on to win the first Tour de France in 1903. Garin covered the 2,428 km (1,500 miles) of the first Tour at an average speed of more than 25 km/hour (16 mph) on a bike weighing about 16 kg (35 lb).

championships at one, five and 50 miles (1.6, 8 and 80.5 km). The Raleigh frame was built like a lightweight of the present day with brazed seat stays and cut-out head lugs. With its sleek lines and light wheels, the total weight was about 11 kg (24.25 lb). This compared with an Ordinary racer of about 14 kg (31 lb) and with regular Ordinaries of twice that weight.

There was a general decline in the public's enthusiasm for both racing and touring between the 1890s boom and the outbreak of World War I. It was perhaps ironic that many of the innovations of the bicycle industry proved valuable in the development of the motor car. Pneumatic tyres, weldless steel tubing and wire spoked wheels were all incorporated in the car, as were various tricycle components such as the differential gear, the freewheel clutch, the William Starley live axle and Ackermann steering.

Also adapted for automobile use was the variable speed gear, first patented by the Sturmey-Archer company in 1902 as a bicycle hub gear. This firm was bought out by Raleigh, who stepped up production to more than 200,000 units a year by 1913, and reduced the cost of the gear from about £3 to £1.

Not able to compete with Raleigh, many other cycle manufacturers turned to car production, including Hillman, Humber, Rover and Singer (in Britain); Pope, Pierce and Lozier (in the United States); and Peugeot (in France). Between 1900 and 1905, 60 per cent of the American bike manufacturers went out of business.

The decline was less pronounced in Europe, where public interest had been retained by an ever expanding programme of road and track races. The major events were sponsored by newspapers in search of bigger circulations and professional teams were sponsored by bicycle manufactureres in search of higher sales. Each promotion tried to be bigger than the previous effort. After the early efforts like Paris-Rouen (in 1869) and Milan-Turin (1876), commercial interests started to call the tune with, first, the 572 km (355 mile) Bordeaux-Paris marathon (1891), then the non-stop 1,200 km (745 mile) Paris-Brest-Paris (1891) race and, capping them all, the mammoth Tour de France (1903).

The first Tour de France lasted 19 days, there being several rest days between the six separate stages that covered a total of 2,428 km (1,500 miles). There were 60 starters and only 20 finishers. Winner Maurice Garin averaged 25.58 km/hour (16 mph) on a safety weighing 16 kg (35 lb). The race was a huge success, and a triumph of organization by Paris sports newspaper *l'Auto* (which still promotes the Tour under its changed name of *l'Equipe*). As motor cars were unreliable, officials and timekeepers travelled by train between stage towns, so the routes of the first Tours were

Le Petit Journal

Le Petit Journal
CHAQUE JOUR 5 CENTIMES

Le Supplément illustré
CHAQUE SEMAINE 5 CENTIMES

Douzième année

SUPPLÉMENT ILLUSTRÉ
Huit Pages : CINQ centimes

DIMANCHE 1ᵉʳ SEPTEMBRE 1901

ABONNEMEN

SEINE ET SEINE-ET-OISE
DÉPARTEMENTS
ETRANGER

MAURICE GAR
Vainqueur de la c

governed by which towns had mainline stations. There is little comparison with modern Tours, that last for three weeks and stop overnight at many towns and villages in France's remote mountain areas.

Despite the public interest in major cycling promotions, the sport was still largely confined to road racing in Europe and track racing in America and the British Isles. But the spread of bicycling to the other continents had started, both through the Olympic movement and through the opening up of new markets by manufacturers such as Raleigh. Australia, South Africa and India were obvious targets, particularly for the cheap, mass produced safety bicycle. China and Japan were also added to the list, and these two countries now support massive indigenous bicycle industries. More surprising perhaps was the inclusion of West Africa, with Nigeria becoming Raleigh's largest overseas customer after World War II.

The bicycle became twentieth century man's most common form of transportation. It was adapted for use by policemen, mailmen and tradesmen the world over. Surprisingly, perhaps, the bicycle also played a significant role in the Boer War as well as the two World Wars. Its use was particularly prominent in Western countries during the depression of the 1930s. In Britain, for instance, there were an estimated 11 million regular cyclists in 1936, using the bicycle to ride to work and many of them using it for touring in their spare time.

Cycle touring was one of the few leisure pursuits available to the working classes, both in Europe and North America. The ranks of the League of American Wheelmen and the CTC swelled noticeably. Membership of the CTC rose from 8,500 in 1918 to nearly 40,000 in 1936. For a short period in Britain, the cyclist's needs were planned for by highway engineers. Concrete cycle paths were built alongside new by-pass roads, but it was a development that was too piecemeal to be effective. Lack of maintenance was another problem and the onset of World War II again pushed cycling into the background of national affairs.

With the World War escalating and extending through the early 1940s, there were fewer and fewer vehicles on the roads of Britain, Europe and America. Fuel was scarce and had to be reserved for essential business. It meant a return to quiet roads, roads which had been built to high standards for the motor car, but which now proved ideal for cycling. Old bicycles were repaired and made roadworthy, heralding a period of new opportunities for the bicycle for utility, touring and racing.

The sport remained at a low ebb in America, less affected by the war, but racing continued in occupied France and the Low

By the mid-1930s, there were more than 10 million regular cyclists in Britain. As this picture shows, student bicycles have never been very smart, the student at Magdalene College, Oxford here placing a typical roadster machine in the concrete bicycle rack.

Fuel rationing after World War II meant that most families – such as this one in Paris in 1949 – used bicycles and tandems for getting out into the country at the weekend. Note the derailleur gear and rear hub brake fitted to this tandem.

Countries. More remarkable was the rebirth of road racing in Britain when, on 7 June 1942, a 96 km (60 mile) massed-start event was held from Llangollen in North Wales to Wolverhampton in the English Midlands. This race's success, followed by many others, led to the formation of the British League of Racing Cyclists (BLRC), a rebel body because road racing was still theoretically banned by the authorities. It was the BLRC with the *Daily Express* newspaper that organized the first ever Tour of Britain in 1951.

In the immediate post-war years, there was a boom in racing in Europe and in touring in Britain. Fuel rationing kept British roads relatively free of traffic, but the reverse was true in America, where the car was king and bicycles were considered playthings of the very young. There was great contrast between the usage of the bicycle in each continent. It was being increasingly used for basic transportation (of goods and people) in countries like China, India and Nigeria; its use declined rapidly in the United States; and there was an emphasis on leisure use throughout Europe.

The lead once held by Britain in the production of accessories and bicycles was gradually lost to European rivals. The derailleur gear (at first offering two gears only) was used initially by continental tourists in the 1920s and the development of lightweight alloy components thereafter remained in the hands of the Europeans.

This meant that in the 1950s and 1960s, lightweight accessory manufacturers in France, Italy, Spain and Switzerland gained most of the increasing business for supplying the European, British and American markets. Their dominance was only questioned when, in the 1970s, Japan expanded its accessory industry and posed serious competition to the European firms.

In Britain, the huge increase in motor car sales between the early

---

Cost of a Bicycle

In 1938 the average bicycle cost a Briton £5.85 at a time when the average weekly wage was only £3.45. It thus took him, on average, 1 week and 3½ days to earn enough to buy a bicycle, assuming he spent his earnings on nothing else.

Forty years later, in contrast, the average 3-speed bike cost £70.95 and the average weekly wage in 1978 was £80.00. It thus took our working man just 4½ days – 4 days less – to earn enough to buy that bicycle.

The Moulton mini-bike gave a fresh look to cycling in the 1960s. Here, inventor Alex Moulton rides his small-wheeled machine, with its open frame and sprung suspension that allowed more convenient travel in towns.

1960s and the mid-1970s brought the bicycle market to its lowest ebb. There were even serious forecasts that the bike was coming to the end of its life as a serious means of transport. One of the few success stories was that of Alex Moulton, an engineer with the British Motor Corporation. Moulton produced a revolutionary design for a mini bicycle, featuring small wheels and a sprung suspension system, which went into production in 1962 and was an instant success in Britain and Europe. It gave rise to a new concept in urban cycling.

The small wheels meant that the machine had ample room for carrying shopping or luggage and, further, the bike's mobility was increased by virtue of its being small enough to fit into the back of most cars. This aspect of Moulton's design paved the way for small-wheeled folding bicycles, which could be carried on trains and packed easily into cars, thus increasing the bicycle's usefulness in an automobile-dominated world.

But overall, the 1960s and early 1970s were difficult times for the British bicycle industry, with the smaller manufacturers having a particularly hard time. The giant TI Raleigh group managed to sustain production with a mixture of traditional roadsters and children's bikes, as did another group comprising Coventry Eagle, Elswick Hopper and Falcon Cycles.

Other once-famous names were not so lucky, although Dawes managed to survive and Viking, having folded previously, were revived under sponsorship from the British government in 1976. This was perhaps indicative of a renewed confidence in the industry. Its ability to adapt to the challenge posed by the motor car was an important aspect of this new-found confidence. As well as the previously-mentioned Moulton, which was eventually bought up by Raleigh, there appeared the equally ingenious Bickerton folding bicycle. The Bickerton was designed with the urban commuter very much in mind, being light, comfortable and small enough when folded to carry almost anywhere.

A key factor in the modern bicycle's world-wide renaissance was the energy crisis of 1973-74. Sunday pleasure motoring was banned in several European countries, leaving the roads free for cyclists. This provided an unexpected platform on which to demonstrate the versatility of bicycling both as a healthy exercise and as an enjoyable pastime. For many people, particularly in the Netherlands and Switzerland, it was the start of regular leisure cycling. It is not coincidental that sales of *sports* bikes increased rapidly in the late 1970s, representing more than 40 per cent of all sales in Britain for example.

The upturn in sales of lightweight bicycles was caused by a

number of factors – increased publicity for cycle racing; the expansion of the keep-fit movement; the availability of rented bikes; and an upsurge of interest in cycle touring. Membership of the Cyclists' Touring Club was close to 35,000 by the end of 1979, the highest figure for more than 20 years. Similar trends were recorded in Europe and North America, with tourists taking advantage of cheaper air travel to explore overseas countries.

Also indicative of the leisure trend was the reintroduction of the tandem to regular production and a step up in the manufacture of smaller lightweight bikes, aimed particularly at the increasing numbers of school-age cyclists. Opportunities for cycle competition at student level greatly expanded in the 1970s, headed by the initiation of an annual Junior World Championship series. This has proved immensely popular and a natural progression towards the Olympic Games and the senior World Cycling Championships. Cycling continues to be the major summer sport in Europe, headed by multi-million dollar professional races such as the Tour de France, with an increasing number of international events throughout the world.

The bicycle entered the 1980s on a note of optimism. Bicycle sales were on the increase in Britain, Canada, the United States and throughout Western Europe. Bicycle manufacture had become one of the main industries in the Far East, with China, Japan, South Korea and Taiwan supplying strong home markets as well as exporting to North America and Europe. There was also a strong base for the trade in the Soviet Union and East European countries. In Africa, Nigeria and South Africa continued as major producers. And the bicycle remained firmly established in India, Pakistan and the countries of South-East Asia.

In the century since it was first made, the safety bicycle retained its familiar diamond shaped frame, a design that has proved to be near perfect. The only real changes have been made in the development of more sophisticated components and materials. The trend has been towards lighter frames and accessories by using aluminium alloys, titanium, carbon fibre materials, and plastics. Extensive trials were made in the 1970s with more streamlined machines, skin-tight clothing for racing and fully enclosed, bullet-shaped bicycles in quest of higher speeds.

But ever since Michaux first laboriously powered an old Drais-ienne up the cobbled slope of the Champs Élysées, it has been the pedal that has provided the key to one of man's most useful ever inventions. And, long after the supplies of fossil fuels have dried up, there will remain the most efficient converter of human energy into forward motion – the bicycle.

World Bicycle Production (Millions manufactured in 1978)	
China	9.00
USA	7.34
Japan	5.87
USSR	5.40
West Germany	2.96
India	2.85
France	2.12
Great Britain	2.08
Italy	1.80
Brazil	1.62
Poland	1.20
Netherlands	1.04
Spain	0.58
Czechoslovakia	0.57
Hungary	0.34
Austria	0.26
Pakistan	0.23
Sweden	0.21
Colombia	0.12
Iraq	0.07
Chile	0.04
Total	**45.70**

Figures not available for Argentina, Canada, Mexico, Nigeria, South Africa, South Korea, Portugal and Taiwan.

3

Choosing Your Mount

Whether you want a trusty beast of burden or a sleek racing steed, your initial choice of bicycle is of the utmost importance; for the newcomer to cycling, it can also be a bewildering choice.

Bike sales are on the increase all over the world and a growing number of manufacturers, with a wider range of models, threatens to swamp the market in the 1980s. A visit to your local bike store or a scan through a cycling magazine will reveal just how many different makes and models are available.

With buoyant home markets, many countries in Western Europe, America and the Far East are well placed for increasing their share of exports. In Britain or North America you may be able to buy a new bike from any one of, perhaps, 20 different countries. Of these, you would be safest choosing a machine built by a well-established firm – probably British, American, French, Italian or Japanese.

If you are a cyclist already, you may be looking to replace your present mount or to buy a second bike for a specialized purpose – commuting, touring or racing. You may even feel ready to build up your own machine by ordering a made-to-measure frame and purchasing the components separately.

The newcomer will almost certainly be more interested in getting value for money from a bike that is as versatile as possible. If so, then your choice will be between a new or second-hand machine and, if buying new, to decide whether to buy a cut-price model from a big department store, or to pay a little extra at a specialist bicycle shop.

It is the purpose of this chapter to help you make up your mind on what bike will best suit your purposes, what points to check when buying and where to buy.

Where to buy

Ideally, a new bicycle should be bought from a specialist shop or store. Only then can you be assured of receiving expert advice on your bike's size, equipment and suitability. With the extra service could come a higher price tag, but study various options before saving a few pounds or dollars on a cut-price bargain. The bargain could well turn out to be a liability.

You may see a 'special offer' advertisement in a magazine or newspaper. If it is from a mail-order establishment, check that it is a genuine offer and that extra payment for postage and packing does not put the price up to what you would have paid in an ordinary shop. Also, you would be ill-advised to buy by mail order unless you can check that the bicycle advertised is made by a recognized manufacturer. The safest method would, therefore, be to

order through a large catalogue mail-order house, which will almost certainly have a sales agreement with a well-known bicycle firm. Whatever mail-order method you choose, make sure that you carry out a thorough examination of the machine as soon as it has been delivered.

First of all, check out the bike's specification against that advertised. If it is supposed to have, say, a 3-speed hub gear, make sure that it has one and is not a much cheaper single freewheel (without gears).

Secondly, check that nothing has been broken or scratched in transit; if it has, then you are under no obligation to accept the bike. You must, however, have a witness to confirm any such damage as, if it is a superficial scratch or a dented mudguard, it may be necessary to prove that it was there when you took possession. Under these circumstances, you may be happy to accept the delivery and make a later claim for the damage.

Finally, check over individual components part by part, as detailed later in this chapter. This could well be the most important phase of

The widest choice of new bicycles is found in a specialist bike shop, where both expensive racing machines and cheaper alternatives are displayed side by side.

The components of a modern bicycle.

1. *Mudguard* (*or fender*)
2. *Valve*
3. *Mudguard stay*
4. *Rear wheel drop-out*
5. *Seat stay*
6. *Rear caliper brake*
7. *Saddle*
8. *Seat post*
9. *Seat tube*
10. *Top tube*
11. *Gear lever*
12. *Handlebar stem* (*or extension*)
13. *Handlebars*
14. *Brake cable*
15. *Brake lever*
16. *Head tube*
17. *Headset*
18. *Front caliper brake*
19. *Fork crown*
20. *Lamp bracket*
21. *Fork*
22. *Front wheel drop-out*
23. *Wheel hub*
24. *Spoke*
25. *Rim*
26. *Tyre*
27. *Down tube*
28. *Pedal*
29. *Crank arm*
30. *Chainwheel* (*or ring*)
31. *Bottom bracket*
32. *Front derailleur*
33. *Pump*
34. *Chain stay*
35. *Chain*
36. *Freewheel block* (*or cluster*)
37. *Rear derailleur*
38. *Rear derailleur gear cable*

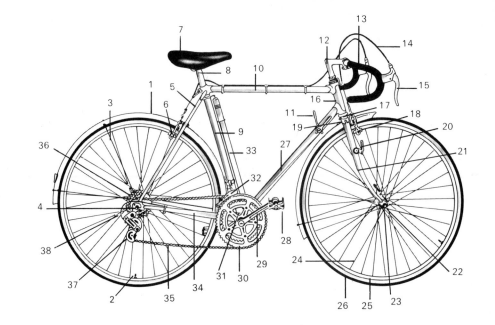

the checking operation because the mail-ordered bicycle will require a certain amount of assembly before it can be ridden. For instance, pedals may need to be screwed into the crank arms and if this is done incorrectly, it may cause one of the pedal threads to be stripped. So, as well as checking that everything is there, always make sure that you know the correct method before starting any assembly job, however small and simple it may seem.

Similar checks will have to be made if you buy from a catalogue showroom or discount warehouse. The one advantage of such a purchase is that you will have a chance to examine several bikes before making a final choice. However, it is unlikely that such an establishment would stock more than one make, and even with a variety of models, the choice of frame sizes is unlikely to be very wide.

Choice can also be fairly limited in a large department store, but you are more likely to receive some sort of advice from the sales assistant. Be careful, however, that you are not steamrollered into buying a machine that appears to have all the features you are looking for, but is cheaper and, therefore, less reliable than similar bikes from a reputable manufacturer. One thing to be borne in mind when buying bicycles and components is that there is no substitute for quality.

The easiest check to make on similar-looking bicycles is to compare their weights. An average-sized adult bike should weigh less than 14 kg (30 lb). Above that weight, the bike will be difficult to ride up hills and at anything other than a slow pace on the level. If you are still unsure which model to choose, ask for a test ride so that you can decide for yourself which bike handles the best and is the easiest to ride.

Because department store bicycles are usually on open display, the chances of superficial damage are quite high. In particular, check for any dents in the frame tubing – a weakness here could lead to a dangerous crack sometime in the future.

It is advisable to make similar checks if buying from a cut-price chain store, which may carry bicycles as one of its sidelines. You may get slightly better sales advice here, but the main advantage is likely to be a wider choice of machine, including an 'own brand' bicycle that costs less than the equivalent 'famous' make.

There can be no substitute, however, for the genuine specialist cycle dealer. If he has an 'own brand', it will most likely be based on a hand-built lightweight frame and be built up with proven, lightweight components. Such a machine would be an ideal buy, as the dealer is putting his reputation at stake. He wouldn't like to hear adverse criticism of one of his bikes as this could soon be echoed in loss of sales.

You will also find a comprehensive selection of production models on sale at the local bike shop. Remember that final assembly of the machine is always carried out at the retail outlet itself – and the specialist dealer will make doubly sure that every component is fitted correctly, and working as it should.

But perhaps the most important advantage of doing business with the small dealer is the personal advice and attention. This may not seem apparent if you go shopping on a hectic Saturday afternoon, so if you are buying a new bike try to make your choice at a less busy time in mid-week. A bicycle is not cheap – the cost being equivalent to that of, say, a single lens reflex camera – so don't rush into buying the one that has the most appealing colour.

The most important features are the bike's size, weight and suitability to your needs. A good dealer will ask what you are going to use it for (utility, commuting, touring, or racing). He should then 'fit' you to the most suitably-sized bike and, finally, give you a test ride. Only then will you be able to get the 'feel' of the bicycle.

If you are not sure that, as a beginner, you want to splash out on a bicycle of your own, then hiring one is a good way of getting started. This method gives you the chance of trying out several different types of bike without the obligation to buy. It may seem an expensive way of getting acquainted with cycling, but such an investment is more than likely to repay itself when you buy the correct machine for your particular needs.

Domestic Sales of Bicycles (in millions)		
Year	Britain	USA
1968	0.65	7.49
1969	0.58	7.05
1970	0.64	6.89
1971	0.75	8.85
1972	0.79	13.90
1973	0.83	15.21
1974	0.93	14.11
1975	1.10	7.29
1976	1.10	7.80
1977	0.91	9.41
1978	1.12	9.38
1979	1.33	11.00

Buying a second-hand bike

The test ride is even more important if you are purchasing a second-hand bike. This is the only way to check that the used machine does not have any badly worn parts – in particular, look for stiff pedals, a loose crankset or even a bent frame. Because of these risks, it is best to buy this type of bicycle through a recognized dealer, who should have checked it over thoroughly before putting the machine on the market.

If you follow up an advertisement in the local newspaper, or similar source, take a knowledgeable friend with you to give a second opinion and to help check the bike over. You will get no guarantee of road-worthiness with a private sale like this, so it is

The tandem has been a popular alternative for couples since the 1880s, when it was usual for the man to sit at the back. Note the levers connecting the handlebars so that the man can steer! Fashions have also changed over the past 100 years.

worthwhile to consider a second-hand deal with an establishment that hires out bikes. Such machines are usually bought new every year, with the used ones being sold off at the end of a season. In this way, you should get a fairly new machine that has had regular maintenance.

A second-hand bike may require a considerable amount of attention. But even the most decrepit looking machine can be transformed by use of a wet sponge, an adjustable spanner (wrench), a screwdriver, new cables and new handlebar tape.

The frame itself should be checked for dents, cracks or chipped paintwork. Any of these defects could indicate major structural

damage, perhaps caused by a crash. If the damage is adjacent to any of the frame's joints, the small dent could quickly become a major fracture. This would necessitate replacing the frame, with costly stripping down and reassembly of all the equipment. If you have any doubts, don't buy.

Spin the wheels to check for any wobbles in the rims or stiffness in the hubs, then check that the spokes are firmly and evenly tensioned; it is expensive to have a wheel completely rebuilt. Other components which should be given visual checks are the brakes, gear mechanisms, cranks, pedals, tyres, saddle, levers and cables. A common fault is a stretched chain: not expensive to replace on its own, but likely to indicate that the bike also needs new sprockets and/or chainwheels. Again, this could be very costly. And the advice would be: don't buy.

Don't let these words dissuade you from buying a second-hand bike because it is, perhaps, the only way that you will get a genuine lightweight bike at a bargain price. A second-hand bike is also an excellent purchase, as a second bike on which to experiment, for the cyclist who wants to learn quickly about bicycle mechanics.

Which bicycle to choose

Just as the amateur photographer will probably be introduced to the hobby by using an inexpensive 'Instamatic' camera, so the cyclist will most likely start riding on a simple, single-gear bike that was an early Christmas present. As the interest develops, so the photographer will progress to more expensive, more sophisticated equipment, and the cyclist will covet a made-to-measure lightweight machine.

To examine in detail the various types of bicycle available, let us begin with the needs of the absolute beginner, and progress, step-by-step, from there to the more specialized needs of the experienced cyclist. Each step entails the bike's becoming gradually lighter and also, unfortunately, the price increasing.

Single-gear bicycles

The most basic type is the single-speed bicycle. This is suitable only for riding on fairly flat terrain, but its uncomplicated nature makes it an ideal choice for the beginner. My young daughter started on a tiny, fixed-wheel version at the age of three, progressing to a larger, freewheel bicycle on her fifth birthday. Other one-geared models include so-called shopping bicycles; heavyweight, upright classic styles; most folding bicycles; and, definitely not for the beginner, fixed-wheel track racing machines.

On a *fixed-wheel* bicycle, the chain gives permanent, direct drive between chainwheel and rear sprocket. The inertia effect of the continuously-moving chain means that the cranks do not stop turning the moment that you stop pedalling. This phenomenon can be used by the skilled rider to slow down and is a recognized form of braking. In Britain, therefore, fixed-wheel bikes need have only one regular brake, instead of the two required – one for each wheel

– on a bike fitted with a freewheel.

For the novice cyclist, however, the chain's inertia can prove troublesome. It could give your leg muscles a nasty strain, or could cause you to crash head first over the handlebars. (This was known as 'taking a header' by Victorian cyclists, who not infrequently fell from their high, fixed-wheel machines – the 'penny-farthings'.) Because of these dangers, the fixed-wheel is best left for use by specialists for track racing (in which it is obligatory), individual time trials or winter training. A more versatile tool is the *single freewheel* bicycle, so called because it allows the rider to stop pedalling while the bike is in motion. This retains the simplicity of the fixed-wheel, but has none of the complications of geared bicycles. For short distance riding on flattish roads, the single free-wheel bicycle is ideal.

In the high-pressure promotion of 10-speed bikes, the advantages of the single-geared machine are often overlooked. It requires experience, skill and agility to make the most of variable gears (called by their French name, *dérailleur*). Most new cyclists are well advised to build up confidence by starting out on a bicycle with a single, low gear. Do not be misled by the patter of a sales assistant pushing the purchase of an expensive 10-speed machine. It is quite possible to buy a new bicycle unadorned with gear levers, cables and derailleur mechanisms.

Children's bikes are generally single-geared. This is for practical reasons as well as to keep the cost down. It is inevitable that the bike will be treated badly, probably being 'parked' by being dropped on the ground, so the simpler the mechanics the better. This should be borne in mind if your child asks for one of the latest racing replica machines, fitted with a derailleur gear and racing-type handlebars. Ask yourself if the child is reponsible enough to treat the bike as a serious means of transport and not as a short-lived craze.

It is not always feasible to fit derailleur or hub gears to an adult's *folding bicycle*, so this type of small-wheeled design will usually offer the one medium-sized gear. My advice is that you should not buy a folding bike unless it is to be used for short journeys in towns. This type of bike's main advantage is that it can be stored more easily where space is limited at home or can be transported in the back of a car – although a conventional bike can be quite easily transported on a roof rack, or even within the car itself (assuming that the bike's wheels are removed).

The machine should always fit the rider, and the only one that is small enough for this Russian toddler is a toy tricycle. A youngster can progress to a two-wheeler from about the age of three.

Hub gears

The next progression in the choice of gears (and price) is the bicycle equipped with a *hub gear*. Like the freewheel, this has only one rear sprocket (the toothed cog on the rear hub), but the 'fat' hub contains a complicated system of epicyclic gears, which will give you a choice of three, four or even five speeds. This means that you will have a range of gears from 'high' to 'low'. The high gear offers more resistance to the pedalling action and thus is used for speed, usually on the flat. The low gear is easier to pedal but will not move you along at such a brisk pace, and is used mainly for hill climbing and 'dead' starts. With a choice of gears, therefore, the rider is better equipped to deal with a variety of terrains.

An important factor of the hub gear is that you can change gear when stationary, something that is not possible with regular derailleur gears. This is a useful point to remember if you expect to do most of your riding in the urban environment. For instance, when stopped at a red light you can change down to bottom gear, for an easier, quicker and safer getaway.

The main difficulties of a hub gear are that it has a limited number of speeds (probably three compared with the usual ten of a derailleur) and that there is a wide gap (or jump) between each gear ratio. The standard 3-speed hub gear by Sturmey-Archer – the original and still the most common make – gives a 25 per cent jump from middle to low gear, and 33.3 per cent from middle to high. These large differences compare with the typical derailleur gap of between 6 and 12 per cent.

This means that when changing the hub gear down from middle to low your legs will suddenly be turning very fast; and on changing up a gear there will be a greatly increased resistance against which to pedal. In both cases, the change could easily break your pedalling rhythm (cadence) and cause a sudden loss of energy.

It is possible to find a hub gear fitted to a small wheeler, or a folding bicycle such as the aluminium-frame Bickerton, but it is more usual to find them on the traditional *roadster* type of machine. This type has a sturdy, steel-tubed frame – with wheels, cranks, chainwheels, pedals, handlebars and brakes also in steel – and because of its weight, is best suited to utility cycling rather than touring.

The roadster may have a fully-enclosed hub dynamo (or generator) and hub brakes. Either dynamo or brakes can be incorporated within the front or rear hub and, like hub gears, are fairly maintenance free. But the concentration of these separate functions within the wheel greatly complicates the bike's servicing; a damaged wheel, such as a broken spoke, can put the whole bicycle out of action.

On the positive side, because they are fully enclosed, hub brakes are immune to bad weather conditions which so severely reduce the performance of standard rim brakes which operate by rubber (or leather) blocks being pulled into contact with the rim and do not grip as tightly when wet. Moreover, hub dynamos are not subject to the noise and possible slipping to which tyre-operated generators are prone. However, the weight of these two hub-enclosed mechanisms tends to make the bicycle feel a much more difficult machine to propel.

Ten-speed tourers and racers

Simplicity and reliability are the two key words to remember when buying your new bike. So don't be misled by glowing publicity for the latest, flashiest machine on the market. Perhaps the greatest confidence trick played by the bike trade in recent years has been the selling of the ubiquitous, so-called '10-speed racer'.

In the American bike boom of the early 1970s, millions of cheap, ill-designed 10-speeds were heaped on an unsuspecting public. Sold in department stores and local gas stations, these practically unserviceable bikes gave bicycling a very poor image. The new

Among the advantages of a folding bicycle such as the Bickerton are its adjustable seat height (making it suitable for different sized riders), its light weight (making it truly portable and easy to ride) and its compactness. This one also has a 3-speed hub gear.

This typical shopper bicycle has 20-inch wheels that allow plenty of luggage space above them. The 3-speed hub gear is operated by a trigger control on the handlebars.

A Tall Story

The tallest cycle (a unicycle) was ridden by Carlho Sem Abrahams in Paramaribo, Surinam, on 26 November, 1977. The cycle itself was 13.97 m (45 ft 10 in) tall but Mr Abrahams managed to ride it a distance of only 7 m (23 ft).

cyclist probably undertook a few trial rides along the nearest, often gravel-strewn, bikeway then discarded the heavyweight 'clunker'. It was perhaps replaced by a pair of lightweight running shoes and the exercise-conscious American became a jogger instead. If you don't want to end up the same way – although there is little wrong with jogging! – then make sure that you buy a reasonably lightweight bike of reputable manufacture. Remember that 'push biking' is hard work, but 'pedal cycling' is a pleasure.

The lower-priced multi-geared bicycle – it will have 5- or 10-gear ratios – is most suitable for commuting or undemanding touring. The low price is achieved by mass production, based on a medium-weight frame built of plain gauge alloy tubing ('plain gauge' means the tube wall is the same thickness throughout its length). No manufacturer produces all the bike's equipment in its own factory. Parts are bought separately from suppliers throughout the world – the most reputable coming from France, Great Britain, Italy, Japan and the United States.

The bigger manufacturers – such as Schwinn and Huffy in the US; Raleigh, Falcon, and Viking in Britain – are able to buy their components in bulk, and therefore can pass on the cost savings to the customer. Other bargains can be found in the ranges of manufacturers that use components all originating from the same country. The French makes of Peugeot, Gitane and Motobecane are good examples of this, producing fairly high-quality machines at relatively low cost, using French-made Stronglight or TA cranksets and Simplex or Huret derailleurs. Various Japanese brands, such as Fuji or Sekai, similarly utilize Japanese-made items such as

Shimano, Sugino or Sun-Tour.

Along with other reputable makes such as Austro-Daimler and Puch (Austria), Atala and Bianchi (Italy), Viscount (Japan and UK), Windsor (Mexico) and Zeus (Spain), there is a standardized appearance about the middle-priced 10-speed. It has mostly light-weight, alloy components, cotterless cranks, wired-on tyres and vinyl-covered, padded-plastic saddle. It will probably weigh between 12 and 13 kg (27-29 lb). And it will probably cost about double the price of an all-steel, 3-speed bike.

The better quality model can be spotted by a number of small details. It will have separate, removable chainrings, rather than have the outer one fixed permanently to the right-hand crank. It should be possible to fit toe clips to the pedals (or they may already be fitted). And the brakes should be adjustable to enable fitment of racing (or sprint) rims (needed for one-piece tubular tyres) or high pressure rims (needed for wired-on tyres).

It is therefore possible to upgrade a basic production model by the comparatively simple replacement of cheap, high-pressure wheels with the much lighter sprint wheels. Other modifications could include the replacement of the plastic saddle with a more

Traditional roadster machines have always been popular in Britain for about-town cycling. The selection in this Cambridge University bike rack have had numbers painted on the mudguards (fenders) so that each machine can be easily identified by its student owner.

comfortable suede-covered or leather seat. On the technical side, a more useful, close-ratio set of gears can be fitted by replacing existing chainrings and/or freewheel sprockets with different sized alternatives. The standard 10-speed bike is usually fitted with a very wide range of gears, most of which will not be required for normal riding (see Chapter 4 for further details on gearing.)

The major hurdle to clear before obtaining a top quality lightweight bike is buying a lightweight frame. For minimum weight combined with high strength and rigidity, the frame should be assembled by hand using special lightweight alloy steel tubes (the more common are produced by Reynolds, Columbus or Ishiwata) and lugs (the specially shaped jointing sleeves). It requires a skilled craftsman to build up a frame using these lightweight components; and even greater experience is required for the manufacture of frames made of welded aluminium alloy, titanium alloy or carbon fibre tubing.

These high-precision frames will alone cost as much as many of the complete 10-speed bicycles. It is therefore logical that such frames will be equipped with the highest quality (and again, most expensive) components to produce a bicycle equivalent to the Jaguar, Ferrari or Rolls Royce of the automobile world. Such components include those made by Campagnolo (Italy), Shimano (Japan), Stronglight (France) and Zeus (Spain). And the complete bike – intended for racing or long range touring – will probably weigh less than 9 kg (about 20 lb) and cost many times the price of the basic 10-speed.

In exchange for the heavy capital outlay, the cycling connoisseur will obtain a true thoroughbred – a made-to-measure bicycle that is the ultimate in looks, overall handling, responsiveness and reliability.

Bicycle Components

To fully appreciate the properties of a new bicycle it is essential to understand how each component functions and how it is constructed. There is an unlimited combination of available parts to form the complete machine, but an expert can tell instantly if the blend is correct. It is the intention of this section to provide the less knowledgeable cyclist with the key to unlock some of the 'secrets' known to the expert.

Frames

To the layman, one bicycle frame looks very much like any other. The main differences he will notice are the colour of the paintwork and (if he picks it up) its weight. But beneath the shiny exterior lies a world of precision-made tubing and accurately dimensioned

jointing. The standard diamond-shaped frame is made up from a total of 24 different tubes, lugs and strengthening bridges. With heavy steel tubing, the average frame will weigh up to 4.5 kg (10 lb), compared with less than 2 kg (under 4.5 lb) for one made of butted alloy steel tubing (which has thin walls and thicker butted ends). With proficient workmanship, the lighter frame will also be stronger than the heavyweight.

When buying a new bike, the all important dimension to know is your inside leg measurement from crotch to the sole of your feet. The measurement will probably be in the region of 73–94 cm (29–37 in). Up to a leg measurement of 78 cm (31 in), ask for a frame size about 25 cm (10 in) less (that is, 48–53 cm; 19–21 in). Subtract 28 cm (11in) for the 80–86 cm (31½–34in) inside leg. And subtract 30 cm (12in) for the 87–94 cm (34½–37in) inside leg, giving a frame size of 57–64 cm (22½–25 in).

This measurement – the frame size – is the distance from the centre of the bottom bracket to the top of the seat tube, where the seat pin is inserted. The other major design consideration is the length of the top tube. For most people, this will be the same dimension as the seat tube, to give a so-called square frame. But for a person who has long arms or tall upper body in relation to the leg measurement, the top tube ideally should be longer than the seat tube. Similarly, for someone who has relatively long legs, the top tube should be shorter than than the seat tube.

To reduce costs, some production models utilize one-piece, solid, front-fork blades, which are not as flexible nor as light as forks made from oval-section tubing. But this kind of cost-cutting is made only at the expense of quality. There are no real short cuts in building an accurately-dimensioned, strong frame. Other economies found on cheaper, heavier frames are seamed tubing of poorer

Two versions of the popular 10-speed sports bicycle. The cheaper one on the left has shallow frame angles, cottered steel chainset, heavy wired-on tyres and rear carrier. The one on the right is more suitable for long distance riding, including racing. It has steeper frame angles, no mudguards (fenders), cotterless alloy chainset and quick-release, lightweight wheels.

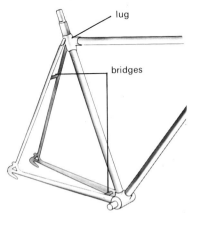

Lugs and bridges give strength to a frame.

53

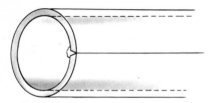

Seamed tubing.

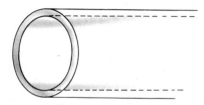

Seamless tubing.

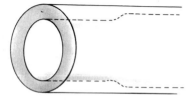

Seamless butted tubing.

quality steel and welding techniques that affect the overall strength of the frame. Lightweight frames are made up of seamless tubing, which is inherently stronger than a rolled and welded tube. In fact, welding is avoided on better frames altogether, the tubes often being butted at each end (the bore of the tube is thickened internally) with the joints brazed together (a less harsh treatment than welding) and the lugs acting as reinforcements.

Main tubes have their ends cut to a predetermined angle (mitred) to give a precise fit; lugs may be filed to shape; and brazing should be done at a minimum temperature and with the minimum of brazing material (probably a silver alloy). The standards of craftsmanship involved in the manufacture of quality frames are usually guarantee enough, but it is as well to check over the frame before purchase. Excess brazing material will reveal itself as small lumps around joints and heavy file marks may be detected.

Probably the most important piece of information to look for on the frame will be a small decal at the top of the seat tube. This will give details of what type of tubing has been used in building the frame. For a lightweight frame, this could be a Reynolds 531 or Columbus, the label saying if the tubes are plain gauge or butted. The latest Reynolds 753 (ultra-thin tubes) or 531 Special Lightweight can be used only by authorized manufacturers. (The '531' and '753' refer to the relative amounts of the principal alloying additives: chromium, manganese and molybdenum.)

You must also check that the frame is perfectly straight, or 'in track'. This can be checked by looking from behind the bike, with the front wheel pointing straight forward, to see if the rear and front wheels are lined up in the same plane. An alternative is to place a long straight edge between the rear drop-out (or fork end) and the side of the head tube, measuring the lateral distance between this and the seat tube. This measurement should be the same on both sides of the bike.

You can also check for correct fitment into the frame of the front forks and bottom bracket (located at the seat tube/down tube junction). The bottom bracket's steel cups should fit squarely into the cylindrical, bottom-bracket shell. The locking ring on the left-hand side of the bottom bracket should be tight; and its axle should turn smoothly, with no tight spots.

Similarly, the headset should be fitted securely into the head tube, and its locking nut should be tight. Turn the forks to check that there are no stiff points, and then rock the bike forwards and back (with the front brake applied) to check that there is no movement of the fork tube within the head tube.

The frame itself must be suitable for the purposes you require, and certain dimensions will determine the uses. The length of the wheel-base (the distance between front and rear hubs), chain stay length (the distance from the bottom bracket to the rear drop-out) and the rake of the front forks (the offset of the fork end to the straight part of the fork) are all inter-connected. A long wheel-base (more than 107 cm; 42 in) results in a stable bicycle more suitable for touring, while a short wheel-base (less than 102 cm; 40 in) gives a more responsive but less stable machine that is best suited for racing.

The racing frame will also feature short chain stays (probably less than 43 cm; 17 in) which allow very little clearance between the seat tube and wheel, meaning that mudguards cannot be fitted. These short dimensions generally indicate that the frame has steep angles. The angle between seat tube and top tube is called the seat angle, and the head tube/top tube combination gives the head angle. These angles are generally the same, producing a 'parallel frame', but the final geometry depends on the theories of the actual builder.

It is not necessary to know the angles – and European cyclists rarely discuss them – but they make a convenient check if they can be measured accurately. A steep, racing frame will have angles of 73 degrees or more while a touring frame will have ones of 72 degrees or shallower. A short rake of the front forks (less than 5 cm; 2 in) will give a bumpier ride than a long rake, because a higher proportion of road vibrations will be directly transmitted through the forks to the handlebars.

To check that the frame geometry is correct for you, sit on the bike and position one foot on a pedal at the point on the crank

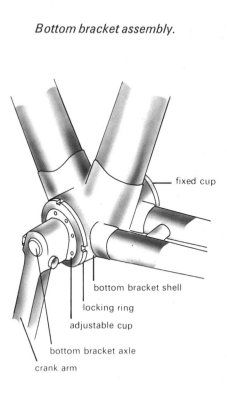

Bottom bracket assembly.

fixed cup

bottom bracket shell

locking ring

adjustable cup

bottom bracket axle

crank arm

Frame dimensions and angles.

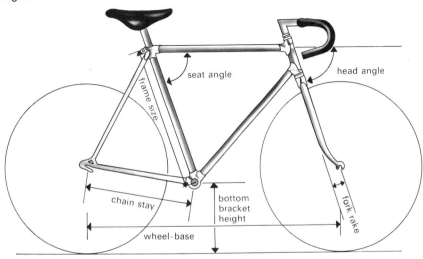

seat angle

head angle

frame size

chain stay

bottom bracket height

fork rake

wheel-base

55

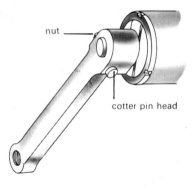

Cottered crankset.

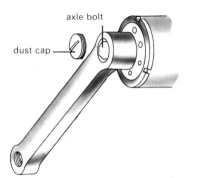

Cotterless crankset.

One-piece crankset.

nut

cotter pin head

axle bolt

dust cap

revolution where it is furthest forward. Then turn the handlebars – your foot should not be touched by the front wheel or mudguard. If they do touch, then there is danger of instability when pedalling around corners. This can also be caused by the pedals hitting the ground. The normal height of the bottom bracket from the ground should be about 28 cm (11 in), less for a short rider, and more for someone using long crank arms.

Some frames have small fixture points (or bosses) brazed on before painting. These are useful items and obviate the need for metal clips to secure brake and gear cables or lights. Eyes for fitting mudguards may be incorporated in the fork ends. Other cosmetic treatment includes chrome-plated forks; this looks nice when it's new, but is unsightly if it starts to peel off and is expensive to replace.

The final finish is a good indication of the care taken in building the frame. One that has obvious bumps and a less than smooth surface probably reflects poor general workmanship. The best frames will be sand-blasted and primed and then sanded again prior to application of the paint. Transfers (or decals) should be applied neatly and some manufacturers like to pick out the delicate line of the frame's lugs by hand painting.

Crankset and chainwheel

The crankset comprises the two cranks, which are fitted to the bottom bracket axle. There are three basic types – cottered, cotterless and one-piece. The most common, and the cheapest, is the all steel cottered set, which uses cotter pins and is fitted to most roadster-type, small wheelers and children's bikes. Cotterless cranksets are normally made of light, aluminium alloy and are made for racing and touring. The quality is necessarily higher than for a cottered set and this is reflected in a price that will probably be five times higher. The third, *one-piece* type, has cranks and axle combined in one long piece of solid steel, and its use is confined to cheaper, usually American, production bikes.

Besides the extra weight of the steel fittings, *cottered cranksets* are made at a low cost and are less precisely assembled than cotterless ones. This means they may not work satisfactorily with front derailleur gears. Also, the cotter pin has to be precisely tapped or forced into position and may need to be filed to shape first – and the pin is often difficult to remove. These possible problems should be weighed up against the low cost of replacement pins and the general availability of spare parts. On a single-geared machine or one fitted with a 3-speed hub gear the cottered crankset is ideal.

There is wide variation in the prices of *cotterless cranksets*, but there is little superficial difference in design and appearance. The extra cost of sets made by firms such as Campagnolo buys a more accurately machined product using the highest quality metal alloys and having the best possible finish.

It is important that both the tapered, square-sectioned ends of the axle and the surfaces of the crank's axle hole are perfectly clean and dry before fitting the two together. This should ensure a perfectly square joint and discourage the crank from working loose. The axle bolt that screws into the bottom bracket axle to fix the crank should not be over-tightened, as this could damage the crank arm. It is important also to screw in the two dust caps so that these threads remain clean to accept the special crank-removing tool.

To ensure that chainwheels are correctly positioned with regard to the chainline, axles come in three different lengths to take one, two (for 10 speed) or three (for 15-speed) chainwheels. If you fit a completely sealed bottom bracket unit (which prevents water and grit from reaching the bearings), be careful to make sure that the axle is of the correct length and that it is of the right section and taper to take your cranks.

Cranks come in a variety of lengths, the usual size being 170 mm (a nominal 6.75 in). A shorter-legged rider will need the 165 mm (6.5 in) length and taller cyclists use the 175 mm (7 in); only in exceptional situations (time trial or hill climb racing) are longer cranks used. These lengths should be stamped on the inside of the cranks, so check that you have the correct size before buying.

The best types of cotterless cranksets are 'five-pin', so called because the chainwheels, which are interchangeable, are fixed to the crank by means of five alloy sleeves and Allen bolts. Chainwheels for use with derailleur gears have teeth 2.38 mm ($^3/_{32}$ in) wide, spaced at 12.7 mm ($^1/_2$ in) pitch.

A slightly wider chainwheel and chain (3.18 mm; $^1/_8$ in) is used for single freewheel, fixed-wheel and hub gears. (Chainwheels come in a variety of sizes and combinations, which depend on the choice of gear ratios; see Chapter 4 for details.)

Pedals

The importance of good pedals cannot be overemphasized. This item of equipment takes a constant bashing from the rider and the weather, and even minor defects in its efficiency can greatly affect your pedalling rhythm. The main considerations are the pedal width, the type of bearing units and the style of design.

There are four basic types of pedal – the rubber platform type (which has a steel body); the double-sided 'rat trap' design (steel or alloy); the single-sided cage or 'quill' pattern (normally alloy); and

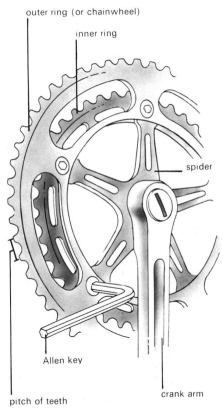

outer ring (or chainwheel)

inner ring

spider

Allen key

pitch of teeth

crank arm

Five-pin cotterless crankset and chainwheel with Allen bolts.

Rubber platform pedal.

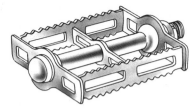

Rat trap pedal.

One-sided cage pedal.

Metal platform pedal.

the metal platform type (steel or alloy). Whatever type is chosen, it is important that the pedal is slightly wider than the broadest part of your foot. A narrow pedal can cause foot cramp, particularly on a longer ride.

The *rubber platform* type gives adequate support to the foot, but it does not accurately position your shoe or stop it from slipping at higher speeds. This design has a low resistance to wear and tear and will not take toe clips and straps, so its use should be restricted to roadsters and small wheelers that will not be used for long rides.

The *rat trap* pedal can be used without toe clips, but the serrated edges of its side plates (with which the foot has contact) can cause discomfort and leave unsightly marks on the sole of a normal walking shoe. But it is lighter than the rubber type and is a good intermediate pedal as toe clips can be fitted. The side plates are also narrow enough to accept the normal pattern of shoe plate (or cleat), the grooved metal plate that can be screwed onto a cycling shoe's sole to prevent the foot slipping.

The *one-sided cage* and *metal platform* types are designed specifically for use with toe clips and they normally have specially tapped locating holes and bolts. Toe clips come in three sizes and you should check that you have the right one: short for shoe size 5 (6½ US or 38 continental) and below, medium up to size 8 (9 US or 42) and long from size 9 (10 US or 43) upwards. Toe straps are fitted so that the quick-release buckle is close to the pedal on the outside.

If you intend to take cycling seriously, then *toe clips* and *straps* are a must. They greatly improve pedalling efficiency and prevent your feet from slipping, particularly when riding uphill. It is not necessary to have the straps pulled tight, so do not be discouraged by tales you may have heard about feet being trapped in toe clips when you are forced to stop suddenly.

There are a number of sealed bearing unit pedals on the market, including the American Phil Wood platform design and the British Barelli pedal, that can be fitted with replacement cages. This is an important consideration because it is quite easy to damage a pedal, and it is less costly to replace just the cage rather than a complete pedal.

Wheels and tyres

A well built pair of wheels is perhaps the bicycle's most vital component. The wheels must effectively transmit the rider's effort to the road and, at the same time, absorb much of the surface vibration as well as support the total weight of the rider. Because of these factors, the correct combination of rims and spokes must be used to prevent repeated spoke breakages or tyre punctures.

A wheel can be produced in a great number of ways, combining different types of hubs, spokes and rims. Hubs can have small or large flanges (to which the spokes are fixed), or incorporate hub gears and brakes. Spokes can be thick (plain gauge) or thin with butted ends and can be made of zinc-plated steel, chrome-plated steel or stainless steel. Rims come in a variety of patterns for use with different types of brake and tyre.

For most purposes, however, it is unnecessary to look beyond the three basic wheel types – roadster, tourist and racing. The roadster wheel will be built for use with heavy, thick-treaded tyres of 1½ inch (38 mm) width and stirrup brakes (with which the blocks pull up from below). These incorporate the *Westwood* rim pattern, are made of steel and have a V-shaped cross-section. Roadster wheels have thick, chrome-plated steel spokes and the rear solid-axle steel hub will probably incorporate a hub gear. This is the sturdiest type of wheel made, and is the most suitable for riding on badly-surfaced roads and for carrying heavy loads.

The tourist, or commuter, using better-surfaced roads may also be carrying certain loads and will need a fairly sturdy wheel, but one that is as light as possible. The ideal tourist wheel will use an alloy rim of *Endrick* pattern which has butted spokes and small-flange quick-release alloy hubs, drilled to accept 36 spokes in each wheel. Check that the spokes are laced so as to cross at least three other spokes; the resultant longer spoke length gives more resilience to absorb shocks from bumpy or pot-holed roads.

The most commonly used tourist type of tyre in Britain and America is the 27 x 1¼ inch high-pressure, *wired-on tyre* (known also as a 'clincher'). This does not have an equivalent size in continental Europe, where the 700C or wider 650B tyres are likely to be used. All incorporate a separate inner tube (probably made of the more resistant Butyl, rather than rubber) and are fixed to the deep section rim by wires incorporated in the tyre side walls. There are various makes of wired-on tyres available, including Michelin, Wolber and (in America) the Schwinn own-brand. Michelin also produce a lighter, narrower tyre (the Elan) which is as light as some racing-type tubular tyres and is inflated to a similar pressure of 6.3 kg/sq cm (90 lbs/sq in).

The lightest, and most expensive, wheel is built up from quick-release hubs, butted spokes and *sprint rims*. These rims have an outer circumference that has a shallow, concave section to accept the circular-sectioned *tubular tyres* (sometimes called 'sew-ups' or 'singles'). These tyres are inflated to pressures in excess of 7 kg/sq cm (100 lb/sq in) and are graded according to their weight. Models

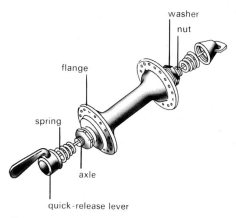

Front wheel hub with small flange and quick-release lever.

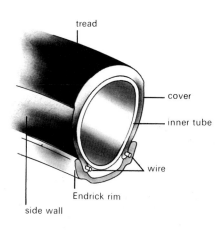

Wired-on (clincher) tyre and rim.

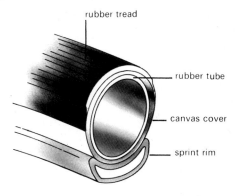

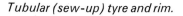

Tubular (sew-up) tyre and rim.

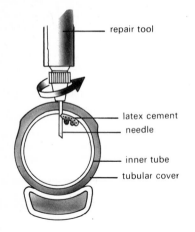

repair tool

latex cement

needle

inner tube

tubular cover

Repairing a 'Liberty' tubular. The needle is inserted through the puncture, the tool is twisted and latex repair solution is injected to seal it on the inside.

notched rivet   spring link

Chain for single sprocket

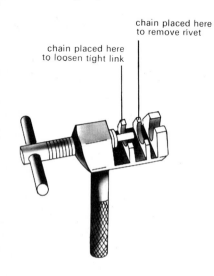

chain placed here to remove rivet

chain placed here to loosen tight link

Rivet extractor tool for derailleur chain.

lighter than about 290 gm (10 oz) should be reserved for racing, but a sprint rim is suitable for touring with heavier tubulars fitted.

There are advantages with both the main types of tyre. The wired-on tyre can have a puncture repaired by the roadside and the thicker tread is likely to last longer than that of the tubular. But others argue that it is easier, and quicker, to remove and change a tubular after a puncture, which can later be mended in the comfort of your own home. However, it is sometimes inconvenient to carry more than one spare tubular, so you could be stranded if you sustain punctures in two tyres.

There has been much experimentation with puncture-proof tyres, but this normally requires filling the tube with a heavy foam, which gives a more resistant, spongy ride. An interesting compromise is the so-called tubeless tubular, such as the Liberty made by Wolber. This type of tyre has no stitching and punctures can be repaired on the rim by injecting latex cement in the area of the puncture using a special needle.

Another consideration is the pump. Make sure that your pump will operate with the type of valve you have fitted – this is normally the Presta (or high-pressure) design (common to both wired-ons and tubulars) which will accept pumps fitted with either a push-on adaptor or the traditional screw-in flexible design.

Chain, sprockets and gears

After tyres, the chain is the item that is likely to be replaced most frequently. When a chain becomes stretched, it will not efficiently transfer the thrust from the chainwheel to the rear sprocket (and the wheel). A stretched chain is also weakened, so it should be replaced before there is a risk of it snapping.

The simplest set-up is the single-sprocket freewheel, which takes a chain of ⅛ in (3.18 mm) inner width. This type of chain is joined together by a spring link, which is fixed by a U-shaped piece of spring steel that clips over a notched rivet. Check that the chain is properly adjusted by measuring the amount of up-and-down movement at a point midway between chainwheel and sprocket. This movement should be about 20 mm (0.8 in).

The longer, *derailleur chain* requires a special tool (a chain rivet extractor) which is used to remove and replace rivets that fix the links and also to loosen tight links by slightly pushing apart the side plates. When fitting a new chain make sure it is of the correct width and pitch to engage with the sprockets. There are now multi-speed freewheel blocks with up to seven sprockets, which need a special chain with flush rivets to operate efficiently.

The rear wheel has to be specially 'dished' (using shorter spokes

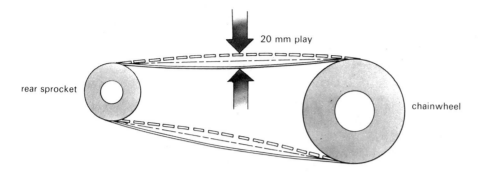

20 mm play

rear sprocket

chainwheel

on the right-hand side) to accommodate the extra width of a derailleur freewheel block (or cluster). It is best to keep 'dishing' to a minimum by using a five-sprocket block which, when combined with two front chainwheels, gives the legendary 10-speed. But it is unlikely that there are more than eight useful gear combinations because the *chain line* is severely distorted when operating from the larger chainwheel to the largest sprocket, and from the smaller chainwheel to the smallest sprocket. This distortion stretches the chain beyond its capacity, which in turn causes excessive wear on gear mechanisms and chainwheel.

When buying a new bike, check that the combination of gears is not impractical. The relevance of *gear ratios* is fully discussed in Chapter 4, but remember that very high gears – say, a 52-tooth chainwheel combined with sprockets of 13, 14 or 15 teeth – are best left for racing. For normal riding, it is preferable to have a smaller outer chainwheel (48 teeth or less) if the smallest sprocket has 14 or 15 teeth. And to avoid big leaps in the gears, there should not be more than a 2-teeth difference between the three smaller (high gear) sprockets.

The word *dérailleur* is derived from the French verb 'to derail', and the derailleur mechanism literally lifts the chain from sprocket or chainwheel and shifts it to the adjacent one. Most derailleurs (front and rear) work on the parallelogram principle, by which a sprung, pivoted cage is pulled into position by a cable linked to hand levers.

The derailleurs work best when the cables are as short as possible. This means that the levers should be fixed to the upper end of the frame's down tube. It may appear more convenient to opt for levers fixed on the handlebar ends or the stem, but this results in protruding parts that could be dangerous in a fall, and they complicate maintenance and adjustment of the handlebars.

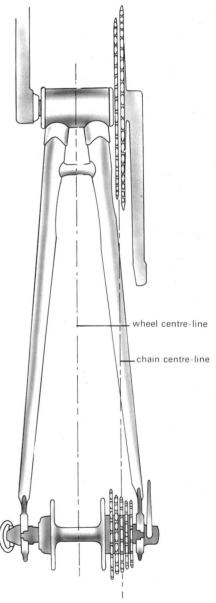

wheel centre-line

chain centre-line

Chain line for derailleurs. The wheel centre-line and chain centre-line should be parallel.

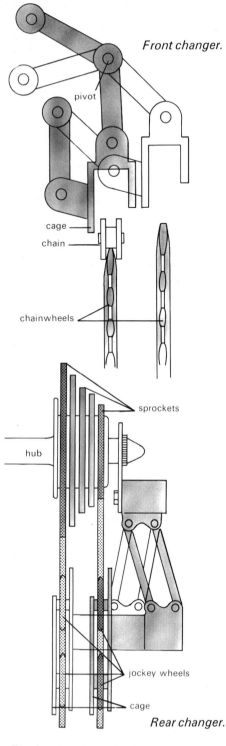

Front changer.

pivot

cage

chain

chainwheels

sprockets

hub

jockey wheels

cage

Rear changer.

The front and rear derailleur gear changers, seen here from behind the rear wheel, operate on the parallelogram principle.

There are many fine makes of derailleur on the market. Most manufacturers produce gears both for touring (with the capacity to handle small chainwheels and large rear sprockets) and for racing (to cope with small shifts of one tooth at a time). Of good value are those made in Japan (Shimano and Sun Tour) and France (Huret and Simplex), while the most precise (and most expensive) are considered to be those made by Campagnolo in Italy.

When buying multi-speed freewheel blocks for use with derailleurs, it should be noted that those made by Shimano are designed for use with their own hubs. The other leading freewheel manufacturers are Maillard (France) and Regina (Italy), both of whom have developed blocks that use titanium to reduce the weight of the potentially heavy 6- and 7-speed models.

Before riding a new bike, the derailleur mechanisms should be adjusted by means of the stop screws (or bolts), as detailed in Chapter 5. These prevent the chain from shooting off the sides of the block or chainwheels into the wheel, or jamming between crank and chainwheel.

Brakes and handlebars
Because there is a close inter-relationship between the brake levers and handlebars, it is wise to discuss brakes and bars at the same

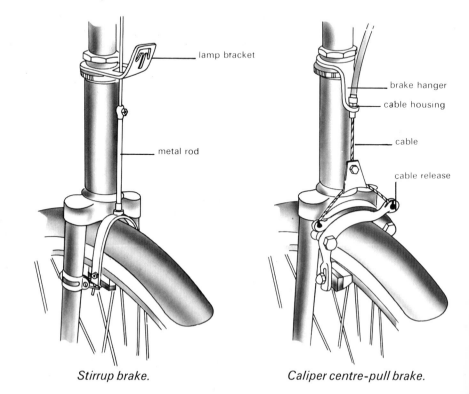

lamp bracket

metal rod

brake hanger

cable housing

cable

cable release

Stirrup brake.

Caliper centre-pull brake.

time. There are six types of hand-operated brake available – three heavyweights (hub, disc and stirrup) and three lightweights (caliper centre-pull, caliper side-pull and cantilever). They are all controlled by cables, except for stirrup brakes, which use metal rods. 'Flat' handlebars (either curved at the ends or almost straight) are used with the heavy brakes due to the type of levers required. Deeper, 'drop' handlebars are associated with cantilever and caliper brakes, which normally use levers with a rubber hood (cover) to give an alternative hand grip.

Some models have so-called *safety levers* attached to the insides of the hoods and extending along the central part of the 'bars, from where they can be operated without transferring the hands on to the hoods. These are difficult items to keep adjusted correctly and an excessive amount of leverage is sometimes necessary to operate them. The answer, if you like to hold the flat part of the handlebars, is to use flat handlebars instead.

Flat 'bars are really suitable, however, for short distance riding only as they offer just the one comfortable position for the hands – on the end grips. For longer rides the body demands to be given a choice; and this is provided by *drop* 'bars – on the hoods for steady cruising, on the tops for pulling uphill and on the drops for riding downhill or into the wind. The most comfortable levers are those

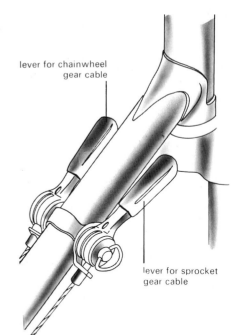

lever for chainwheel gear cable

lever for sprocket gear cable

Derailleur gear levers fitted on the down tube.

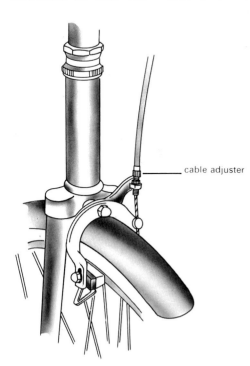

cable adjuster

Caliper side-pull brake.

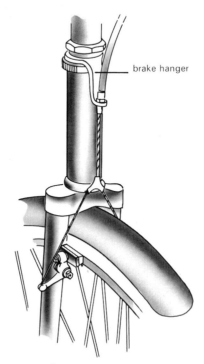

brake hanger

Cantilever brake.

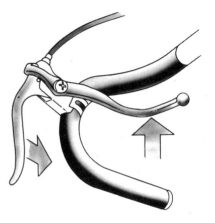

Dual or 'safety' brake levers.

63

Mathauser profiled brake block, designed with a curve to fit the rim. The shoes also feature heat-transfer fins.

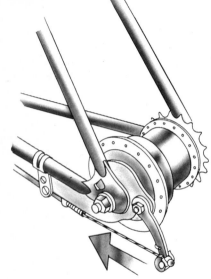

Hub brake, showing how the lever operating the brake inside the hub is pulled by the cable.

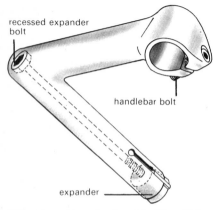

recessed expander bolt

handlebar bolt

expander

Stem (or extension), with Allen fitting, showing the expander bolt.

that have a fully enclosing rubber hood, such as Campagnolo, Shimano, Weinmann or Universal.

There is little to choose between the merits of *side-pull* or *centre-pull caliper brakes*, both of which function adequately if correctly adjusted. But simple, cheap (usually chrome-plated) side-pulls tend to pull to one side, leaving one brake block dragging on the rim. Centre-pull brakes are usually heavier as they have bulky mechanisms and require special hangers fixed to the headset and seat bolt.

The best centre-pull brakes are considered to be those made by Mafac (France), but the Swiss manufacturer Weinmann is equally reputable and Shimano (Japan) have recently perfected a centre-pull that does not need the frame-mounted hangers. However, the most effective cable-operated brakes are the *cantilever* version. These work on the centre-pull theory but have longer brake arms, that pivot about bolts screwed into special bosses brazed on to the forks, providing greater leverage.

But with all brakes that depend on grip between the rim and the brake block, the key factor is the rim/block material combination. Most rubber blocks pull up well in the dry, but wet weather makes them almost ineffective in stopping chromed steel rims. This problem has been solved by the British manufacturer Fibrax, who produce a particularly effective chromed leather block.

Smooth-sided alloy rims are relatively effective in wet or dry conditions, but rims with a grooved side should be avoided. The water collects in the grooves and acts as a lubricant, on which the brake blocks slide. In contrast, a patterned or slotted rubber block is more efficient than a smooth one, and extra-long, profiled blocks such as produced by the American firm Mathauser are even better.

There are no wet weather problems with hub and disc brakes, but this advantage must be measured against their extra weight and the frequent difficulty of obtaining spare parts from your local dealer. A further problem is that hub brakes tend to overheat when used on long downhill runs. The same can be said of coaster brakes, which are operated by pedalling backwards and are fitted to some cheaper American bicycles.

Stems

Handlebars are fixed to the frame by means of the stem (or extension), shaped like a figure 7, which slides into the front fork tube and is fixed by a long expander bolt that screws into a cone-shaped nut at the base of the stem. This bolt may have a standard hexagonal end for adjustment, or a recessed Allen key fitting to give a neater appearance. On some cheaper bikes, the forward extension of the stem is very short, thus restricting the rider into a hunched up position which can be uncomfortable on a long ride.

The optimum length of the extension (measured from the centre of the handlebars to the centre of the top of the expander bolt) depends on the individual's riding position, as discussed in the next chapter, but is most likely to be in the 70–120 mm range (about 3–5 in). Someone with exceptionally long arms may require a stem over 150 mm (6 in); at this length, the extension should be of steel which is more rigid than the usual alloy.

It is advisable to choose stem and handlebars of the same make. This should ensure that there is no incompatibility between the diameter of the handlebars and that of the stem's clamp.

Saddles and seat posts

Feeling comfortable on a bike, especially on longer rides, ultimately depends on a wise choice of saddle. It is not just a seat in which you sit, but the firm base from which the entire pedalling action begins. Your pelvic bones rock gently from side to side, between 60 and 100 times a minute, so there has to be some 'give' in the saddle. But it must not be so soft that you start to bounce up and down, thus losing considerable power.

It is also imperative that the back of the saddle is wide enough to provide support for the pelvic bones, and narrow enough at the front so that the insides of your thighs are not chafed when pedalling.

Most of these conditions are met by some of the heavy-duty saddles, such as the Brooks B90/3 that has a well sculptured, thick leather top and is heavily sprung; but this weighs up to 2 kg (4.4 lb) or more, which is unacceptable for normal riding. In contrast, the Brooks racing models, such as the B17 or the Professional, weigh less than 650 g (about 1.5 lb) and are contoured to give a firm, comfortable position.

Although leather saddles eventually give a perfectly shaped seat, they need to be 'broken in' until the rider has moulded the surface sufficiently to prevent soreness. This can be partially overcome by pre-treating the leather to soften it, and both Brooks and Ideale sell such saddles. One answer to the 'breaking-in' problem is to buy a moulded nylon/plastic saddle which has foam padding and a leather (or suede) covering.

Leather-covered nylon saddles are ideal for racing and serious touring and there is a large number of manufacturers specializing in this product. They include Avocet (US), Milremo, Royale, Unica, Concor and Cinelli (Italy) and Brooks (UK). Most lightweight saddles have a double wire base, which fits into a special *seat post* (or pillar) or into the standard saddle clip and seat pin, which is much cheaper.

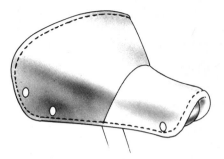

Mattress saddle.

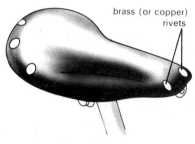

brass (or copper) rivets

Leather racing saddle.

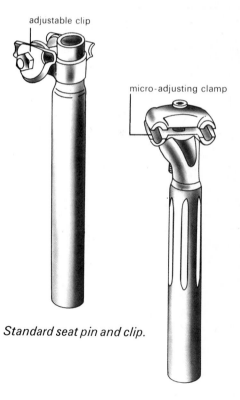

adjustable clip

micro-adjusting clamp

Standard seat pin and clip.

Seat post (or pillar) with micro-adjuster.

65

Carrying heavy loads is a common task for rickshaw cyclists in the Far East. Here, an Indian in Calcutta transports a formidable load of canes and matting on his specially adapted tricycle.

The seat post is the most rigid support for a saddle. There is no possible twisting movement at the top (as is possible with a clip) and fine adjustment of the saddle angle is obtained by means of a neat Allen key-operated clamp. Campagnolo, Shimano, Zeus and others produce such seat posts, but make sure that yours is not too short. There should be about 10 cm (4 in) or more of post showing above the frame, and a similar length within the seat tube. The correct height for the saddle is discussed in the next chapter.

Accessories

Before the bicycle is ready for the road, a number of accessories need to be bought to make it more functional. These items can be categorized into those for carrying things and those for improving safety or protection. The choice of accessories depends on what type of cycling you will be doing and how much cash you have available: bike accessories aren't cheap.

Carrying things

Pictures frequently appear in the press of seemingly overloaded bicycles belonging to travellers on the way, perhaps, from Japan to America via Europe. In countries like Nigeria and China, the bicycle is one of the most common means of transport, including the transport of bulky loads. Yes, a bicycle can be a beast of burden but it is important, however, that any load is well balanced and does not interfere with your pedalling or your all-round vision.

Specialized bags, panniers and racks for touring are described in Chapter 6. For normal about-town riding, it is sufficient to have a simple rear carrier, which should be firmly bolted to the two mudguard eyes and the rear brake bridge. This can carry a normal holdall bag, strapped down with elasticated cords.

Specialized handlebar bags and open-top baskets have their uses, but they restrict the number of hand holds on the 'bars, unless a special support is fixed to move it a few centimetres forward. Never carry things in your hands when riding, and only use a shoulder bag or back pack for short trips. A heavy load on your back is uncomfortable and it also makes your centre of gravity dangerously high.

The best place to carry a drinking or feeder bottle (called a *bidon*) is in a wire cage fixed to the down tube. Some bikes have these already attached, but it is a good thing to buy if you envisage using the bike for trips into the country or longer tours.

On any trip, you will require a puncture repair outfit (or spare inner tube, or tubular tyre) and a pump. For Presta-type valves, you can buy a pump fitted with a push-on adaptor that will fit inside the frame, along the seat tube, without using clips. For pumps with a standard connection it is best to use pump pegs that hold the pump at either end. The best place is on the seat tube – between this and the rear wheel if there is enough clearance.

It is possible to buy special tubular carrying bags that will strap behind the saddle which also hold enough tools for emergency repairs – don't forget your tyre levers if you have wired-on tyres. If you buy one of the padlocks that has a very long chain, this can be wrapped around the seat cluster below the saddle, but it would be

The shape of the basic cyclometer (or distance recorder) has changed little in the twentieth century. This advertisement proclaims the instrument here to be dustproof, waterproof and positively accurate!

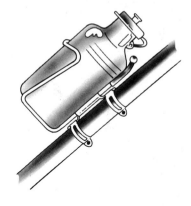

Down-tube cage and drinking bottle.

Possible positions for the pump.

The early headlights were operated by burning acetylene oil. The usual modern method is a dry cell battery or tyre-operated generator.

Babies can be safely carried on a bicycle in a seat mounted above the rear wheel. The supports should be securely bolted to the bicycle frame. The upper age limit for a child using a seat like this is about four years old.

less cumbersome to carry it in a bag. Padlocks are discussed in the next chapter.

Gadgets available to give you information while riding include speedometers, cyclometers and watch holders. Cyclometers record distances ridden and are best fixed to the base of a front fork. Huret now market a belt-driven meter that is fixed to a quick-release hub and records trip as well as cumulative distances. Even more esoteric is a magnetically-operated speedometer (that gives instant read-out of speed, cadence and distance) which fixes to the handlebars. But beware – it costs about the same as a cheaper bike! The best method of fixing a pocket watch to the bike is with a special, adjustable metal clip that bolts on to the handlebars.

Safety and protection

Riding at night can be the most dangerous time for a cyclist. It is essential that you can be seen clearly, and there are legal requirements in most countries to carry fixed lights as well as reflectors. In Britain, there are official British Standard numbers (BS 3648 on red rear lamps) that are stamped only on lamps meeting the current design standards. Lamps must be fixed front and rear, with a reflector on the back of the bike as well. Regulations vary from state to state in America, but it is usual for the cyclist to require a front-showing white light and rear-facing reflector, at least. Some states demand reflectors on pedals and on the wheels to add – by means of movement – to the cyclist's visibility.

Standard battery lamps – preferably fixed to the seat stay and front fork – are adequate for most purposes, especially if you will be riding under street lights. To give you a better view of the road ahead, a dynamo (or generator) is desirable. This type does not function when you stop, which can be dangerous in traffic, but a model is available which incorporates a battery system to avoid this problem.

Hub-mounted generators were mentioned earlier; the other type is operated from a tyre. One of the best available has a driving wheel that is in contact with the full tread of the rear tyre. This generator is mounted just behind the bottom bracket instead of on a seat stay and operating off the tyre's side wall. One of the lightest set-ups, by Soubitez of France, works off the side wall and has a front lamp that fixes to the front mudguard. This cancels out the usual argument against generators, which many consider too heavy. Others think that wheel drag is another deterrent to their use.

Use of reflective Scotchlite-type tape, stuck to rear facing bags or clothing, is also sensible. Other aids to make the cyclist more conspicuous are reflective over-vests and flags. A high masted pennant fixed behind the rider would not be worthwhile in town; but on long, straight, undulating highways such a device is a good warning for fast-moving motorists. In Scandinavia, short horizontally mounted pennants are frequently used to make motor traffic give cyclists a wider berth.

As a daytime warning, a handlebar-mounted bell is as good a device as any to alert jay-walking pedestrians. But a well-timed shout is probably more effective, particularly to warn off straying dogs or other animals.

Accessories that protect you or the bicycle include mudguards (fenders), 'tyre savers', saddle covers and handlebar sleeves. Some new bikes are fitted with very short 'racing' mudguards. These are virtually ineffective and are little more than cosmetic features. In contrast, a full mudguard and mud flap protects vulnerable parts of the bike (such as the bottom bracket) as well as the rider and any other cyclist who is following immediately behind. So they are recommended for use when riding in town and for touring.

Plastic mudguards weigh little and the increased wind resistance at speeds below 32 km/hour (20 mph) is only marginal. Aluminium mudguards are a good alternative, as they will retain their shape longer than the plastic type. When fitting new mudguards, make sure that the top ends of the fixing stays do not protrude excessively – a pair of wire cutters (or small hacksaw) will quickly trim them.

Tyre savers are small U-shaped pieces of plastic-covered wire that fix to the brake bolts and flick away any small stones that are picked up in the tyre treads and thus go some way to avoiding punctures. They can be effective, but the constant drag on the tyres can irritate the rider and also wear away the tread in time.

The last two items concern the rider's comfort. A *saddle cover* that slips over a new seat is useful for protecting clothes (particularly from an oil-treated leather saddle), and can give extra padding on a hard plastic seat. To give the hands a better hold and a softer grip, several firms now market padded leather or suede *handlebar sleeves*. These slip around each arm of the handlebars and are stitched in place. Normal handlebar tape is available in suede as well as in cotton or plastic. I have found adhesive cotton tape, such as Tressorex, to give the best grip.

Another item you will almost certainly require is an effective padlock. Bicycle thefts are prolific throughout the world, with a flourishing (but illegal) international trade in stolen bikes. Details of recommended padlocks can be found in the following chapter, which deals at length with the many ways in which you can become more proficient at cycling and how you can use your bicycle for improving your health and fitness.

Flags like this one can be mounted on the rear carrier or frame of a bicycle so that they project towards overtaking traffic. Widely used in Scandinavia, they are intended to increase the distances at which vehicles pass a cyclist.

Following pages: The proficient cyclist knows how to get the best out of his machine and how to carry out basic maintenance and repair. The road is then open to safe and enjoyable bicycling.

69

Know Your Machine

4

Cycling Proficiency

Proficient cycling means more than learning how to ride a bicycle in a straight line without wobbling. It means establishing an efficient riding posture, learning how to operate brakes and gears smoothly, developing your physical fitness and stamina, knowing where to position your bike when riding in heavy traffic, and acquiring the thousand and one skills that experienced cyclists seem to possess instinctively.

There is a lot of nonsense written and spoken about learning to become a safe cyclist by learning safety codes. This is putting the cart before the horse because you must first learn the basic skills and gain confidence in your new-found ability. A so-called 'safe' cyclist is not necessarily a skilful cyclist, but a skilful cyclist will certainly be a good, safe cyclist.

For instance, some safety codes (such as Britain's *Highway Code*) suggest that busy highway intersections can be negotiated by the cyclist dismounting at the edge of the road and wheeling the bike across the road to make a turn. Such an ultra cautious approach would show that you considered yourself to be no more than a pedestrian on wheels rather than part of the general traffic flow. Nine times out of ten, the exception being very busy roads, the correct manoeuvre at the intersection would be to begin thinking about the turn about 400 metres (or yards) beforehand, keeping aware of the traffic around you, signalling clearly your intentions if you have to change traffic lanes and finally making the turn as quickly and smoothly as possible.

The previous chapter told you how to buy a bicycle and what accessories you may need. Having made your choice, the next step is to learn how to ride the bike efficiently. Most people develop the necessary sense of balance as children, and it is preferable to be taught the basics of cycling at as young an age as possible. Three- and four-year-olds will adapt to balancing and pedalling a bike far more readily than an adult.

Learning to ride a bicycle

When teaching the very young, first adjust the bicycle so that both feet reach the ground when the child is sitting in the saddle. Choose a flat stretch of pathway for the first lesson, getting the child used to the new experience by pushing him (or her) along with one hand at the back of the saddle and your other hand holding the head tube of the frame. Let the child do the steering.

Gradually increase the speed from a slow walk to a brisk trot, still keeping hold with both your hands. It may take two or three sessions, or perhaps a dozen, before you reach that brisk trot. The next step is to remove the front hand, so that you are only pushing

Saddle-height is correct when the heel (on flat-heeled shoes) just reaches the pedal with the leg outstretched.

the bike, not guiding it as well. Depending on how confident the child is, gradually reduce the strength of your push so that the child's pedalling takes over as the bike's motive power.

The last phase of the operation is to continue running alongside the child, but intermittently releasing your grip from the saddle until you are satisfied that the child is proficient at balancing, steering and pedalling. Even when the child realizes that he is finally 'doing it on his own', continue your moral support and encouragement from alongside – until he tells you to 'get lost'!

You should also help the child in a similar manner when the small, toy bicycle is replaced by a larger one. This is particularly important if the new bike is fitted with a freewheel and caliper brakes as these both involve learning new operations.

To teach yourself how to ride a bike – if you have never ridden one, or if you think you have forgotten how to – it is best to ask a friend for assistance. Using a traffic-free area, perhaps a local park, get your friend to hold your bike upright during the first few attempts at mastering the techniques of balancing and steering. If possible, choose a slight downhill slope for these attempts. You can then freewheel to obtain enough speed, without your friend having to push as well as hold your bike.

When learning, it is best to keep the saddle at a height low enough for you to reach the ground with both feet when sitting on the bike. But as you become more confident you will find that such a cramped position does not allow you to pedal smoothly. To correct this, raise the saddle height by increments of about 1 cm (0·4 in) until you feel comfortable and in control.

Finding the ideal posture

A well-balanced, efficient riding posture is one of the keys to proficient cycling, and the sooner you perfect your position the more quickly will you progress. Even if you consider yourself a fairly experienced cyclist, you can benefit from checking your position at regular intervals. This is how it is done.

With a friend holding your bike upright, sit on the saddle and place your heels on the pedals. Wear low or flat-heeled shoes that you would normally use for cycling. Sitting upright, turn the pedals without rocking from side to side. If you feel a pull at the back of your knees when the pedals are at the bottom of their stroke, then the saddle is too high. If your legs are bent at the bottom of the stroke, then it is too low. If the saddle is at the right height, your legs should just straighten. (To turn pedals when stationary, you can pedal backwards with a freewheel. A fixed-wheel bike will require removal of the chain.)

Lateral position of the saddle is correct when a vertical line through the pedal axle falls just behind the knee cap with the foot in normal riding position and the cranks parallel to the ground.

Handlebars and stem are positioned correctly when the knees just brush the inside of the elbows.

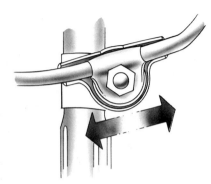

Both lateral position and tilt of the saddle can be adjusted.

Ball of the foot should be over the pedal axle.

Once the saddle height is determined, stick a short length of adhesive tape on the seat post (pillar) where it emerges from the frame. This will prove a useful reference point during the next stages of the operation. The saddle should be level, with no tilt forwards or backwards, before you check its lateral positioning. Sit on the saddle again, with your friend holding the bike upright and place the soles of your feet on the pedals. Now position the cranks parallel with the ground and get your friend to check the position of your forward knee relative to the pedal. A vertical line through the pedal spindle should also pass through the centre of your knee joint, just behind the kneecap. If possible, check this with a plumb line – a heavy object joined to a long piece of thread will do.

Once this forward-and-back adjustment of the saddle is fixed, tighten the saddle clip or pillar bolts and re-check that the height is correct with the heel-on-the-pedal routine.

With the saddle position fixed, the next step is to adjust the handlebars. With straight 'bars, there is little choice of position, but do make sure that the grips are at the same height as the saddle, or slightly lower. For drop handlebars, the height of the central part should be level with the saddle for touring purposes, or up to 5 cm (2 in) lower than the saddle for racing. In either case, the handlebars should not be tilted excessively – the bottom part of the 'bars should be almost parallel with the ground.

The best check for the forward-and-back position of the handlebars is to sit on the bike, with your feet and hands in the normal riding position. When you turn the pedals, the outsides of your knees should just brush the insides of your elbows. If, looking from the side, there is a big gap between knee and elbow then you are too

stretched out and will need to fit a shorter stem for the 'bars. Conversely, too much overlap of knees and elbows will mean fitting a longer stem.

The aim of the ideal riding posture is to be sitting as comfortably as possible while pedalling efficiently in as streamlined a position as bicycle aerodynamics allow. The arms are gently flexed, able to absorb road vibration and support part of the weight of the upper body, yet relaxed enough to allow you to pull on the handlebars. And the legs are never stretched or bent during your, hopefully fluid, pedal action.

Youngsters can learn the basic pedalling and turning operations in cycling on tricycles, such as these seen in a children's cycle ground at Rhyl in North Wales. Even adults can benefit from practice on off-road locations, especially when learning the basic skills of balance.

Cadence and pedalling
Your speed of pedalling, or cadence, measured in revolutions per minute (rpm), is dependent on several key factors: your physical strength and fitness; your position on the bike; the weight of the bike and the size of gear being used; and your cycling skill. Of these various factors, only two are variable once you are in motion – your position and the size of gear. The weight of your bike, your fitness and your skill are already determined, and improvements will only come with time.

How you place your foot on the pedal is critical; it is why most experienced cyclists (racers and tourists) use some form of shoe

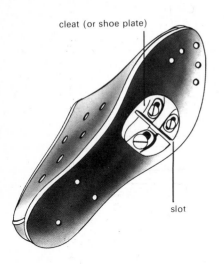

cleat (or shoe plate)

slot

Cycling shoe and cleat (or shoe plate). The slot fits over the back plate of the pedal.

plate and toe clip to position the foot accurately. What is the best position? In order to transmit energy effectively, the best position for your foot on the pedal is to have the ball of your foot placed firmly and directly above the pedal spindle. This is both mechanically efficient and comfortable. Novice cyclists are often seen riding with the pedals pushed against the heels of their shoes, thus leaving the pedal spindle beneath the arches of their feet; this is inefficient, uncomfortable and should be avoided.

Once you have set your bike up to give the optimum riding position and you have learnt with which part of your foot to push the pedals, you must discover the best way to pedal. There are two schools of thought on which is the most effective method of turning the pedals – 'toes down' and 'ankling'.

The 'toes down' method is the more natural way and is used by the majority of experienced cyclists, particularly for racing. Throughout each revolution of the chainwheel, the position of the foot remains unchanged relative to the pedal, the toes always being lower than the heel.

In contrast, 'ankling' entails dropping the heel below the level of the toes as the pedal approaches the top of its revolution. At the same time, the lower foot starts to claw back on its pedal (with toes pointing down). In effect, one foot is pushing down as the other is pulling up. The aim is to overcome the theoretical dead spot, when the cranks are in the six o'clock position.

This second method demands rather exaggerated movement of the ankles and requires hours of practice. Extra stress is placed on the muscles of the foot, shin and calf by the alternating push-pull process and these muscles will constantly ache until they become accustomed to the new technique.

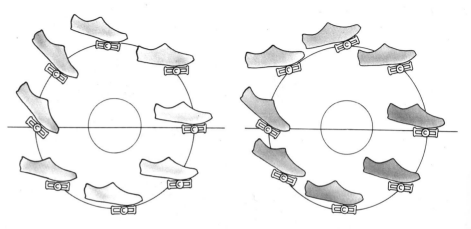

'Toes-down' method of pedalling.   *'Ankling' method of pedalling.*

Ankling is most effective at low cadences (50 to 60 rpm) and when you need to apply further pressure to the pedals, such as on a long, gradual climb. However, at higher cadences (100 rpm and above), the feet tend to flap when you are attempting to ankle. The toes-down method is far more effective at these speeds, the impetus overcoming any dead spots. In any case, at 100 rpm the theoretical dead spot is a split second phenomenon, lasting about 0.03 of a second.

Gears and gearing

The benefits of a good pedalling technique are most apparent when cycling conditions are the most difficult – riding against the wind or climbing steep hills. One answer to the problems posed by these difficulties is to use brute strength and force round a big gear; but the experienced rider will make intelligent use of his derailleur gears, maintaining a fairly high cadence. For this section, however, we will assume a general-purpose cadence of 75 rpm. Racing and touring cyclists require variations on this and advice on specialist gearing can be found in Chapters 6 and 7.

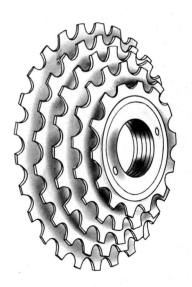

Five-speed block (or cluster).

For example, a touring cyclist riding along a flat road at a modest 25 km/hour (15.5 mph) using a medium gear of 5.5 m (68.8 in) requires a cadence of about 75 rpm. In contrast, a rider travelling at the same speed, but with a cadence of 50 rpm, will need to use a gear in excess of 8.0 m (100 in), which would require a 50 per cent greater force to be applied to the pedals. Also, a sudden gust of wind or change in gradient is less easily overcome by a cyclist labouring in a high gear.

The essence of skilful cycling is to conserve energy. It is clearly inefficient to waste energy by rocking from side to side in an attempt to push round a big gear. Keep your gears low and you will be able to sit more firmly in the saddle, allowing you to concentrate on turning the pedals smoothly. Make use of the conditions, using a big gear only when the wind is at your back or when the road points downhill. Do not fight the wind or the gradient when they are against you. They can more easily be overcome by using lower gears and developing a good riding technique.

Cadence and gear control are essential parameters. The car driver must learn that low gears need to be engaged when starting or when driving up a steep hill – selecting too big a gear will stall the engine. You are the engine on a bicycle, and if you select too high a gear in adverse conditions then your 'engine' will stall; in other words, you will have to dismount and push the bike up the hill.

Just as the car driver has to keep his engine's revs up, so the cyclist must maintain a steady cadence. For the expert, this will mean a rate of perhaps 100 rpm, which allows the racing cyclist to ride along a flat road at 40 km/hour (25 mph) in a gear of 6.7 m (84 in), or the tourist to maintain 32 km/hour (20 mph) in a gear of 5.3 m (66 in). In contrast, the novice turning the pedals at 50 rpm would ride at a very modest 20 km/hour (12.5 mph) in the 6.7 m (84 in) gear.

Your first aim should be to practise pedalling in low gears (about 5 m, or 62 in) on flat roads until you can attain a cadence of, say, 75 rpm. To take an accurate check, you will need a straight stretch of traffic-free road about 500 m (550 yd) in length, counting the number of your pedal revolutions (say, each time your right foot reaches the bottom of its stroke) in one minute. For example, 75 revs of your 5 m (62 in) gear will carry you 375 m (410 yd) in the minute.

Learning to maintain a high cadence is essential if you are to use your gears successfully, particularly derailleur gears. There is a direct link between cadence and gear size, formulated as:

$$\text{Gear size (in metres)} = \frac{\text{Speed (km/hour)} \times 1000}{\text{Cadence (rpm)} \times 60}$$

Once you have determined your optimum cadence (in this case 75 rpm), the best gear to use at a given speed can quickly be found. The formula becomes:

$$\text{Gear size (m)} = \frac{\text{Speed (km/hour)} \times 1000}{75 \times 60} = \frac{\text{Speed} \times 2}{9}$$

Applied to your actual riding, you can calculate the ideal range of gears for your type of riding. On the flat, your normal speed for commuting is likely to be 24 km/hour (15 mph), so, in our example, the correct gear is

$$\frac{24 \times 2}{9} = 5.3 \text{ m (or 66 in)}.$$

Downhill, or with a strong tail wind, you could ride at 35 km/hour (22 mph) in a gear of 7.8 m (97.3 in), and up a fairly steep hill at 15 km/hour (9.5 mph) in a gear of 3.3 m (41.5 in).

When calculating the range of gears on your bike, or when deciding on the sizes you want, you must remember that there are always two unusable gears in a derailleur set-up. These are the two gears with the most distorted chain cross-over – with the chain on the inner (or smaller) chainwheel and the outer (smallest) rear

Sensible cycling means making sure that you can be easily seen by other road users at night. This rider has reflectors on both wheels and rear mudguard, fixed front and rear lights, another lamp strapped to his knee, and a reflective bib.

sprocket; and on the outer (or larger) chainwheel and the inner (largest) sprocket. In these extreme positions, the chain cannot efficiently transfer power, as much of the energy is being wasted in overcoming the friction caused by the chain sideplates rubbing against the teeth of chainwheel and sprocket.

In a 10-speed set-up, therefore, there are only eight effective gears. Returning to the example of the rider with a 75 rpm cadence who requires a high of around 8 m (100 in) and a low of 3.3 m (41.5 in), we can calculate the ideal range of metric gears by first determining the gap, or step-up, between adjacent gears. Assuming eight effective gears, there will be seven step-ups of

$$\frac{8.0 - 3.3}{7} = \frac{4.7}{7} = 0.68.$$

Therefore the range of gears should be 3.30, 3.98, 4.66, 5.34, 6.02, 6.70, 7.38, 8.06. Referring to the gear table, it will be seen that such an exact combination is impossible; therefore, the optimum has to be taken as a guide to produce a typical, practical combination of gears, as shown in the table here.

	Sprockets				
	14	15	16	22	28
Outer Chainwheel 52	8.00	7.47	7.00	5.09	*
Inner Chainwheel 42	*	6.03	5.66	4.11	3.23

*=ineffective gears

METRIC GEAR TABLE FOR 27-INCH WHEEL

NUMBER OF TEETH IN CHAINWHEEL

NUMBER OF TEETH ON SPROCKET	54	53	52	51	50	49	48	47	46	45	44	43	42	41	40	39	38
13	8.95	8.79	8.62	8.45	8.29	8.12	7.96	7.79	7.63	7.46	7.29	7.13	6.96	6.79	6.63	6.46	6.30
14	8.31	8.16	8.00	7.85	7.70	7.54	7.39	7.23	7.08	6.93	6.78	6.62	6.46	6.31	6.16	6.00	5.85
15	7.75	7.61	7.47	7.33	7.18	7.04	6.90	6.75	6.61	6.46	6.32	6.18	6.03	5.89	5.75	5.60	5.46
16	7.27	7.14	7.00	6.87	6.73	6.60	6.46	6.33	6.20	6.06	5.93	5.79	5.66	5.52	5.39	5.25	5.12
17	6.85	6.72	6.59	6.46	6.34	6.21	6.08	5.95	5.83	5.70	5.58	5.45	5.32	5.20	5.07	4.94	4.82
18	6.46	6.35	6.23	6.11	5.99	5.87	5.75	5.63	5.51	5.39	5.27	5.15	5.03	4.91	4.79	4.67	4.55
19	6.12	6.01	5.90	5.78	5.67	5.56	5.44	5.33	5.22	5.10	4.99	4.88	4.76	4.65	4.54	4.42	4.31
20	5.82	5.71	5.60	5.50	5.39	5.28	5.17	5.06	4.96	4.85	4.74	4.63	4.53	4.42	4.31	4.20	4.10
21	5.54	5.44	5.34	5.23	5.13	5.03	4.93	4.83	4.72	4.62	4.52	4.41	4.31	4.21	4.10	4.00	3.90
22	5.29	5.19	5.09	5.00	4.90	4.80	4.70	4.60	4.51	4.41	4.31	4.21	4.11	4.02	3.92	3.82	3.72
23	5.06	4.97	4.87	4.78	4.68	4.59	4.50	4.40	4.31	4.22	4.12	4.03	3.94	3.84	3.75	3.65	3.56
24	4.85	4.76	4.67	4.58	4.49	4.40	4.31	4.22	4.13	4.04	3.95	3.86	3.77	3.68	3.59	3.50	3.41
25	4.65	4.57	4.48	4.40	4.31	4.22	4.14	4.05	3.97	3.88	3.80	3.71	3.62	3.53	3.45	3.36	3.27
26	4.48	4.39	4.31	4.23	4.14	4.06	3.98	3.90	3.81	3.73	3.65	3.56	3.48	3.40	3.32	3.23	3.15
27	4.31	4.23	4.15	4.07	3.99	3.91	3.83	3.75	3.67	3.59	3.51	3.43	3.35	3.27	3.20	3.12	3.04
28	4.16	4.08	4.00	3.93	3.85	3.77	3.69	3.62	3.54	3.46	3.39	3.31	3.23	3.16	3.08	3.00	2.93

IMPERIAL GEAR TABLE FOR 27-INCH WHEEL

NUMBER OF TEETH IN CHAINWHEEL

NUMBER OF TEETH ON SPROCKET	54	53	52	51	50	49	48	47	46	45	44	43	42	41	40	39	38
13	112.15	110.07	108.00	105.92	103.84	101.77	99.69	97.61	95.54	93.46	91.38	89.31	87.23	85.15	83.07	81.00	78.92
14	104.14	102.21	100.28	98.35	96.42	94.50	92.57	90.64	88.71	86.78	84.86	82.93	81.00	79.07	77.14	75.21	73.28
15	97.20	95.39	93.59	91.80	89.99	88.12	86.40	84.60	82.80	81.00	79.20	77.40	75.60	73.80	72.00	70.20	68.40
16	91.12	89.43	87.75	86.06	84.37	82.69	81.00	79.31	77.62	75.94	74.25	72.56	70.87	69.19	67.50	65.81	64.12
17	85.76	84.17	82.58	81.00	79.41	77.82	76.23	74.65	73.06	71.47	69.88	68.29	66.70	65.12	63.53	61.94	60.35
18	81.00	79.49	77.99	76.49	74.97	73.50	72.00	70.50	69.00	67.50	66.00	64.50	63.00	61.50	60.00	58.50	57.00
19	76.73	75.31	73.89	72.47	71.05	69.63	68.21	66.79	65.37	63.95	62.52	61.10	59.68	58.26	56.84	55.42	54.00
20	72.90	71.55	70.20	68.85	67.05	66.15	64.80	63.45	62.10	60.75	59.40	58.05	56.70	55.35	54.00	52.65	51.30
21	69.42	68.14	66.85	65.57	64.28	63.00	61.71	60.42	59.14	57.86	56.57	55.28	54.00	52.71	51.43	50.14	48.86
22	66.27	65.04	63.81	62.59	61.36	60.13	58.90	57.68	56.45	55.23	54.00	52.77	51.54	50.32	49.10	47.86	46.64
23	63.39	62.21	61.04	59.86	58.69	57.52	56.34	55.17	54.00	52.83	51.65	50.48	49.30	48.13	46.95	45.78	44.61
24	60.75	59.62	58.49	57.37	56.24	55.12	54.00	52.87	51.75	50.62	49.50	48.37	47.25	46.12	45.00	43.87	42.75
25	58.32	57.24	56.16	55.08	54.00	52.92	51.84	50.76	49.68	48.60	47.52	46.44	45.36	44.28	43.20	42.12	41.04
26	56.07	55.03	54.00	52.96	51.92	50.88	49.84	48.81	47.77	46.73	45.69	44.65	43.61	42.57	41.54	40.50	39.46
27	54.00	53.00	52.00	51.00	50.00	49.00	48.00	47.00	46.00	45.00	44.00	43.00	42.00	41.00	40.00	39.00	38.00
28	52.07	51.10	50.14	49.17	48.21	47.25	46.28	45.32	44.36	43.39	42.43	41.46	40.30	39.53	38.57	37.61	36.64

Although not ideal, this combination gives the required range of gears with the smallest step-ups (approximately 0.5) between the high gears, when the biggest power output is required, and the largest step-ups (0.9, 1.0) between the low gears, when a big jump is less critical. At least, that is the theory; the sensible use of the available gears is up to the rider.

Learning to be proficient at changing gear, as with most other cycling skills, requires constant practice. It is possible to buy gear levers that 'click' into position — such as Shimano's 'Positron' system — but the first priority is to maintain the derailleurs and cables in good working order (see next chapter).

Uphill and down

The greatest boon of variable gears is that they enable you to climb hills more easily. The sequence of operations is straightforward. When approaching the hill, keep your cadence high to give your bike the impetus to tackle the first slopes. Quickly change down to a lower gear to maintain your cadence, but do not be tempted to immediately engage the lowest gear. This should be kept in reserve for hills that are particularly steep (more than 12 per cent, or 1-in-8) or when the hills are very long. The aim is to conserve energy, sitting in the saddle, turning as high a gear as is comfortable. Too low and you will be wasting energy by pedalling too fast; too high and you will soon have to ride out of the saddle, standing on the pedals.

It is a considerable asset to be able to stand on the pedals – or to 'honk' in cycling vernacular. The French term it, more picturesquely, *en danseuse*, or 'dancing' on the pedals. This is almost impossible to do effectively on a bike fitted with straight handlebars. On a sports model, with drop handlebars, grip the brake hoods and ease yourself forward so that your weight is balanced between your arms and legs. In this position, you are ideally placed for pulling up on the bars, and pushing down vertically on the pedals. Honking is particularly useful for maintaining your speed over, say, a humped back bridge over a canal or railway; while riding out of the saddle for short periods on a long climb is of great benefit in relieving pressure on the seat.

Gear sizes

When American and British cyclists talk about a gear of say 66 inches, they are referring to what would have been the diameter of the front wheel of an ungeared Ordinary (or penny-farthing) bicycle to create an equivalent gear on their bicycle. It is calculated by dividing the number of teeth on the chainwheel (say, 44) by the number of teeth on the rear sprocket (say, 18) and multiplying by the diameter of the wheel (probably 27 inches). The gear size, in this example, is $44 \div 18 \times 27 = 66$.

The metric system is more logical because the gear size refers directly to the distance travelled by the bicycle for each revolution of the pedals whatever the size of the wheel. Looking at the table, we see that the 44 by 18 gearing will move the bike 5.27 m each time the pedals are turned through 360 degrees. To get the same answer using the English system, the 66 inches must be multiplied by $\pi(3.142)$ and then converted to metres (here, $66 \times 3.142 = 207.4$ in $= 5.27$ m).

The metric table (left) for the standard 27-inch wheel shows gears from a very low 3 m to a very high 9 m.

Climbing a steep or long hill is often made easier by getting out of the saddle and standing on the pedals, or 'honking'. This is a picture of a Tour de France competitor climbing an unpaved Alpine pass road in the 1930s.

10·56. "YOICKS!" SPRIGGINS LEARNS WHAT A "CROPPER" MEANS.

A Punch *magazine cartoon of 1869.*

Once you have passed the crest of the hill, but not before, you can think about changing up through the gears in preparation for the drop down the other side. Don't worry if your legs are aching, and your breath is short, by the top of a climb. It is a well known fact that the crest is the best place to launch an attack in a cycling road race because it is where most riders are, both physically and psychologically, feeling at their weakest.

There is also the prospect of freewheeling down the other side of a hill, one of the most exhilarating experiences in cycling, particularly touring. There is considerable skill involved in descending smoothly and safely. Keep a constant look-out on the road ahead, working out the best line to take when negotiating a bend or passing a parked vehicle. Before any such manoeuvre, you should apply the brakes gently, the rear one marginally earlier than the front brake. On long, straight descents it is sometimes necessary to use intermittent braking: a regular, momentary application of both brakes, which will slow you to a safe speed and also help prevent the wheel rims from overheating – a common problem with prolonged braking on descents. Sudden changes of direction or sharp braking should always be avoided when descending hills.

Riding in traffic

A proficient cyclist will constantly think ahead so that unexpected emergencies do not arise. When riding in traffic, you should think of yourself as part of the general flow. Change down to a lower gear before stopping so that you can start off in a smooth manner, without wobbling. Do not ride too close to the side of the road; remain about one metre (at least 1 yard) clear so that you avoid drain covers and the debris that inevitably settles in the gutter. Taking such a line also gives you room to manoeuvre if a motor vehicle comes by you dangerously close.

Basic information on riding in traffic should be learnt at school age. In Britain, the well established National Cycling Proficiency Scheme gives a good grounding in the subject, although the practical test is not carried out on the road. Parents should see that more experienced cyclists ride with their children until they become confident at sharing the road with motor traffic. Remember that, with few exceptions, a bicycle is regarded as a normal vehicle all over the world.

As such, a bicyclist should follow to the letter the rules of the road. Failure to do this is frequently apparent in the United States, where many parents (even some police officers) misguidedly tell child cyclists to ride along the side of the road facing oncoming traffic. The consequences are often disastrous, particularly at night

When riding in traffic, the cyclist should be part of the vehicle flow, not a separate entity like a pedestrian. Essential moves should be (left) *keeping well away from parked cars to avoid a suddenly opening door, and* (below) *giving clear hand signals so that your movements are obvious to the other road users.*

or along narrow roads, when car drivers simply do not have time to avoid hitting the cyclist who is approaching at a closing speed of perhaps 100 km/hour: 20 for the cyclist, 80 for the car (62 mph; 12 and 50 respectively). Road safety is a major problem in America and will probably not be solved until there is a nationally organized training scheme as exists in countries such as Britain and the Netherlands, or until there is a nationally distributed publication such as France's *Code de la Route* or Britain's *Highway Code* .

The *Highway Code* has a section for pedal cyclists and it contains some essential advice that could apply to cycling in any country. The most important points are as follows:

Make sure your cycle is safe to ride. At night you must have front and rear lamps and a rear reflector. Your brakes, lamps and reflector must be kept in proper working order. Make sure your tyres are in good condition and are properly pumped up. Do not ride more than two side by side. Ride in single file on busy narrow roads. You must not ride on a footpath or pavement (sidewalk) by the side of the road. (Unless it is a special cycle path, of course.)

Remember that you cannot be seen as easily as larger vehicles and that you should always give clear arm signals to let drivers behind you know what you intend to do, especially at round-abouts (traffic circles) and junctions.

When you are riding:
★ always keep both hands on the handlebars unless you are signalling
★ always keep both feet on the pedals
★ do not hold on to another vehicle or another cyclist
★ do not carry a passenger unless your cycle has been built or altered to carry one
★ do not ride close behind another vehicle
★ do not carry anything which might affect your balance or become entangled with the wheels or chain
★ do not lead an animal
★ wear light-coloured or reflective and fluorescent clothing.

Defensive cycling

If every cyclist took heed of these commonsense rules, and also learnt to ride proficiently and skilfully, there could be big reductions in the numbers of cyclists injured in traffic accidents. As it is, about 20,000 cyclists are injured every year on British roads, and about three times that number in the US. Statistics show that the largest percentage of cyclist-involved accidents take place at intersections, and most of these accidents are caused by motor vehicles turning across the path of the cyclist.

You should therefore be particularly wary of cars that are turning into, or emerging from, side roads. Be prepared for the motorist not seeing you and continuing with his turn as if you did not exist. Before I knew that such irrational behaviour took place, I twice got hit by cars turning across the road in front of me when cycling in my home town. On another occasion, a car overtook me and immediately turned into a side road, taking me with it.

To avoid having accidents such as these, I now make sure that I am in a position to avoid hitting cars that make these inexplicable movements. This is called 'defensive cycling' and is the basis of most current theories on safe cycling. For example, if a car overtakes you shortly before a side road junction, immediately slow down until you can see that the car is continuing straight on. As for vehicles coming in the opposite direction, be prepared for their not giving a correct signal. Observe the vehicle's and the driver's actions. Eye-to-eye contact between you and the driver is possible if it is daylight – then you can be sure that the driver has seen you. If not, look at the front wheels of the vehicle because this is your first indication if the car is about to make a turn.

Equally, you should never make unsignalled turns yourself. Always use your eyes and ears, as well as your brakes and gears, when approaching intersections. The more experienced rider will avoid as many danger spots as possible by careful planning of his route before setting off. This is of particular importance to the cycling commuter because roads are at their busiest during the periods of each trip.

In towns, it is generally safer and more pleasant to use the quieter roads that run parallel to the principal highways. If possible, avoid excessively steep or long hills. By studying contour maps, and experimenting with different routes, you may find that a hill can be missed by using a road that skirts the high ground. It may be a longer distance, but the actual time of the journey may be of similar duration to the one along the seemingly direct route.

You will probably have even greater choice when undertaking a trip between towns. Accident statistics prove that high-speed main roads are dangerous for cyclists, so always use a quieter alternative if possible. Again, the distance may be longer, but the pleasure will be infinitely greater riding along a peaceful country lane.

Security and locks
One thing you should never forget is to ensure that your bicycle is safe and secure at the end of a ride. At home, you should store it in a dry place that can be locked up. A basement or garage is ideal, but you may have to settle for a garden hut, a verandah or even your hallway. Elsewhere, you should always try to store the bicycle under cover and padlock it to a suitable immovable object.

Bicycle theft is a major problem throughout the world. Tens of thousands are stolen in major cities every year. It is big business to the thieves, who generally transport the stolen bikes to distant towns or even overseas, selling them where they won't be recognized.

There are several precautions that you can take to prevent your bicycle becoming another crime statistic. Keep a full description of your bike – size, colour, makes and types of equipment – so that it can be traced if it should be stolen. Always insure the bike, just as you would any valuable piece of machinery. And don't forget to make a note of the frame number, which may be stamped under the bottom bracket shell, at the top of the seat tube or on the rear drop-out.

When leaving your bicycle in town, try to find somewhere undercover to park it; this may be inside your workplace or perhaps in a specially designated building. You should have a sturdy lock to discourage thefts still further, and remember to chain the bike to something immovable such as iron railings or a parking meter post (provided the chain cannot be lifted over the top of the post!).

There is a wide variety of padlocks and chains on the market, and it is best to study all options before buying. The most expensive are

the most effective and the manufacturers of the 'Citadel', a case-hardened metal, U-shaped padlock, even offer a US $200 guarantee should the bicycle be stolen. Just as important as buying an effective lock is how it is locked. The chain, cable or metal loop should pass through one wheel as well as around the frame and around a solid post or railings. If your bike has quick-release hubs on the wheels, chain both wheels to the frame and the immovable object, or take the front wheel with you. Also, remove any pieces of equipment such as pump, spare tyre, lamps or tool kit. In short, make the bike the least attractive possible to the prospective thief. In towns, it is a good idea to leave the bike in a place that can be seen by passing pedestrians – do not chain it up where the thief can work in private.

Clothing
Besides looking after your bicycle, you must also look after yourself if you are to get the most out of your cycling. This means keeping healthy, improving your fitness and dressing sensibly.

It is important to wear shoes that have firm soles; flexible ones lead to inefficient transfer of your leg power from foot to pedal. The shoes should also fit tightly. It is important, if you use toe clips and straps, that the shoes are not too wide. It is possible to buy shoes made specifically for cycling, but an alternative is the type of running shoe that has a hard sole.

If you wear a warm-up suit, the legs should fit snugly, otherwise there will be a danger of their snagging in the chain or chainwheel. With normal trousers (slacks) use ankle bands or clips to stop them flapping; or tuck them into your socks. Do not attempt to ride long distances while wearing denim jeans because the combination of stiff material and thick seams will cause great discomfort.

If you commute regularly to work, then it is advisable to cycle in a separate change of clothing, especially if the trip is more than 10 km (6 miles). It is more comfortable to ride in clothes designed for the job, just as it is more pleasant to change into clean clothing for your day at work. Moreover, wearing specific clothes for the journey to work will encourage you to cycle more energetically and benefit from the greater exercise.

The ideal cycling outfit is composed of stockings (to the knee), knickerbockers (or so-called plus-ones), a long T-shirt or undershirt, sports shirt or cycle racing jersey, plus a track-suit top or woollen pullover in cold weather. In summer, wear ankle socks, shorts and a shirt. In winter, you will need some thick gloves (woollen or the type used for skiing), perhaps an extra pair of stockings and some form of headwear (woollen pom-pom hat or cloth cap). Many experienced cyclists like to use, even in the summer, a pair of cycling mitts (similar to car drivers' fingerless gloves), which prevent your hands slipping on the handlebars and also protect the hands if you should fall.

Wet-weather wear depends upon your personal preference. A long, plastic cycling cape plus leggings and hat gives the greatest protection, but they can be awkward to ride in when it is windy. An alternative is a short, jacket-like plastic cape, mainly used for racing. See Chapter 6 for more details.

In hot weather, it is dangerous not to wear some form of light headwear as protection against the sun. Similarly, apply sun tan oil or sun screen to arms, legs and face to prevent sunburn. There are few outdoor pursuits like cycling, in which you are out of doors for such long periods – the fresh air and exercise are, of course, two of the pastime's chief attractions. But you will get even greater enjoyment from it if your body is properly prepared.

You can prepare yourself for cycling by eating sensibly and keeping in good shape generally. Avoid fatty foods and excess sugar (confectionery, for instance), and reserve five or ten minutes each day for a routine of simple exercises (such as sit-ups, stretching and chin-ups). Do this and you will find that your cycling will improve – and so will your overall fitness and health. Cycling should be an integral part of your life-style, and whatever degree of proficiency you achieve will be a reflection of how much time and effort you put into it.

This French bicyclist presents a commendably smart appearance in his cold-weather cycling garb.

5

Maintenance & Repairs

One of the chief features of the modern bicycle shop is a small sign that is stuck in the window or behind the sales counter. It will read something like 'No repairs accepted', or 'Three weeks delay on repairs'. The reason for the notice and for the dealer turning away business, is that bicycle repairs are time-consuming. It is not an economical proposition to employ an experienced mechanic on routine repair work that is unlikely to show a profit – even if such a person can be found.

As a compromise, some bike shop managers allow you to do your own repairs on the premises using the shop's extensive range of tools. But even this service may be withdrawn when customers become too numerous or maybe damage or misplace the tools. Another little notice then appears: 'Tools will no longer be lent to customers'. It may be a short-sighted policy, but there is no sentiment of remembering 'the good old days' in a trade that is selling (and making handsome profits on) millions of bicycles each year.

The mechanics of a bicycle are basically simple. Repairs are logical, if sometimes laborious. But more importantly, maintenance is routine and not time-consuming. Prevention is very definitely better than cure when it comes to keeping a bike in good working order. And the time to learn this is as soon as you have acquired a new or second-hand bicycle.

Some manufacturers and big chain stores supply a small maintenance handbook with a new bicycle. This is a useful starting point for getting to know your bicycle. Further knowledge can be gained by reading books that deal with the subject in detail. But no theory can replace the practical work on your own machine, which should be regularly cleaned, checked over, adjusted and studied.

One of the first lessons to be learned is that you should never rush a job: allow yourself an hour for even a simple checking operation. Whether it is just cleaning the bike, replacing a cable or repairing a tyre, the job will inevitably take longer than you expect. The aim is to set up the bike in perfect adjustment ... and then to keep it that way by regular cleaning and maintenance.

If possible, you should work on your bike in a basement, shed or garage that has artificial lighting. Then, you will not try to rush a job when the daylight starts to fail. By working in a specially equipped environment you won't be interfering with other members of the household, nor will you be distracted by outside interference. And, if you have to break off from working, you can leave your bike and the dismantled parts ready for the next day.

It pays to be neat, logical and patient. Have small containers at hand to place loose ball bearings, clean cloths ready to keep you and the components clean of grease and grime and keep all your tools in a special box or drawer. Sometimes, you won't have the correct tool or part to complete a repair and if this happens, it will mean another trip to the bike shop.

Then, you will have to make a decision on whether to complete the job yourself or to ask the dealer to do it. And the answer to that could depend on the attitude of your particular dealer. Maybe there will be one of those little signs in the window: 'No repairs accepted' . . .

Regular maintenance

There are no set rules about how often you should carry out a full maintenance check on your bike. In the Tour de France, for example, team mechanics have to wash, strip down and re-assemble ten bikes every night for almost a month. That's because the professional racers are on their machines for up to seven hours non-stop every day, racing through all weathers and over mountain passes as high as 2,700 m (9,000 ft). A faulty gear or a broken cable could spell disaster – a crash over a precipice or, at best, the loss of a few minutes of all-important time. Either could result in a big loss in the rider's, and the team's, income.

An experienced mechanic at work in a specialist bicycle shop.

In contrast, your daily ride to the local train station, for example, is not a matter of life and death; but a breakdown causing you to miss your commuter train may be equally important in the context of your daily life. It's not suggested that you service your bike as regularly as the Tour de France mechanic, but the oil can and a cleaning cloth should be used at least once a week to keep things running smoothly, as well as looking good. And it's a sensible habit to make a quick check of the tyres at the end of every ride – a small piece of glass in the tread could mean a flat tyre in the morning.

You should make a more comprehensive check of the bicycle at regular intervals (say six times a year), particularly after a period of wet weather or before a long tour. Don't leave this major service until the night before you want to use the bike. Do it a couple of days before so that you can give the bike a short road test to pinpoint any remaining gremlins. This is vitally important if you have fitted any special accessories, such as a new luggage rack or panniers.

A full list of recommended tools appears later in this chapter, but it is not suggested that all these should be bought before you venture into the world of bicycle mechanics. Almost certainly, you will acquire specialist tools only when the time comes to carry out a repair that would be impossible without that tool. For your regular maintenance, you will require little more than the tools that find their way into most homes: adjustable spanner(s) (US: wrenches), screwdriver(s), pliers, wire cutters, hammer, punch, scissors and metal file. If you have a bench and vice (vise), so much the better.

With a new bike, you may be given a multi-purpose spanner (wrench) that fits most of the nuts and bolts on the bike, including bottom bracket locking ring and pedals. New pedals are sometimes supplied with a tool for removing the end dust cap. Among the items you should buy from the bike shop are a set of metric spanners (wrenches) and Allen keys, alloy tyre levers (tire irons) for wired-on tyres, puncture repair outfit (plus needle and thread for tubulars) and, if you have derailleur gears, a chain rivet extractor and freewheel remover. Cotterless cranks require a special spanner/extractor for tightening bolts and removing cranks – this tool's design depends on the brand of crankset fitted.

With your tools assembled and cloth, grease and oil can handy, you are ready to start work. It is possible to buy a bike stand, as used by professional mechanics, to firmly hold the frame at a convenient working height, but it is an expensive convenience. It is more usual to turn the bike upside down and stand it on a large area of cloth, sacking or plastic sheet, perhaps supporting the handlebars with a shoe box that has slots cut in the sides. If you

want to work on the bike right way up, hang it from, say, a roof beam by means of ropes or cables hooked under the two ends of the top tube.

For this example, let us assume that it is a 10-speed bike without mudguards. The sequence of maintenance operations is basically the same for any machine, although much simpler for bicycles fitted with a single- or hub-gear (only one chainwheel and one sprocket). You will have been riding the bike, and you will know whether you have worn brake blocks, frayed handlebar tape or perhaps a tyre that needs replacing. So before starting, remember to buy any new parts required.

Your first operation is cleaning the bike. The wheels are best cleaned separately; to remove them, push both gear levers forward so the chain is on the small sprocket and inside chainwheel. The rear wheel is removed by undoing the hub quick-release (or by

For trouble-free action, a rear derailleur should be kept in proper adjustment and fitted neatly. This classic Campagnolo gear mechanism features a flexible alloy outer cable and a plastic cover to prevent the inner cable end from fraying. The two sprung adjusting bolts are seen clearly.

Holding back the rear derailleur arm to release the rear wheel.

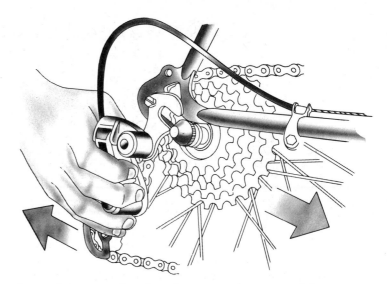

Disconnecting the hub gear cable

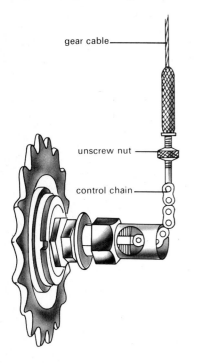

gear cable

unscrew nut

control chain

Right: *Mass production of bicycles began in the late 1890s, when many small manufacturers were bought out by their more progressive rivals. This print depicts frame building at a large American factory during this period.*

unscrewing wing nuts by hand, or track nuts with a spanner or wrench) and pulling the wheel forward while holding back the rear derailleur arm. Remove the front wheel by releasing its quick-release lever, wing nuts or track nuts. Put the wheels together on one side. (For hub gears, you will first have to disconnect the gear cable from the control chain before removing the rear wheel.) Using the chain rivet extractor (page 122), remove the chain and place it on a sheet of newspaper or hang it from a nail, out of your way. (For hub gears, prise off the clip on the spring link to remove the chain.)

It is also advisable to remove the brakes. First undo the cable locking nuts with a small metric spanner (wrench) for side-pull mechanisms, or press the brake blocks together to release cable loops for centre-pull. Another metric spanner (wrench) will undo the nut of the pivot bolt, front and rear. Don't lose any of the shaped seating washers or nuts when lifting off the brake mechanisms, and replace them on the bolt before putting the brakes to one side.

Now the washing operation can start. If the bike is really filthy, the first stage is best done with warm, soapy water and a large sponge or cloth. Have a small bucket or bowl of water ready, with a couple of squirts of dish-washing liquid mixed in. This should help disperse any grease that has attached itself to the frame and chainwheels. Wash everything (except saddle and handlebars, which can wait), not forgetting the previously removed brakes and wheels. If you have been more conscientious and have cleaned your bike after every ride, you will need to give it just a once-over wipe with a damp cloth at this stage.

Particular attention should be paid to the handlebars and saddle.

If you have cotton handlebar tape, this can be cleaned with a small scrubbing brush: it's surprising how much grease and oil congregates on the 'bars. Plastic tape is best cleaned with a soft cloth and spirit. If fabric tape has started to fray, this can be taken care of with a pair of scissors. To retape the 'bars, see the detailed instructions later in this chapter.

Leather saddles can be washed, underneath as well as on top, and a light coat of dressing, such as Brooks' Proofide, should be applied while it is still damp. If the leather is particularly dry, apply one or two further coats later on, but don't forget to buff up the top surface before riding. Plastic saddles require only a wipe over with a soapy cloth (not forgetting underneath), and a suede covering can be smartened up with a light, preferably nylon-tufted, suede brush.

A clean, damp cloth should now be used to wipe over the frame and other parts previously washed with soapy water. If there is any rust or oxide on the components (including the wheels and brakes), it is best to use a mild metal cleaner to remove it – but check that the cleaner won't corrode the metal. Next use a metal polish on the frame and other metal parts. I prefer a wadding-type polish which a clean cloth will buff up to an impeccable finish.

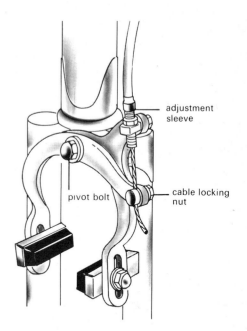

adjustment sleeve

pivot bolt

cable locking nut

Loosen the cable locking nut to release side-pull brakes.

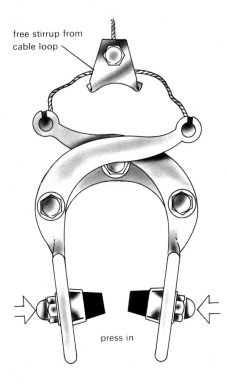

free stirrup from cable loop

press in

Releasing centre-pull brakes with the wheel loosened.

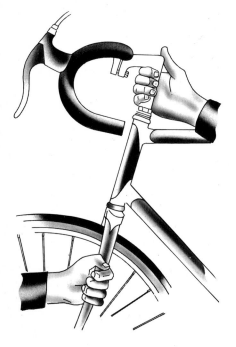

Checking the headset.

Before continuing, wipe the grime from your hands using a petroleum-based cleaner. You can now check over the bike without leaving greasy fingerprints everywhere. First, check the headset by holding the front forks with one hand and the stem with the other: there should be no rocking movement backwards and forwards. If there is, the upper ball race will need tightening (page 100). Also turn the forks to check for any tightness – a tight spot could mean the ball races or bearings need replacing.

A similar set of checks should be made on the bottom bracket. Is there any play when you hold the two cranks and try to rock them laterally? Are there any tight spots when the cranks are spun? Again, the first adjustment should be to undo the locking ring on the side opposite the chainwheels and slightly tighten (or loosen) the adjustable cup by hand. Then retighten the locking ring (see under 'bottom bracket', page 104).

With the appropriate Allen keys and spanners (wrenches), check the tightness of all main bolts and nuts including crank bolts (or cotter pins), chainwheels, derailleur bolts, seat pillar and handlebar stem. Also check that the pedals are tight, remembering that the one on the left-hand side of the bike has a left-handed thread.

When you have finished cleaning and polishing the wheels, which can be a particularly tedious but rewarding task, lift each one in turn holding it by the axle ends. Then spin the wheels to check for any tightness in the hubs. To adjust the hub bearings, use two extra-thin cone spanners (wrenches), making fine adjustment by hand once the lock nut is freed. With the wheels still out, closely inspect the treads of the tyres, looking for any slits or bulges. A slit on the cover of a wired-on tyre can normally be repaired by affixing a patch on the inside, but a bulge on the side wall generally means a replacement is necessary. As for tubulars, it is sometimes possible to extend their lives by inserting a tread-stopping compound in any nicks found in the tread.

If you find one of the wheels is buckled, check the spokes for possible breakages and also for slackness. It is advisable to take a badly buckled wheel to a competent wheel-builder rather than risk making a mess of the job yourself. But if a buckle is apparent where there is slackness on one side of the wheel, you can be almost certain that it can be trued up by tightening the appropriate spokes with a nipple key (also called a spoke spanner or spoke wrench).

With the brakes already off the bike, it is possible to clean and polish them thoroughly. If the brake blocks are worn, replace them (page 114). You may consider improving your bike's braking ability by fitting completely different blocks – chrome leather ones if you have chromed steel rims; soft rubber, patterned blocks (usually red)

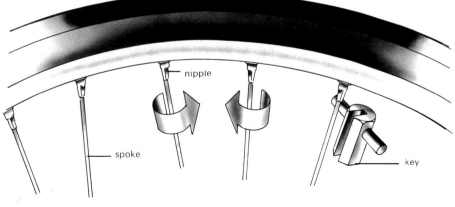

nipple

spoke

key

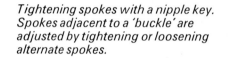

Tightening spokes with a nipple key. Spokes adjacent to a 'buckle' are adjusted by tightening or loosening alternate spokes.

if you have alloy rims; or the extra-long, profiled shoes and blocks as marketed by Mathauser, which can be bought to fit any rim size.

Replace both wheels in the frame and refix the brakes, remembering not to overtighten the lock nuts. With both items in place, you can fix the brake blocks in correct alignment: just the slightest of gaps between each block and the rim, and the blocks making 100 per cent contact with the rim when the brakes are applied. To achieve this, it may be necessary to adjust the length of cables with the barrel adjuster (see page 116) as well as to position the blocks accurately.

Before replacing the chain, inspect the jockey wheels of the rear derailleur mechanism. If they feel loose, with considerable up and down play on them, it is possible to adjust them slightly (by tightening their cones) if they are of the ball bearing variety. If not, make a mental note to buy replacement jockey wheels as soon as possible. The chain itself – unless it is stretched or has loose rivets and needs replacing – should be cleaned with paraffin (kerosene) and an old tooth-brush. This is the best combination for removing all the accumulated grease and grit. An alternative is to soak the chain in a tray of paraffin (kerosene), and then hang it up to drip dry, but this second method can destroy all the chain's lubricants and reduce its effective life.

When ready, refit the chain by threading it through the rear derailleur and around the inner chainwheel. When you have rejoined it with the rivet extractor, check that there are no stiff links (they can be freed by use of the second notch on the extractor tool) and then lubricate it with a very light coating of oil. Use a special cycle oil, or a thin, general-use oil. This should also be used to lubricate (sparingly) the derailleur jockey wheels, the freewheel, brake pivots,

Testing the bottom bracket for lateral movement.

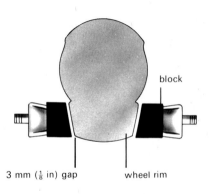

block

3 mm ($\frac{1}{8}$ in) gap   wheel rim

Correct position for the brake blocks.

95

brake levers and exposed sections of gear and brake cables. (For single or hub gears, refit the chain, using the spring link and pushing into place the locking clip. A few spots of thin, high quality oil is sufficient to lubricate a hub gear.)

Before taking the bike down from its supports, or while it is standing upside down, run through the gears while turning the cranks. If the derailleurs do not shift the chain cleanly onto the outer sprockets or chainwheels, then adjust the appropriate stop screws on the front and rear mechanisms. Next, put the bike back on the ground. Test the brakes one at a time, to confirm that the blocks are still correctly aligned with the rims. Give the frame and metal components a last polish with a dry cloth. Then, check the pressure in the tyres and, finally, go for a short test ride.

If you are ever in any doubt about a certain repair, then get some expert advice before you proceed. Similarly, if you don't have the correct tool for a job, wait until you can get it. It is not worth risking a thread being stripped or, say, a pedal being forced into a crank at the wrong angle.

However, don't expect every job to go as smoothly as the textbook. It is sometimes necessary to use penetrating oil to ease off a stubborn nut. And, however good your preparations, you will sometimes lose a vital screw, washer or nut. To finish the job you may have to use temporarily something that is not quite the correct size. It is therefore always helpful to keep a special container for bits and pieces that some day may come in useful.

From these regular maintenance sessions will emerge the need to carry out more complex repairs or complete replacement of certain parts. Never be afraid to tackle a new job once you have gained sufficient experience in bicycle maintenance. Just remember three basic rules: be prepared (with the correct parts and tools); be methodical; and be patient (it never pays to rush).

Service and repair
It is the aim of regular maintenance to prevent serious trouble before it materializes. However, components will inevitably wear out with constant use. As you get to know your bike you will also get experienced at spotting the tell-tale signs – such as a bulging tyre, a slack chain or a clicking pedal. Sometimes, it will be possible to repair the damaged item. In other cases, complete replacement will be necessary. For you to decide what to do – to repair or replace – you will need to know how to dismantle the item, how it works and how it was made: only then will you be able to decide which course of action is best. And when you have decided, you will want to know how to effect the operation.

Correct route for the chain through the rear derailleur.

On the following pages you will find a run-down on all the major components that make up the modern bicycle, starting with the frame and working through to optional accessories. These details are complementary to the description of components given in Chapter 3, which should be read in conjunction with this section. (Please note that 'left-hand' and 'right-hand' refer to when both rider and bike are facing forward.)

Frame

The frame tubes and forks have no moving parts, so it would seem that there is little to wear out or to replace. But breakages do sometimes occur, perhaps due to metal fatigue or poor workmanship. A frame, particularly the forks, absorbs most of the vibration caused by an irregular road surface. This includes the occasional, massive stress caused by riding over a deep hole or unexpected bump. These forces are accentuated where the frame is weakened – by a dent or by corrosion.

Water can get inside the frame's tubes at various points. The most common ingress is at the top of the seat tube. This is open to the atmosphere when a conventional seat post and clip is used, but the problem can be solved by plugging the top of the post with a piece of wood or a handlebar end stop (rubber or plastic). This should be fitted before fixing the saddle.

Some modern seat posts (or pillars) are fluted down the sides. This was initially done as a weight-saving device, but it resulted in water entering the frame via the flutes. Consequently, this fluting now stops well short of the base of the post. Water can still trickle down, however, if the post is fitted too far down the seat tube. The answer is to avoid this type of seat post unless you have a well-established riding position, which is not going to require major adjustment.

Another place where water can ingress is at the bottom bracket. Certain racing frames have weight-saving slots cut out from the base of the bottom bracket shell. If so, there should be a protective shield fitted inside the bottom bracket. Other frames have a lubrication point positioned in the bottom bracket shell to facilitate regular oiling from outside. However, most bracket bearings nowadays are fitted with grease and the lubricator is redundant or missing. Again, the resulting hole should be plugged, perhaps with a blob of hard-setting epoxy glue. In any case, when a bottom bracket unit is being replaced, the insides of the frame tubes should be inspected and any dampness or corrosion removed.

The last place where corrosion is possible is inside the fork tube. Most frames have a hole under the fork crown where the front

Seat post can be plugged before fitting the saddle.

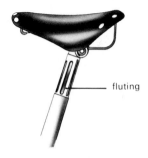

fluting

Seat post flutes should not extend below the top of the seat tube.

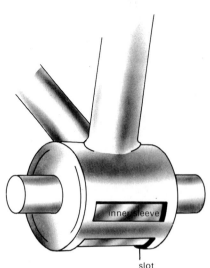

inner sleeve

slot

A slotted bottom bracket shell should have a protective inner sleeve.

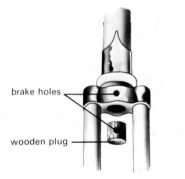

brake holes

wooden plug

Inserting a wooden plug into the fork tube.

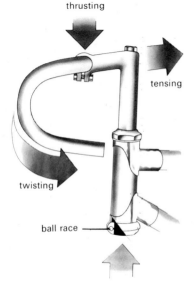

thrusting

tensing

twisting

ball race

Forces on the headset ball race.

Assembling the headset.

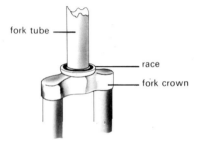

fork tube

race

fork crown

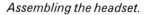

Bed down the fork crown race.

brake is mounted. Spray off the front tyre will find its way through this hole and up into the fork tube. The traditional, continental method of filling this hole is (before fitting the brake) to insert a short length of broom stick or appropriately sized dowelling. This should sit tight in the tube and it has to be drilled through the brake holes before fitting the brake. Many experts think that this wooden plug gives invaluable extra support for the brake, and helps reduce 'juddering' when braking hard.

However well you care for your bike, keeping the frame clean and polished, it is inevitable that the paintwork will get scratched or chipped. Such marks should be carefully painted over with hard-setting enamel paint of the same shade as the frame. Never allow them to become rusty – as this will be a source of weakness as well as being unsightly. An exception to this general rule is the area of paint in contact with the cones on each side of the wheel hubs. Here, the paintwork needs to be broken so that the hub axles are held firmly in the frame, so remember to keep the fork ends clean and dry.

When fitting new wheels, you may find that there is not sufficient width between the rear drop-outs or fork ends to accommodate the new hubs. Do not attempt to force the frame apart to accept a wider hub as the width can probably be reduced by removal of a packing washer. But it is best to check with an experienced mechanic and avoid any permanent damage to the frame.

Headset

The headset fixes the front forks into the frame's head tube. It comprises two head races, fitted to each end of the head tube and incorporating ball bearings that allow the forks to be turned smoothly. Precise fitting and correct adjustment of the headset bearings is essential if this component is to have a long life. The headset ensures a firm joint between the front forks and the rest of the frame, but must also allow smooth steering. There are no constant rotational forces (to which bearings in the bottom bracket and hubs are subject) so there are few frictional forces to cause wear. But there are considerable compression forces transmitted up the forks and, if the adjustment is too loose, there are resultant lateral forces. These are the ones that can cause pitting of the head races.

If the head races are tightened too much, the compressive forces will cause wear when the forks are turned. This wear can be made worse by the tensional and torsional forces imposed by the rider pulling and twisting on the handlebars. There is also an additional downward thrust caused by the weight of the rider when riding uphill out of the saddle. On a traditional, unsealed headset the wearing process of these forces is accentuated by dust and water working their way into the ball races. This ingress is resisted by correct adjustment and by the grease packed round the bearings. But too much grease will attract grit. Most of these problems are eliminated by use of a modern sealed headset unit which, in theory, should never need replacing. In fact, one recently developed headset (by Avocet) is guaranteed for life. This unit uses cylindrical bearings in place of balls.

When buying a headset – as with all parts that fit into frame tubes – check whether your frame has English, Italian or French threads. They all have slightly different dimensions. Using the wrong one could strip the thread on the fork tube. Whenever the headset has to be dismantled, always put a wide cloth or newspaper underneath to catch any loose ball bearings. Take apart each race separately, keeping the fork tube held in the head tube. This way you can extract, count and place in a container, each set of ball bearings separately. You will then know how many ball bearings to put back when you reassemble the headset. The number of ball bearings will vary with different makes of headset assembly and different sizes of tubing. You will require an extra-wide adjustable spanner (wrench), probably a 300 mm (12 in) one, to undo the locking ring of the upper end of the headset assembly. The ball races can all be unscrewed by hand, except those which are force-fitted into the tube ends.

Whether the headset is sealed or has conventional bearings, fitting is basically the same. Even if you never venture into taking your headset apart and replacing it, it is necessary to know the set-up so that regular adjustment can be made properly. Starting with bare head tube and forks, slide the fork crown race over the fork tube and bed down squarely. Next, push the head races into the top and bottom of the head tube. These may have to be bedded down by placing a wooden block over the end and tapping gently with a hammer. Lightly grease the races and place the ball bearings (or caged ball race) around the fork crown race. Slide the fork tube carefully into the head tube and marry the two lower races, making certain that no loose ball bearings drop out. Place the upper bearings on the lightly greased head race and bed down. Slide the adjustable head race over the protruding fork tube, carefully positioning it at the top of the thread before screwing it onto the fork tube. Make sure that the threads are married as it is easy to strip threads with large diameters. The threads should be lightly greased to facilitate ease of removal. Don't tighten the race completely, wait for adjustment.

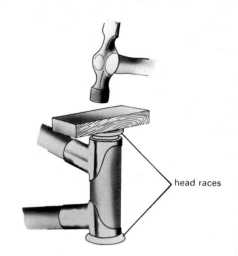

Bed down the head races.

Place the bearings on the head race. Slide the fork tube gently into the head tube.

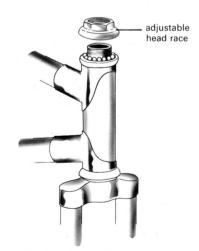

Place the bearings in the crown race.

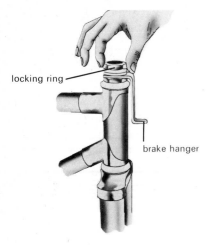

Screw the locking ring on by hand before final adjustment.

Slide the packing washer (or brake hanger for centre-pull brakes) over the fork tube and bed down squarely on the adjustable race. Then take the locking ring and carefully screw it on to the fork tube by hand. The headset is now ready for final adjustment. The adjustable race must not be too loose or too tight. Screw it down by hand until tight, then unscrew by about a quarter turn. Check that there is no slack by trying to rock the forks. Keep hold of the adjustable race and screw down the locking ring, first by hand and then using the spanner (wrench). Be careful not to overtighten with a long-handled spanner (wrench).

The headset is correctly adjusted when the forks will turn smoothly around the full 360 degrees (no brakes or handlebars yet fitted) and when there is no slack when the forks are rocked forward and back. It is difficult to get this right the first time and, after using the bike a few times, you may find that it has worked loose. One way to combat this is to screw the adjustable race down tight by hand, then to tighten the locking ring and finally to slacken off the adjustable race. In effect you are screwing the adjustable race up towards the locking ring, but this remedy is successful nine times out of ten.

Bottom bracket

The mechanical efficiency of the bicycle depends largely on the bottom bracket smoothly converting downward pedal thrusts into forward motion. There are three aims in the maintenance of the bottom bracket: to eliminate lateral movement; to resist the compressive forces imposed by the cranks; and to eliminate friction between the bearings and the bottom bracket axle.

A vital factor in preventing lateral movement is frame stiffness. On many, cheaper, frames there is excessive 'whip' (as this lateral movement is termed) caused at high speeds – when the stresses are at a maximum. This is one reason why a racing bicycle requires a stiffer frame than one used for touring or utility riding.

The aim of the proficient cyclist is to impose a constant pedalling force at right angles to the cranks. But, inevitably, a bad riding position or jerky pedalling will cause much of the pedal thrust (as well as the weight of the cyclist) to be taken directly down the cranks. These alternate forces – first down one crank, then the other – impose bending moments along the axle that have to be absorbed by the bearings and the cups of the bottom bracket. Again, these forces will be magnified by poor adjustment of the cups.

Friction is the main cause of wear in the bottom bracket – cups, axle and bearings – especially if the unit is not lubricated correctly and regularly. Most bikes have the bracket bearings seated on

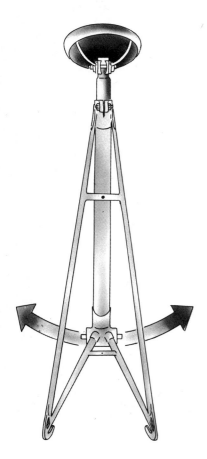

Frame 'whip'.

grease, which both reduces friction and prevents water and grit infiltrating from the outside but, to be effective, this grease has to be changed about once a year. Alternatives are sealed bottom brackets (which are expensive) or the heavy (and now little used) oil bath units.

The theory of a sealed unit is to prevent any intrusion of water or grit, either from the frame tubes or along the axle. It achieves this by very precise fitting, the close machine tolerances and use of high quality alloy dictating the higher cost. This unit includes (as does an oil bath unit) a metal sleeve which fits inside the bottom shell.

In an oil bath unit, the bearings and axle are immersed permanently in oil, which discourages the ingress of unwanted pollutants. This is maintained by regular topping up of the oil via the lubricating point, while the sealed unit should be maintenance free. If either of these units needs closer attention, any such work should be performed by an experienced mechanic or the unit should be returned to the manufacturer. But let us return to the more common, adjustable bottom bracket.

Assuming that both cranks have been removed (see next section), the first move is to loosen the locking ring on the left-hand side of the bracket. This has a notched circumference and should be undone with a C-shaped spanner (wrench), which encircles the ring and engages with one of the notches. In the absence of such a tool, it is possible to loosen the locking ring by placing a flat-ended punch at an angle to the side of a notch and tapping gently with a hammer.

With the locking ring removed (it has a normal, right-handed thread), loosen the adjustable threaded cup using a peg spanner (wrench). This has short projections that engage with two of the round indentations in the cup's outer face. Again, a punch (pointed this time) and hammer can be used, but with the greatest care, as there is danger of damaging the notches or indentations, and also of causing damage to the cups and bearings.

Before unscrewing the adjustable cup, make sure there is a cloth or newspaper ready to catch the ball bearings and then tilt the frame to the left. Keep hold of the axle where it emerges from the right-hand, fixed cup while you remove the adjustable cup and bearings. Now, pull the axle out from the left-hand side, being sure to catch the bearings that will follow. Remove the last of the bearings left in the bracket, then clean the inside of the still fixed right-hand cup with paraffin (kerosene).

Inspect the fixed cup (still in position), by shining a lamp through from the open side of the bottom bracket shell. If there are signs of corrosion or 'pitting', it will have to be replaced. (It usually has a left-handed thread but some European makes are right-handed.) It

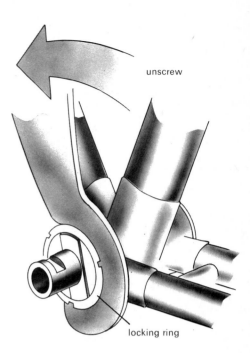

Loosening the locking ring with a C-spanner (wrench).

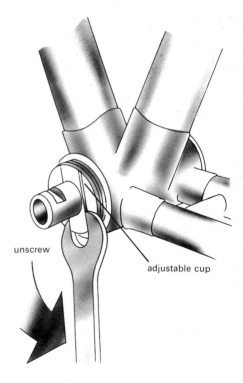

Unscrewing the adjustable cup.

101

should be removed using the correct spanner (wrench): possibly a peg type unless it has flats on the edge to accept a wide, adjustable type.

The adjustable cup, axle and ball bearings should also be closely inspected after cleaning. The balls and the tracks made by them in the cups and on the axle should be bright and unpitted. If just a few of the ball bearings are corroded or pitted, then replace the whole set. Mixing old (worn) and new bearings would cause unequal distribution of stresses, which would increase the likelihood of pitting. Similarly, if it appears that just one cup is unusable, both cups should be replaced.

When buying replacement parts for the bottom bracket, take the old parts with you so that the shop assistant can check that the new ones are of the right dimension: cups should have the correct threading (English, French or Italian), axles should be of the right length (a double chainwheel needs a longer axle than a single one), ball bearings should be of the correct diameter (probably 6.5 mm, ¼ in), and you should have the right quantity (the same number as you took out). An alternative is caged ball races, which are ready mounted and spaced.

Assembling a bottom bracket from scratch is straightforward, but must not be rushed. First check that the inside of the shell is perfectly clean and dry, and then smear a thin layer of grease over the threads inside the frame. Using a high quality light grease, spread a thick layer inside each of the bottom bracket cups, making sure there is an even covering.

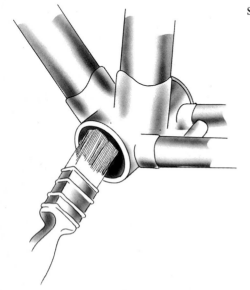

Cleaning inside the bottom bracket shell.

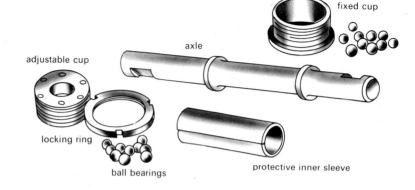

Bottom bracket assembly.

Next, take the fixed, right-hand side cup in your hand and screw it carefully into position, remembering which way it is threaded. The large diameter and the fineness of the threading make it dangerously easy to cross-thread the cup, so make sure you are in the correct groove before tightening. Screw it in with your hand, and tighten it with an adjustable or peg spanner (wrench) on the last few turns. It should bed down perfectly flat against the frame.

The correct number of ball bearings (of the right diameter) should be placed, using your fingers, into the fixed cup; with caged bearings, wait until you insert the axle before placing them. The cage is simply slipped over the right-hand end of the axle and bedded down onto the curved, raised ball race. If used, the cylindrical protective sleeve should now be inserted to sit snugly inside the bottom bracket shell.

To get the axle to slide into position correctly, hold it with one hand while inserting a finger from the other hand into the fixed cup from the outside. This finger will guide the axle through without dislodging any of the ball bearings. Make sure that the long end of the axle goes in first.

The other set of bearings should now be placed in the well-greased adjustable cup (or the second caged race slipped over the opposite end of the axle). Then hold the axle in place with one hand, using the other to screw into place the (right-hand threaded) adjustable cup. Again, beware of cross-threading and do not force the cup into place with a spanner (wrench). If possible, use only your hand to screw the left-hand cup into position.

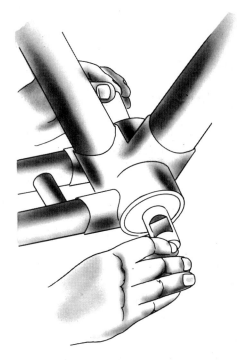

Guiding the axle through the fixed cup.

The bottom bracket assembly and crankset, located at the junction of the seat tube and down tube, are subject to considerable stress and require regular maintenance.

103

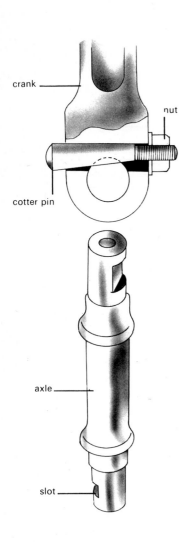

crank

nut

cotter pin

axle

slot

Cottered crankset, showing the axle in end cross-section (top) with the cotter pin in position.

Final adjustment of the bottom bracket takes place with the fixed cup bedded down, the adjustable cup hand tight and the locking ring (right-handed thread) screwed into position. The adjustable cup should be screwed in or out until there is just the slightest lateral play (movement) in the axle, which should rotate easily. Now, hold the cup in this position with a peg spanner (wrench), and fully tighten the locking ring, first by hand and then with a C-shaped spanner (wrench).

If the axle does not turn freely, or if there is excessive lateral play, slacken off the locking ring and try again. Always tighten the locking ring before checking the adjustment. Once you are satisfied that everything is correctly spaced and tightened, you can continue to fix the cranks, chainwheels and pedals into place. However, check the bottom bracket again after a test ride (and subsequent outings) until you are certain that everything has bedded down permanently.

Cranks and chainwheels

The majority of bicycles have the cranks fixed by cotter pins, which are short lengths of cylindrical steel, threaded at one end and with one side flattened into a wedge shape. If the crank is to fit squarely onto the bottom bracket axle, the cotter pins must fit perfectly into the slots formed on each end of the axle.

It is because of the inexactness of cotter pins that most serious cyclists use cotterless cranks. These are either of a square or splined pattern and should always fit squarely. The appropriately shaped ends of the axle fit directly into holes machined in the cranks, and are fixed by bolts screwing into the axle. This should result in an homogeneous joint that cannot cause wear to the axle ends or cranks.

The less common one-piece cranks combine both crank arms and a bottom bracket axle, so adjustment is effected solely by tightening (or loosening) the bracket cups.

Cranks have to be removed whenever work has to be done on the bottom bracket assembly. For a cottered crankset, you will need a hammer (or wooden mallet), punch, spanner (wrench) and two blocks of wood. One of these should have a V-shaped notch about 8 cm (3 in) deep cut in its side. This block is placed under one crank, with the nut pointing upwards and the cranks horizontal. The crank should be evenly supported by the wooden block, with, perhaps, a brick to support the block itself.

The nut of the cotter pin should be undone using an appropriately sized spanner (wrench) and unscrewed until its top is flush with (but no higher than) the end of the cotter pin's threaded end. The pin itself can be loosened by now giving a smart blow to this end, using a wooden mallet or an intermediate block of wood to minimize the danger of damaging the threads. The nut should be removed and the extraction of the cotter pin completed by gentle use of a punch and hammer. Repeat for the other crank, making sure that the crank is again fully supported by the wooden block.

If the locking nuts on the pins should prove stubborn to remove, a few drops of penetrating oil may loosen the thread. If that fails, try using a long-armed ring spanner (wrench) to give extra leverage. Such problems can be avoided if grease is smeared on the cotter pin threads before fitting.

When the cranks are detached they should be checked for trueness against a straight edge. Bent cranks can be straightened by a qualified mechanic, but steel cottered cranks are relatively cheap and can be bought separately. Therefore replacement is the best answer. The new crank should, of course, be the same length as the old one.

To reassemble, first slide the cranks onto the axle with the cotter holes aligned with the axle slots. Each of the cotter pins should be pushed into its hole, ensuring that it is inserted in the right direction. This is such that when a crank is pointed vertically upwards the threaded end of the cotter pin should point backwards. If threads are damaged, then replace with a new pair of cotter pins.

If new cotter pins do not lie squarely in the hole, the remedy is to file down the flat side of the pin to the correct angle. Never grind the axle slot. This bedding angle can only be checked by fitting the washers and nuts and tightening the nuts sufficiently to pull the pin into contact with the axle slot. The assembly can continue if, when viewed from the side, the cranks are in the same line.

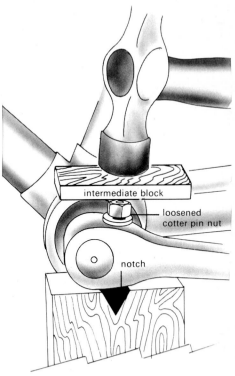

Removing the cotter pin.

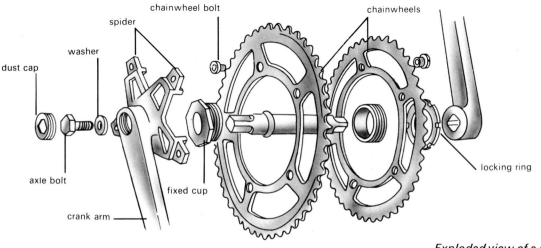

Exploded view of a cotterless crankset.

Removing cotterless cranks.

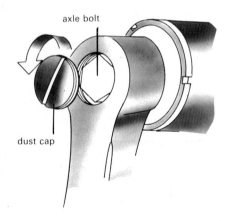

Unscrew the dust cap.

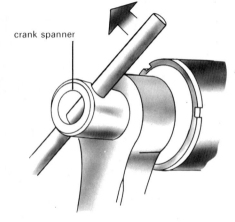

Unscrew the axle bolt.

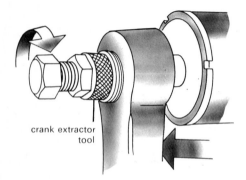

Insert the tool and screw in to remove the crank.

The notched wooden block should alternately support each crank as the cotter pins are driven home by sharp blows on the domed heads. (A wooden block and hammer should be used, as before.) The nuts can then be further tightened with a spanner (wrench), but not overtightened. A stripped cotter thread would mean starting the operation all over again. Again, the tightness of the cotter pins should be checked (and adjusted) after each of the next few bike rides.

Cotterless cranks are more straightforward, assuming that you have the correct crank extractor tool and spanner (wrench), which should come supplied with the crankset. The removal sequence begins with the unscrewing of the dust caps that cover the axle bolts. These bolts are removed using the spanner (wrench), while holding firm the opposite crank. Next, undo the inner part of the extractor tool as far as it will go and screw the outer barrel into the threads left by the dust cap. This should be screwed by hand into the crank as far as possible. Next, tighten down the inner bolt of the extractor tool, using the special spanner (wrench) supplied with the tool. This forces the crank off the axle. Repeat with the other crank.

When the cranks are off, check that there are no signs of cracking around the pedal holes or the axle holes. If there is, then the crank should be replaced – the danger of a crank snapping off is too big a risk. Also the cranks should be cleaned with spirit and thoroughly dried before reassembly.

To refit cotterless cranks, slip each one carefully onto the square- (or spline-) sectioned axle end to ensure that each is a perfect fit. The axle bolts (with washers) should then be screwed into their holes and the cranks clamped into place. It is not necessary to bed down the cranks by use of block and hammer.

Finally, screw in the two dust caps, placing a spot of grease on the threads before inserting. Again, check the cranks' tightness after road testing the bike. If a bicycle is used repeatedly with a loose crank, the crank could become permanently damaged, requiring replacement.

Regular checks on the trueness of chainwheels should also be made. This is straightforward for the normal steel cottered cranksets on which a single chainwheel is permanently fixed to the right hand crank. To check its trueness, turn the cranks slowly, noting the gap between the chain stays and the chainwheel throughout its revolution. It should not vary, but if the gap has a definite maximum and minimum mark these clearly.

The chainwheel can now be straightened, using a long-handled adjustable spanner, (wrench), by alternately pulling and pushing at the two marked points. This tool can also be used for straightening any bent teeth on the chainwheel.

A cotterless crankset usually has separate chainwheels (two for 10-speed derailleur gears) that bolt onto a three-, five- or six-legged 'spider', which is part of the right-hand crank. Removal of these chainwheels (or rings) is facilitated by unscrewing the three (five or six) bolts which are fitted into alloy sleeves. An Allen key is the usual tool required. Once the bolts are extracted, the rings can be lifted off, manipulating them over the spider and crank.

Refitting is the reverse of this last operation, then aligning the holes in the rings with the holes in the spider. Each bolt should be only partially tightened before bedding each down in rotation. Their tightness should be tested after each of your subsequent test rides.

Straightening teeth on a chainwheel.

Pedals

The pedals are perhaps the most abused components on the bicycle. They are subject to continual, irregular forces imposed by the rider's feet. Their working environment is close to the road surface, being exposed to persistent attacks by rain, dust, mud and salt. They may even receive hard blows from the side, caused by the bike falling over, or a pedal hitting the kerb when cornering. And yet they must still function efficiently, converting the downward thrusts of the cyclist into a smoothly turning motion.

Regular maintenance includes checks for lateral play (not too tight) and turning (no tight spots). If the pedal does not spin evenly, it could mean that its axle (the spindle) has been bent. This may demand replacement of the whole pedal, although a competent mechanic can sometimes straighten it. This involves stripping down the pedal; holding the crank in a vice; screwing in the bare spindle and cone; placing an appropriately sized piece of steel tubing over the cone and shoulder of the tapering spindle; and carefully removing the bend by gently pulling on the tube end.

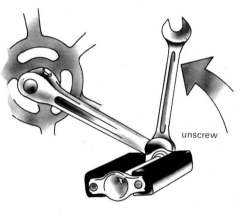

Removing a 'tight' right-hand pedal.

As with the bottom bracket, the bearings in the pedal must be re-greased at regular intervals, unless you have sealed units. This overhaul should take place every six months if the bike is used most days. First unscrew the pedals from the cranks, remembering that the left-hand one has a left-handed thread. If one is difficult to remove, turn the cranks until the 'difficult' one is pointing forward in a horizontal position. Place the spanner (wrench) on the flat of the pedal spindle so that you have to push it down towards the crank to unscrew the pedal. This way, it is possible to get more leverage. The bike should be on the ground for this purpose with the wheels fitted.

With the pedals removed, the ideal method for dismantling them is to have the spindle flat gripped in a bench vice. Otherwise, hold

Exploded view of a rat trap pedal.

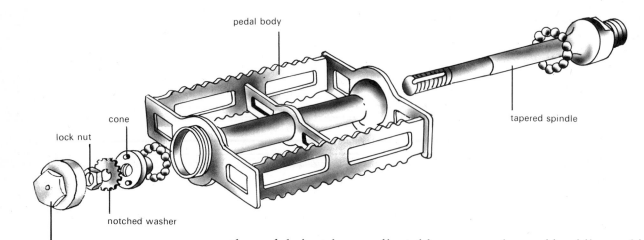

Exploded view of a rat trap pedal.

pedal body

tapered spindle

cone

lock nut

notched washer

dust cap

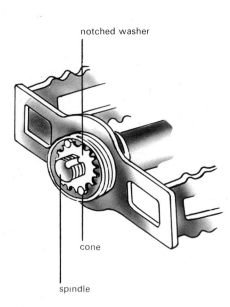

notched washer

cone

spindle

Notched washer engages with the cone and spindle notch.

the pedals in a large adjustable spanner (wrench) while working on them. (Remember to place a cloth underneath to catch the ball bearings.) The first thing to remove is the dust cap on the outer end of the pedal: this may require a special spanner which should be supplied with the pedal because some caps do not have conventional flats, but knurled rims. It could also be a push-on dust cap, which will have to be gently prised off.

It is normal for both dust caps to have a right-hand thread, as do the locking nuts, which are now exposed. Unscrew this nut, then lift off the shaped washer. This leaves you with the cone, under which are the ball bearings. So unscrew this carefully (right-hand thread), catching the balls and placing them in a small container.

Next, lift the main body of the pedal off the spindle, this time catching the ball bearings from the other side and placing them in a separate container. You are now left with just the tapered spindle. Clean this, as well as the cones, bearings, washers and nuts with paraffin (kerosene). Keep the different sets of ball bearings in separate containers. Check all parts for corrosion, pitting or cracking and the spindle for straightness. Replace all the balls if any are faulty.

To reassemble the pedal, first pack with grease the two ball cups (on each end of the pedal body) and place in the correct number of balls. Smear grease on the spindle and carefully slide it through the pedal barrel, taking care not to dislodge any balls. Now, screw on the cone hand-tight and slide on the washer. Some washers interlock with the cone, so carefully unscrew the cone until the notches line up. Then, screw on and tighten the locking nut. Check that the pedal turns freely. If not, undo the locking nut, slightly slacken off cone and then retighten the locking nut. Finally, refit the dust cap.

The fitting, or replacement, of toe clips can form another facet of the pedal's overhaul. Being made of light, aluminium alloy or spring steel, toe clips are liable to bending or cracking if mistreated. And, like the pedals, because they are close to the road surface they are also more prone to corrosion than most other components, so pay greater attention to keeping them dry and polished.

They are attached to the body of the pedal by one of two methods: with short bolts, washers, spacer and nuts fitted through the pedal's front plate; or, with the more expensive models, by bolts directly into bosses sunk into the front plate. To remove them, simply unscrew these bolts with the appropriate tools – Allen key, metric spanner (wrench) or screwdriver.

When refitting, it is essential that you have the right size of toe clip (short, medium or long) and that the loop for the toe strap is placed centrally above your shoe when it is squarely on the pedal. This is no problem with pedals such as the Campagnolo Strada as there is only one position for the toe clips, the correct one. Otherwise, fit the different parts in the correct order and screw the bolts hand-tight. You will now be able to slide the clip sideways until it locates centrally. Fully tighten when satisfied that it is central and, finally, thread in the toe straps.

Inserting a packing piece to lengthen a toe clip.

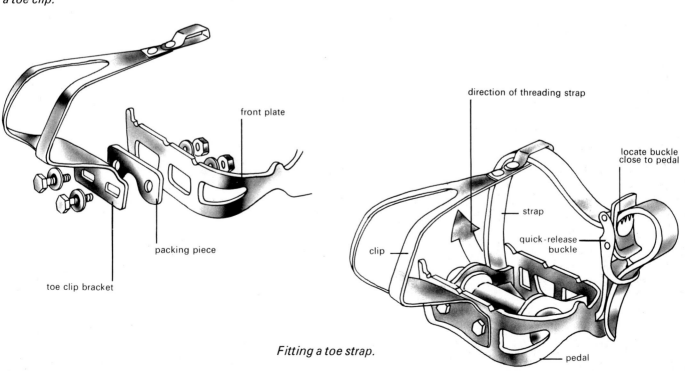

front plate

packing piece

toe clip bracket

direction of threading strap

locate buckle close to pedal

strap

quick-release buckle

clip

pedal

Fitting a toe strap.

If the longest toe clip is too small for your foot – there should be a gap of about 5–6 mm (¼ in) between the shoe end and the clip – it can be lengthened by inserting packing pieces. These should be placed between the front plate and the toe clip bracket, as shown,

When fitting a toe strap, start threading it through the outside plate of the pedal body, pulling through the strap until the buckle is as close to the pedal as possible. Continue threading under the pedal, up through the inner plate and finally through the top loop on the toe clip. Straps are often too long, flapping dangerously. If so, cut off the end of the strap and bind with two or three thicknesses of adhesive cotton tape.

The binding on the end of the strap will stop it slipping out of the buckle and also make it easier to grab when you want to tighten the strap. The chrome leather from which they are made should be kept supple by regular application of saddle polish. A dry, hardened toe strap is likely to snap if pulled at hurriedly. A spot of oil on the buckle pivot will ensure that the strap can be released quickly in an emergency.

Handlebars and stems

Being static, the stem and handlebars would appear to require little maintenance. But it is not unknown for handlebars to fracture – probably adjacent to the central bulge or ferrule – or for a stem to become jammed in the fork tube. It is therefore important to keep the 'bars clean so that any tell-tale cracking can be spotted before it gets dangerous. And a spot of oil inserted inside the fork tube, from below, should insure that the stem does not jam solid.

To release the stem, you loosen the expander bolt at the top (normal hexagonal head or recessed Allen fitting), unscrew it two or three turns. Gently tap the end of the bolt with a wooden mallet (or cushioned by a wood block) to release the expander bolt from the split end of the stem inside the frame. The stem (and handlebars) can now be pulled out of the fork tube, perhaps clamping the front wheel to the floor between your legs and pulling the 'bars upwards with a twisting motion.

When refitting the stem, smear some grease on the thread of the expander bolt to avoid 'jamming' problems. Some expander cones have two small projections which should be fitted into the slots of the stem's split end. This prevents the cone turning with the bolt.

The operation most frequently required is likely to be retaping of the handlebars. With constant use (and misuse), handlebar tape tends to fray (cotton variety), to wear thin and break (plastic) or to come loose and unwind itself. Never attempt to re-use old tape because it will have stretched, faded or distorted. Plastic tape can

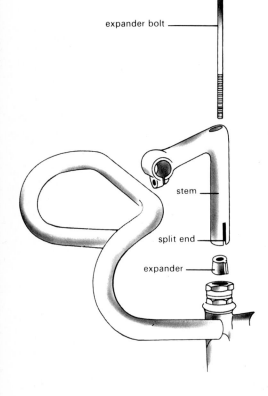

expander bolt

stem

split end

expander

Exploded view of handlebar stem.

easily be unwound, first removing the handlebar end plugs and slackening the brake levers. To remove adhesive cotton tape, it is sometimes necessary to cut it away by carefully making an incision the length of the 'bars with a craft knife or hooded razor. The tape can then be peeled off more easily.

If for some reason you have to change the stem or handlebars, you will have to remove all the tape and the brake levers. With any tape removed, you then loosen the bolt fixing the handlebars (hexagonal or Allen fitting) and pull the 'bars from one end through the end of the stem. It may be necessary to prize open this opening with a wide-headed screwdriver, once the bolt has been removed. Check that the bolt is not bent, or that its thread is not stripped, before re-using it. Replace if necessary, ensuring that the bolt's small projection slots into its gap in the stem head. Check that the handlebars are central with a measuring tape before retightening the bolt.

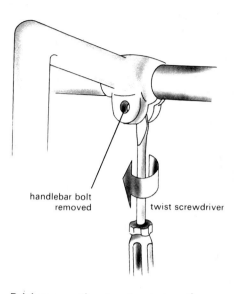

Prising open the stem to remove the handlebars.

There are a number of theories as to the best method of taping handlebars – do you use non-adhesive plastic or adhesive cotton tape? do you begin taping at the ends or the middle? do you cover the 'bars with one or two layers? You will find conflicting answers to these questions whether you read specialist books or listen to the advice of experienced cyclists. Plastic is easier to keep clean, but becomes slippery if lubricated by rain or sweat. Cotton tape is more difficult to clean, but provides a good grip, with or without cycling gloves. Final choice is dependent on your personal preference – but make sure that it is taped correctly, whether plastic or cotton.

Non-adhesive, plastic tape is thin and clings more tightly to the metal tube of the handlebars. Therefore, some cyclists find it more comfortable to have two thicknesses of tape. Before you begin, snip from the end three 6 cm (2½ in) lengths of tape and position them (with adhesive 'Sellotape' or 'Scotch' tape) on each side of the brake lever hoods where they meet the handlebars. This will prevent an unsightly gap between adjacent windings of tape. If your brake levers have rubber hoods, roll these back before you start taping. You will need a separate roll of tape for each side of the handlebars.

Start taping about 5 cm (2 in) from the edge of the stem, sticking the tape end to the metal with a short length of adhesive tape. Hold the roll firmly, keeping it about 10 cm (4 in) away from the handlebars. Keep the tape taut as you begin wrapping the plastic tightly around the bar, methodically overlapping each turn by about 5 mm (¼ in). Maintain this overlap on the outside of the curved sections; it will of course be much more of an overlap on the inside.

When reaching the brake lever hood, take the roll from the back of the bar at an angle to the base of the hood. Make one loop

Binding with non-adhesive tape:

Use adhesive tape to position the handlebar tape over the brake hood clamps. Start taping about 5cm (2in) from the stem. Keeping the tape taut, overlap each turn by about 5mm ($\frac{1}{4}$in). When you reach the brake hood clamp, take the roll up at an angle to the back of the bar. Make one loop around the clamp. Bring the roll down at an angle to the back of the bar. Make another loop to cover any gaps. Continue taping the bar to the end. Overlap the end by about 10cm (4in) to push inside the tube. Insert the end plug.

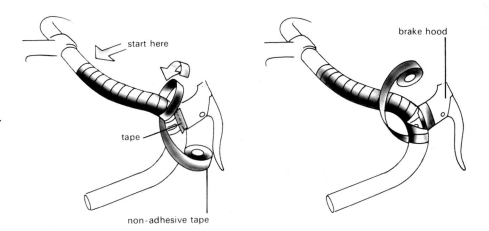

start here

tape

brake hood

non-adhesive tape

around the hood, then take the roll up at an angle to the back of the bar on the opposite side. Make a further turn around the bar, above the brake hood; then bring the tape down at an angle around the bar, pulling it firmly in a turn at the base before continuing with straightforward taping.

If there are any loose sections of tape, or if any metal shows through, undo the taping up to a point just above the defective part. Remind yourself to keep the tape taut the whole time and it will probably work out well at the second attempt. When reaching the end of the 'bars, leave about 10 cm (4 in) to push inside the tube before inserting the end plug.

End plugs are made of rubber or plastic. Slightly tapered, the rubber ones are pushed into the end with a screwing motion. Plastic plugs normally have a split end with an expander bolt that is tightened by a screwdriver from the outside. If you have handlebar-mounted gear control levers – which fix into the end of the 'bars – it is advisable to saw off about 5 cm (2 in) from the handlebar ends to compensate for the extra length of the levers. If you don't, there is a danger of banging your knees on the levers when pedalling out of the saddle.

With adhesive cotton tape, again snip off two lengths to stick either side of the brake lever hood, but begin taping from the handlebar end. By working upwards, the overlaps cause the edge of the tape to point outwards and downwards. This discourages the edge from folding over and fraying, which can happen if your hands are constantly pushing down on an exposed tape edge.

An alternative, if much more expensive, method of 'taping' the 'bars is with a soft leather sleeve. This slips onto, and around, the handlebar, being fitted loosely and then tightened by means of a draw-string. This is tied at the end and is pushed into the handlebar

A Brooks Professional 'Select' leather saddle in its presentation box.

end before inserting the end plug.

The reason for covering curved handlebars with tape is that they are likely to be gripped in various positions – on the drops, on the bend, above the brake hoods and on the top. The same does not apply to straight or upturned handlebars, where there is normally just one position for the hands. Then, plastic or rubber grips are all that are required. Such grips sometimes work loose and slide round when gripped. If so, pull them off and either roughen the surface of the metal and apply a hard setting adhesive, or increase the thickness of the bars with adhesive tape, before refitting the grips.

Saddle and seat post

The seat post (or pillar) is a cylindrical tube that is clamped into the seat tube of the frame by means of (a) a binder bolt and nut that pulls together the two sides of the split-ended seat tube, or (b) an Allen bolt set into the seat tube end, or (c) a metal clip around the top of the seat tube.

The saddle is clamped to the top of the seat post by a chunky metal clip and positioned by a square-section bolt with threaded ends. Or, if the saddle has a base with two steel wires, an adjustable seat post (or pillar) can be used. This incorporates an adjustable top clamp that holds the two wires in channels. Correct positioning of the saddle is discussed in the section on riding position in Chapter 4.

Most saddles incorporate an adjustable hexagonal nut that screws onto a long, threaded bolt under the nose of the saddle. If the saddle sags, then this nut should be tightened to restore the intended profile of the leather. If the saddle is hard and unyielding, slacken off the nut to provide more suppleness.

Leather saddles are normally fixed to a metal base plate by large, copper rivets. These rivets sometimes work loose. If so, remove the

When binding with adhesive tape, begin at the handlebar end.

Screwing on grips for straight handlebars.

113

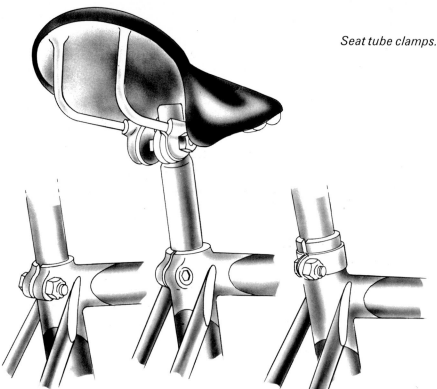

Seat tube clamps.

Binder bolt and nut.   *Allen bolt set into seat tube.*   *Metal clip and bolt.*

offending rivet completely and get a skilled mechanic or the manufacturer to fit a new one.

Brakes

When caliper or cantilever brakes are applied there are three different forces at work: tension in the brake cable caused by hand pressure on the lever; friction between the rim and brake block; and rotational forces on the brake pivots. Each force leads to both short and long term maintenance jobs. This principle applies equally to rim and hub brakes, except that the frictional forces for the latter are within the hub, between brake drum and pad. For disc brakes, the friction is between disc and brake pads.

The friction between rim and brake block of the caliper brake soon wears down the rubber (or chrome leather) of the brake blocks. To keep the blocks as close to the rim as possible, small adjustments can be made with the barrel adjuster. This is located where the cable is fitted to the brake arm (side-pull), fixed to the brake hanger (centre-pull) or on the brake's lever. First loosen the small locking nut, adjust the threaded barrel as necessary, and retighten the locking nut.

To replace the brake blocks, first let off any quick-release mechanism (a button on the lever or a cam on the barrel adjuster)

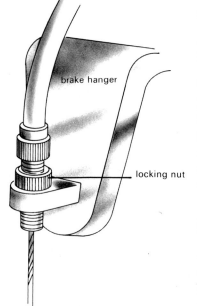

brake hanger

locking nut

Barrel adjuster.

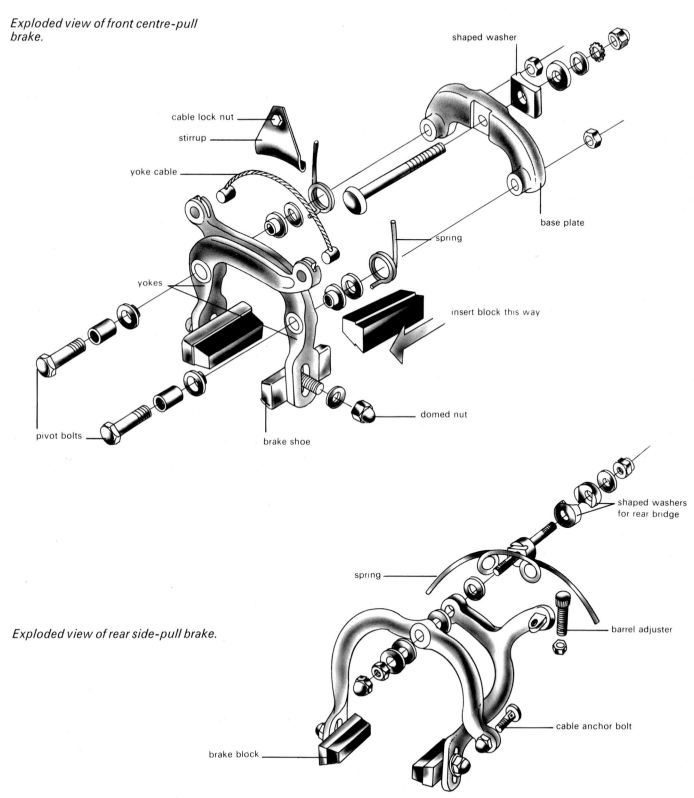

Exploded view of front centre-pull brake.

shaped washer

cable lock nut

stirrup

yoke cable

base plate

spring

yokes

insert block this way

pivot bolts

brake shoe

domed nut

Exploded view of rear side-pull brake.

shaped washers for rear bridge

spring

barrel adjuster

cable anchor bolt

brake block

115

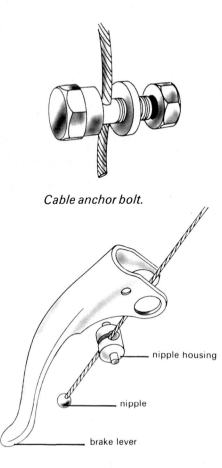

Cable anchor bolt.

nipple housing

nipple

brake lever

Brake lever cable housing.

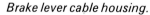

inner cable

outer cable

pivot

brake hood

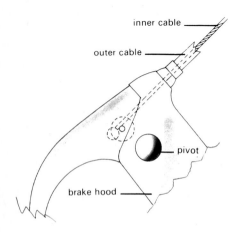

Lever with cable bedded down.

or release the cable completely on centre-pull brakes. This will relax the brake arms, bringing the brake shoes away from the rim. Next, unscrew the nuts (possibly domed) to slide out the brake shoes and blocks. The blocks can sometimes be pulled from the shoes by hand. If not, you can clamp the metal shoe in a vice and pull or push the block out with a pair of pliers; or, if you don't have a vice, use two pairs of pliers.

When refitting the shoes and blocks, check that the open end of the shoe is pointing backwards; otherwise, when the levers are pulled on, the rotating rim would pull the blocks from the shoes. If the brakes should 'squeal', the remedy is usually to angle the blocks to the rim by gently twisting the brake arm, so that the front end of the block engages with the rim marginally ahead of the rest of the block. Also ensure that the rims are always dry and clean, and that the blocks fully grip the side of the rim.

The other item likely to need frequent replacement is the brake cable. This is subject to both steady tensional forces when descending hills, and to sudden heavy stresses caused by hard braking. The result is a gradual stretching of the cable, and possible fraying where kinks may have developed (possibly at the cable's exit from the brake lever or next to the locking nut at the brake end).

The cable should be replaced before these tell-tale signs make it liable to snap unexpectedly. The infiltration of water between the inner cable and its cover will inevitably cause corrosion – hence the need for regular greasing.

To remove a cable, undo the locking nut with the appropriate metric spanner (wrench) and then release the other end from the brake lever. This end has a soldered nipple, which should be pushed away from its housing so that the cable can be pulled clear through the adjacent slot. You can now hold the cable at the nipple end and pull it from its outer cover. Check this cover for any kinks, and closely inspect the ends. If either end is pinched in, a new opening can be made by snipping off a few millimetres with a pair of wire cutters.

Kinks in the inner cable are more serious. They prevent the cable from operating smoothly and, in time, can erode some of the cable's strands. The best solution is to replace the outer casing, as well as the inner cable. It is easier to replace the cables on both brakes at the same time; if one needs replacing the chances are that it won't be long before the other does, as well. Check the cable clips (if used) at the same time and replace if there are signs of rust.

When refitting the cables, you have to decide which brake you connect with which brake lever. There have been moves in both Britain and the US to legislate that on all new bikes the front brake is operated by the right hand lever. I have found the opposite to be the preference of most experienced cyclists. The reason is that the right hand is constantly used for operating the gear levers. So the more effective front brake is best operated by the left hand.

Once you have made your choice, cut the new outer cover into the correct lengths by measuring against the old cover. If doing it from scratch, make sure that the cut lengths will provide long, sweeping curves for the cable. The rear cable is best housed in one long section from brake lever to brake mechanism. With centre-pull brakes, avoid making too tight a loop from the last cable clip (or brazed-on stop) on the top tube to the rear brake hanger. The top points of the two cables should be level where they loop up from the brake levers.

As you thread through the inner cable (from the lever end), smear it with grease. Any excess will congregate at the near end of the outer cable (cover), so don't worry about over-greasing. Once the cable is right through, fit the nipple into the lever slot, pull it up tight and bed down the outer cable into its housing on top of the lever hood.

For the next step, the help of a friend would be useful. The blocks must be held against the rim of the wheel as the cable is pulled taut through the lock nut and the nut tightened. If there is no one available, it is possible with practice to hold the blocks tight with one hand and tighten the nut with the other. Failing that, you may be able to use a 'third hand' tool, a C clamp or string. Final adjustments can then be made with the barrel adjuster.

The last operation with new cables is to snip off the ends with sharp wire cutters, leaving about 5 cm (2 in) for possible readjustments. The cut end of the inner cable can be soldered or fitted with a small nylon cap to discourage fraying.

It should rarely be necessary to completely dismantle the brakes. The most likely reason would be 'spongy' action of the brake mechanisms, which could be caused by a build-up of grease and grit (clean with spirit), a stretched cable or the spring being corroded or faulty (replace). If you have to do this, be methodical and remember the correct sequence of the parts as you dismantle it.

Wheels and freewheels

Building a wheel is perhaps as skilful as building a frame, and in each case the amateur should not contemplate doing the work of an expert. It is an art to lace up the spokes of a bicycle wheel and to tighten them to the right, even tension. Too tight, and the spokes will be overloaded, making them liable to breakage. Too loose, and the whole wheel is likely to collapse.

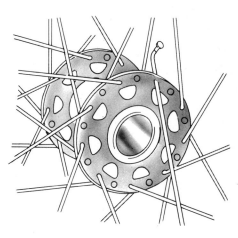

Removing a broken spoke from the hub.

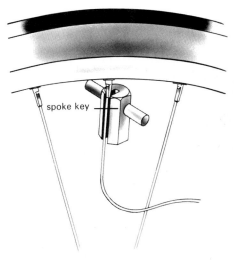

Removing a broken spoke from the rim.

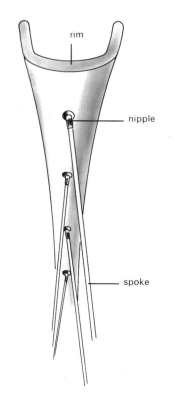

rim

nipple

spoke

Alternate spokes connect with opposite sides of the hub.

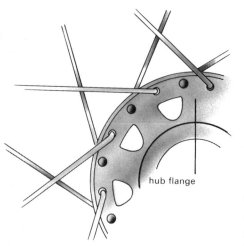

hub flange

A poorly built wheel is also an inefficient conductor of the rider's efforts into forward motion. Energy can be wasted through friction in the hub bearings as well as through incorrect spoke tensioning. Both of these tendencies are increased with heavier loading of the bike, which means that your wheels are going to need more frequent attention if you have a big build or if your bike is subject to carrying fully laden bags or panniers.

The jobs you will most likely be required to do are replacing broken spokes and regreasing the hubs. To remove a broken spoke is a simple operation. The part nearest the hub is held at right angles to the hub flange and then pushed out of the spoke hole. If this is on the right hand flange of the rear wheel, then it will be necessary to first remove the freewheel (see below).

It is possible to remove the other part of the spoke without taking the tyre from the rim. This is done by holding the nipple firm with the spoke key, then bending the broken end of the spoke, which is grasped tightly in your other hand. Keep hold of this end, pulling it away from the rim, and at the same time turning the spoke key (and nipple) clockwise. If the nipple is stuck – probably due to corrosion – then you will have to remove the tyre (and tube) and push out the spoke and nipple.

You will need a replacement spoke of the same gauge and the same length as the old one. It is as well to buy, say, a dozen new spokes of the correct dimension, so that you always have some at hand. A spoke that is too long will inevitably pierce the inner tube, while one too short will be impossible to fit.

To re-thread a spoke, you must first unscrew the nipple, then push the threaded end through the hole in the hub flange. Make sure that you push it through from the correct side (the spokes alternate from inside to outside – see illustration). It may be necessary to carefully bend the spoke to avoid spokes on the opposite side of the wheel before the replacement can be pulled through completely and its spoke head bedded down into the hub flange.

Nearly all wheels are spoked tangentially, which means that the spoke is fitted at a tangent to the hub flange. Each spoke will intersect either three or four other spokes on its way to the rim. Check this, and the way the spoke should be laced between the others, by studying the path of the spoke two away from the one being replaced.

If the tyre has been removed, push the threaded end of the new spoke through the spare hole in the rim. Smear grease on the thread and then screw on the nipple – first by hand and then with the spoke key – until it is evenly tensioned with those adjacent to it. Check the wheel for trueness by spinning it on its axle. And then, if necessary, file down any excess length of spoke emerging from the nipple.

If the tyre remains in place, deflate it before bringing the new spoke up to the rim and screwing on the old nipple. Don't do this unless you are certain that the replacement spoke is of the same length as was the broken one. It might be possible to check this by turning back the tyre and tube to expose the nipple.

Unless you have sealed bearing hubs, which should be virtually maintenance-free, both hubs should be regreased about once a year or about every 8,000 km (5,000 miles). This involves dismantling the hubs and examining all ball bearings and ball races, replacing any items that are worn or pitted.

Start with the front hub, as its make-up is less complex than that of the rear hub. It comprises a fixed axle (known as the spindle), on to which is mounted the hub shell (a hollow cylinder). This spins on the spindle, being mounted on two sets of ball bearings that are located between ball-race cups (fixed in the shell) and cones (which screw on to the ends of the spindle). Dust and water are discouraged from entering the ball races by circular dust caps pressed on the outer edges of the hub shell. This arrangement is common to both quick-release and regular hub units. The main difference between quick-release and regular units is that the spindle of a quick-release unit is hollow, having a fine skewer passing through it with a lever cam mechanism at one end, which performs the task of tightening normally done by the screwing-on of track nuts or wing nuts.

To dismantle, first remove the wheel from the forks and unscrew the outer track nuts or wing nuts. On hubs with quick-release mechanisms the quick-release skewer should be removed completely from the axle. All threads are normal, right-handed ones.

Before continuing, place a wide cloth underneath the wheel to catch any ball bearings that fall out during the next stages. One of the two cones may be fixed, screwed up to a shoulder on the spindle. The other is adjustable (on the left-hand side for the rear hub) and is fixed in position by a locking nut. This should be unscrewed first, using a special cone spanner (wrench), which is narrower than usual.

Next, lift off the succeeding, notched washer. Carefully note how it engages with the spindle and/or cone, so that you will know how to reassemble the hub. The cone can now be unscrewed and removed, which will allow the spindle (plus fixed cone and lock nut) to be extracted from the hub shell.

To remove the freewheel block, it is necessary to have a special removal key. This is usually cylindrical in shape, with a central hole to slip over the spindle and two projections which engage with slots

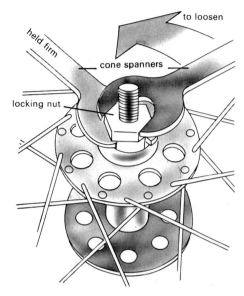

Removing the hub locking nut.

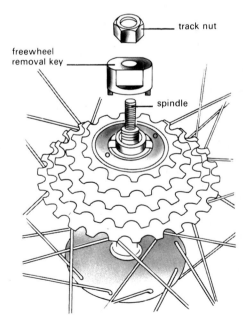

Removing the freewheel block. The freewheel tool's projections engage with slots in the block.

119

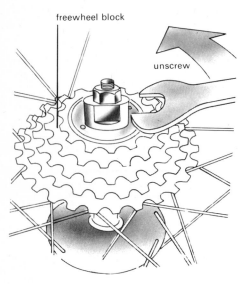

freewheel block

unscrew

Tighten the track nut before unscrewing.

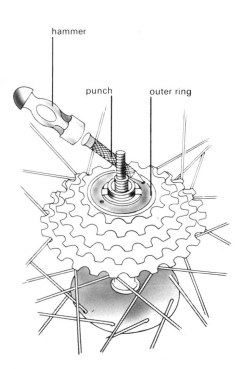

hammer

punch

outer ring

Tapping loose the outer ring.

in the freewheel body; alternatively, some makes have splines on the key and freewheel body. This key should be pushed into position with the hub's track nuts removed. If you have a quick-release hub, take off the two helical springs before replacing the skewer and its locking cone. Now, replace the track nuts and screw them down tight (or tighten the quick-release), fixing the removal key hard up against the freewheel.

There are two flats on the key, and you will require a wide adjustable spanner (wrench) or vice to fit across them. The freewheel can now be loosened, gaining enough leverage by firmly holding the wheel's rim in one hand while exerting pressure on the end of the spanner (wrench). The track nuts (or quick-release skewer) will have to be loosened before the freewheel can be completely unscrewed by the key.

Maintenance of the freewheel itself should be limited to the insertion of small amounts of oil during the regular maintenance session, or to the changing of worn sprockets. If the freewheel should fail – either by jamming solid or freewheeling in both directions – it usually means that it is time to replace the whole unit. Actual repairs to the freewheel mechanism require delicate skills and should only be tackled by an experienced mechanic.

If you are tempted to investigate a faulty freewheel, it is best to work on it still fixed to the wheel. You will require a small pointed punch and hammer to unscrew the outer ring, tapping this loose in the direction indicated on the body itself. Inside are some paper-thin packing rings, which have to be lifted off after removal of a toothed ring and some small ball bearings. After this come two pawls held in place by very delicate springs. A faulty spring should be replaced, as it is likely to be the cause of any problems occurring with a freewheel. Before reassembly the internal mechanism should be cleaned and lightly lubricated.

With the hub spindle out, shake out those ball bearings that have remained in the ball race cups. Thoroughly clean all parts that have been removed, using spirit and clean rag, and check the ball bearings for signs of cracking or pitting. Replace if necessary. Also clean the hub shell, inside and out, closely inspecting the ball-race cups. It should not be necessary to remove the dust caps for this inspection but, if it is, lever them out with the greatest care.

If any ball bearings are damaged, replace the whole set. Before starting the refit, make sure you know the order in which the various parts are assembled. Pack the ball-race cups with grease and put further smears on the various screw threads. Now, screw up the fixed cone as far as it will go and fully tighten the locking nut. Insert the spindle part way into the hub shell, with enough space to place the correct number (and size) of bearings in the cup.

Turn the wheel over, holding the spindle in place and then drop in the ball bearings to the other side. The adjustable cone should then be screwed on, hand tight, leaving the hub ready for final adjustment. This should be done with the washer dropped back in its initial position, and then slackening or tightening the cone to respectively eliminate stiffness or shake. The locking nut is then finally placed in position and screwed tight, making sure that the cone is not displaced. For rear hubs, the freewheel block has to be removed for working on the hub. You may find spacers on the hub spindle to allow the optimum chain line with derailleur gears.

Another job that few people relish tackling – and that includes most bike shop mechanics – is dismantling and repairing a hub gear. There are so many different types in use and on the market, that it is best to get a full breakdown on your gear's particular parts and assembly from the manufacturer. This will probably be in the form of a large, exploded type drawing of the mechanism, with each part being labelled with a specific serial number.

The same advice applies to coaster brakes, hub brakes and generators. These items are designed in the hope that virtually no maintenance will be required. If you have problems with any of these products when they are still reasonably new, then be sure to have them returned to the manufacturer for repair or replacement.

Derailleur gears and chains

To judge by the high number of multi-speed bicycles that are ridden with defective gears, it is safe to assume that the derailleur is the component most frequently in need of repair. Probably 90 per cent of the problems which arise are due to lack of knowledge, poor adjustment or lack of maintenance. The other 10 per cent can be caused by a faulty chain, a stretched or kinked cable, warped chainwheel or worn rear sprockets. Very few problems are caused by the derailleur itself, the most likely being a slipping control lever,

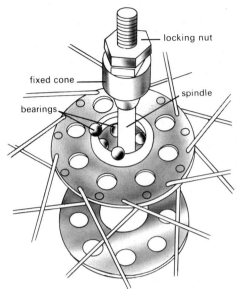

Replacing ball bearings with the spindle held loosely in the hub.

Sprockets are best removed using two sprocket removers and turning them in opposite directions. (Only one tool is shown here for clarity.) The sprocket remover has a chain which wraps around the sprockets to grip them.

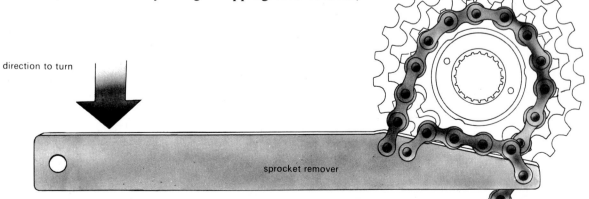

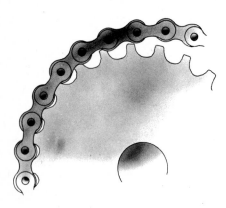

Worn sprockets and stretched chain cause the chain to 'ride up'.

a loose jockey wheel or an ageing tension spring.

The first checks you should make when the gears are not operating smoothly should be with the chain, cables, chainwheels and sprockets – not with the derailleur mechanisms.

A chainwheel that is warped or has bent teeth can be made to run true with careful manipulation. But worn rear sprockets generally means that the freewheel needs renewing completely, unless just one sprocket (the most used one) is causing problems. In this case, the answer is to replace just the sprocket: this usually means unscrewing the outer sprockets using a special tool – a sprocket remover – not the easiest of jobs.

Cable problems have been dealt with in the earlier section on brakes. These problems are simply exacerbated by the longer derailleur cables; a rear gear operated by handlebar control levers has a cable about 1.5 m (nearly 5 ft) long. As with brake cables, keep them well greased and avoid tight curves – particularly the bottom ones from down tube to front changer, and from chain stay to rear changer. The most frequent adjustment should be keeping the cables taut.

For the rear changer, shift the lever so that the chain is on the smallest (outer) sprocket and the cable is at its loosest. Undo the locking nut (or bolt) that fixes the cable to the derailleur; pull through this the rear end of the cable as tight as it will go (possibly gripping it with pliers); then retighten locking nut (or bolt). Some types have a channel in which to seat the cable, others have a hole through which it is threaded.

The procedure for the front changer is similar, except that the cable usually is loosest when the chain is on the smaller chainwheel. When the cable has been pulled tight and refixed, shift the chain onto the big chainwheel, and back to the smaller one, making sure that the cable adjustment has not affected the lateral 'throw' of the derailleur. The throw is controlled by means of spring-loaded stop screws or knurled ring adjusters: these can be located by watching where the derailleur body is stopped as you shift it from the outer to inner chainwheels or sprockets.

Some derailleurs have hatch plates located on the rear cage so that it is possible to lift the chain away, allowing you to remove the gear mechanism without taking the chain itself from the bike. But the chain has to be removed periodically to clean it properly, and this is also the ideal time to clean and check over the derailleurs.

A chain rivet extractor tool (or, more correctly, a bearing pin extractor) is shaped like a small clamp; it has a screw with a hard metal pin at the end which engages with the dimpled end of a chain rivet (bearing pin) and forces this out of the chain when the bolt is screwed in. For this operation the chain seats on the notch closest to the tool's back plate.

It is very easy to bend the chain plates by not centring the extractor pin on the rivet, or by forcing the rivet completely from the chain. I advise you to use the extractor tool on two adjacent rivets, pushing them just through the top chain plate, which can then be lifted off. This leaves free the lower plate (and both rivets), which can be lifted out from the chain, with no danger of bending any parts.

To rejoin the chain after cleaning it, you simply slip the plate and its two rivets back into place on the chain; seat it on the extractor tool, with the loose plate at the back; then push each rivet in turn back into place. Be careful not to force the rivets through too far. If there is any tightness in the link when refitted, seat it back on the extractor tool, but on the second slot, closest to the screw. Engage the pin with the tight rivet and a small amount of pressure will 'spread' the plates and loosen the rivet.

When fitting a new chain, you may have to remove several links so that the slack can be taken up comfortably by the rear derailleur's tension spring. Check this by temporarily fitting the chain with the derailleurs shifted to the smallest sprocket and smaller chainwheel. If the chain hangs loose, it will have to be shortened by probably two or three links. Any further slack can be taken up by tightening the derailleur's roller cage spring – but this is only recommended as a last resort. (As there are so many derailleur mechanisms on the market it is best to seek expert advice on the means by which your particular roller cage spring is adjusted.)

Before removing any links, check the tension in the chain with the derailleurs shifted onto the largest sprocket used and larger chainwheel. The chain should not be so tight that the rear changer is pulled so far forward that there is no play left in the roller cage. If you cannot draw a compromise between the chain being too short in this position, and too long in the other, then you will have two choices. The first is to buy a new rear derailleur that can cope with a wider range of gears; the second is to fit a smaller 'big' sprocket and smaller chainwheels to give you the same gear sizes, but requiring less extreme position of the chain.

With the chain removed, the precise condition of the derailleurs can be determined. Check the rear one first. It may look complicated, but its operation is basically simple. To remove the derailleur from the frame, unscrew the bolt (or nut) that locks the cable in place. You will need an Allen key, spanner (wrench) or screwdriver. Now, pull the cable away, taking care not to unravel the strands. The mechanism itself is either bolted directly to the frame (if it has

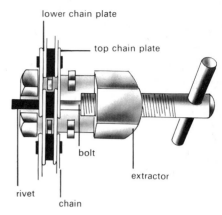

Using a chain rivet extractor to push out a rivet. Screw down the tool's bolt with the chain in this position.

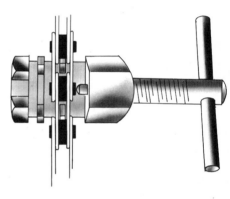

Using a chain rivet extractor to loosen a tight link. Tighten the bolt with the chain in this position.

Three types of rear derailleur.

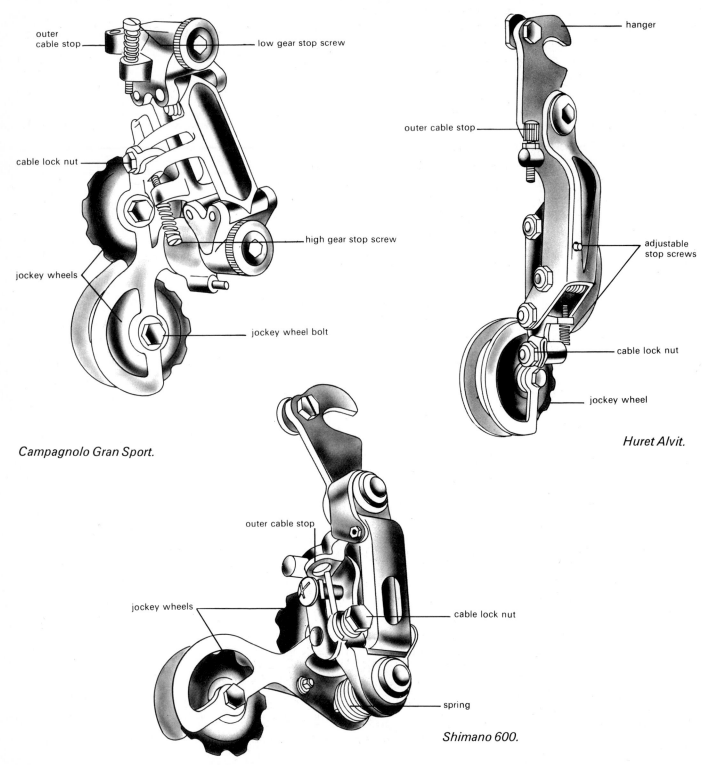

outer cable stop

low gear stop screw

hanger

outer cable stop

cable lock nut

high gear stop screw

adjustable stop screws

jockey wheels

jockey wheel bolt

cable lock nut

jockey wheel

Campagnolo Gran Sport.

Huret Alvit.

outer cable stop

jockey wheels

cable lock nut

spring

Shimano 600.

a special boss), or it is clamped into the rear fork end. A metric spanner (wrench) or Allen key is required to loosen the respective fixing bolts.

The rear derailleur performs two basic functions: moving the chain sideways onto each of the sprockets, and keeping the chain taut. The first is done by means of a parallelogram shaped frame, pivoted at the top and bottom. It is spring-loaded and will automatically move away from the wheel if not countered by the control cable, which pulls the parallelogram back towards the spokes. The chain is kept in tension by a cage that pivots on a spring-loaded bolt which engages with a housing mounted on the lower end of the parallelogram. The chain runs on two jockey wheels that are fixed into opposite ends of the cage.

Details vary tremendously from one manufacturer to another, and even from one model to another in the same range. But each follows the above pattern, and you should closely study your own derailleur to be certain how yours actually functions. The parts most likely to need replacement are the two jockey wheels and the spring that controls the sideways movement of the parallelogram

The jockey wheels will jam up with grease and grit if not cleaned regularly. To remove them, unscrew the metric headed bolts that fix them into the cage. This should be done by holding the cage in one hand and, preferably, using a dome-headed Allen spanner (wrench) to release the bolts. Complete the job by hand holding the jockey wheel itself as you extract the bolt. Take careful note of where the various washers and sleeves are fitted. Some wheels are mounted on ball bearings with adjustable cones, like a miniature hub. These will need repacking with grease once all the parts have been washed clean with spirit.

The spring in the parallelogram is generally fixed with a pivot bolt that can be undone with a screwdriver. Again, make sure you know how it is fitted before completely removing it.

The front derailleur is less likely to get damaged than the rear changer, and it is rarely necessary to replace any parts. It works on the same parallelogram principle, except that the metal-sided cage physically pushes the chain from one chainwheel to the other. The lateral throw is much more limited, and the parallelogram is consequently more compact.

The most likely cause of trouble is gumming up of the parallelogram's spring and pivot bolts with grease and grit. This can only be shifted thoroughly by dismantling the mechanism, a job which should be tackled after close inspection of the specific model on your bike. The basic moves are: release the cable locking nut and pull the cable clear; then unscrew the bolts that fix the derailleur's

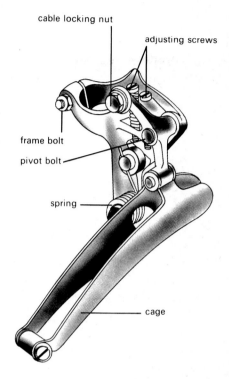

Typical front derailleur.

Correct adjustment of the front and rear derailleurs' stop screws is essential to the smooth operation of the gears. In effect, on the rear derailleur, these screws prevent the chain being shifted off the largest sprocket into the wheel, and off the smallest sprocket into the frame. Rough adjustment of both sets of screws should be made with the bike turned upside down (so that you can see where the screws 'stop' the derailleur). Final adjustment (to eliminate unwanted sounds) may be required after a short test ride.

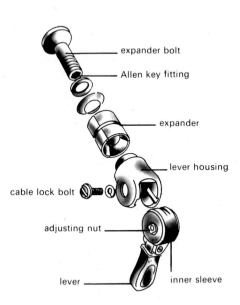

Exploded view of handlebar end gear control lever.

- expander bolt
- Allen key fitting
- expander
- lever housing
- cable lock bolt
- adjusting nut
- lever
- inner sleeve

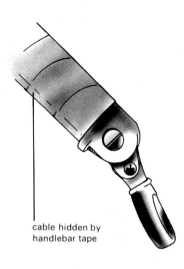

cable hidden by handlebar tape

Lever and cable in place.

bracket to the seat tube; and finally, undo the bolt that will release the cage from the parallelogram.

On some designs, this third bolt will also release the main spring, so take the usual precautions of unscrewing it carefully and noting where each sleeve and washer is fitted. Thoroughly clean the whole assembly with spirit, and make sure it is properly dried before reassembly. Do not use grease for lubricating the pivots – it will attract dust and grit. Simply put a few drops of oil on each pivot bolt as it is refitted, and wipe clean any excess when the job is completed.

To reposition the front changer on the bike, loosely clamp it back onto the seat tube. Then carefully swivel it until the cage side plates are parallel to the chainwheels and the bottom edge of the cage is just clear of the teeth on the largest chainwheel. Final adjustment will have to wait until the cable, chain and wheels are back in place. Lateral play is normally adjusted by means of spring-loaded screws set into the rear part of the fixing bracket.

The gear control (or shift) levers need not be removed when overhauling the other parts of the system. They are fixed by a tension screw that passes through the lever pivot-hole (and various washers) into a boss. This may be brazed to the frame downtube or may form part of a clip that is clamped to the downtube. The most complicated set-up is the lever unit fitted to the handlebar ends. In this case, the lever slots into a housing that is fitted into the handlebar by an expander bolt. The cable has then to be threaded through the lever before this is clamped into place with a specially shaped sleeve and locking bolt.

When threading new cables into any type of lever, be very careful not to pull it through hurriedly and perhaps cause the cable to spiral. It is much better to feed it through slowly around the cable slot on the lever, making sure that the cable nipple beds down firmly into its housing.

The lever tension screw is correctly adjusted when the lever is tight enough to hold the chain on the biggest sprocket or large chainwheel, but not so tight that it is difficult to shift the lever. As with brake cables, avoid any sharp curves when fitting new outer cable covers.

For handlebar-end levers, the neatest method is to fix the cables before taping the bars. The line of the cable should be from the lever, along the bottom of the drops, on the inside of the curved part beside the brake lever hood and finally breaking away from the underside of the central section of the handlebars about 15 cm (6 in) from the stem. It will then loop to a frame clip on the downtube, at about the same spot where the levers are usually fitted.

The Flying Bicycle

At dawn, on a calm June morning in 1979, a Californian biologist, Bryan Allen, started pedalling a bike-like machine along a hardboard 'runway' placed on a concrete quay at The Warren, Folkestone in England. After one false start, in which one of the machine's 50 mm (2 in) diameter plastic wheels shattered, Allen pedalled the propeller-driven *Gossamer Albatross* into the air and then continued to fly his 33 kg (72 lb) aeroplane across the English Channel to land on the beach near Calais, France almost 3 hours later.

This first man-powered Channel flight won Allen, and an American back-up team headed by the Albatross' inventor Dr Paul McCready, a prize of £100,000 donated by British industrialist Henry Kremer. Allen was a proficient amateur racing cyclist as well as a hang-gliding enthusiast, so he was well qualified to achieve success. Two years previously he had helped to win his team the £25,000 Kremer prize to fly the man-powered *Gossamer Condor* (shown above) over a mile-long (1.609 km) figure-of-eight course.

The wingspan of the Albatross was the same as that of a DC-9 jet airliner, about 30 m (100 ft). It took a constant output of about 0.3 horsepower from Allen, who sat inside the craft's transparent polythene and aluminium-framed fuselage. He used conventional bicycle components such as saddle, pedals, cranks and chainwheel fitted to a carbon fibre tubed frame. The difference was that the chainwheel turned a long, urethane chain, which was geared through two further chainwheels to a rear-mounted propeller.

Repairing a tyre puncture.

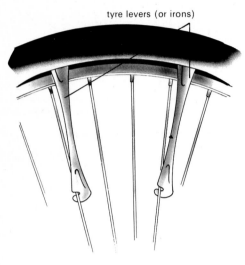

tyre levers (or irons)

Remove the wired-on tyre cover using tyre levers.

Immerse the inner tube in water to locate the puncture.

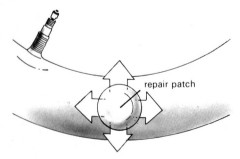

repair patch

Press the patch down firmly, working outwards, to remove any air bubbles in the rubber solution.

When the cables are completely fitted and adjusted, clip the ends off with wire cutters about 5 cm (2 in) away from the cable fixing bolt. A flapping cable end could catch in the spokes (rear mechanism) or scratch the inside of your left-hand crank (front).

Tyres and punctures
There are three types of puncture repairs: to tyres with separate inner tube and wired-on cover; to sewn-up tubular tyres; and to Liberty-type tubulars. The methods of repair are shown in the following sequences of illustrations.

Wired-on tyre
Before removing the tyre from the rim, pump some air into the valve and feel round the tyre to see if the air is coming from an obvious hole in the cover. If so, you will not need to remove the complete tyre from the rim, only the section by the puncture.

If the puncture is not easily discovered, you will have to remove the tyre. First, undo the valve locking ring and deflate the tyre. Insert the spoon end of a tyre lever (tire iron) between the rim and tyre cover, working it under the fixing wire and being careful not to pinch the inner tube. Hook the notched end of the lever around an adjacent spoke. Repeat with a second lever about 10 cm (4 in) away from the first, and hook it to a spoke as before. The wired-on cover may now be loose enough to remove the rest by hand. If not, use the third lever a further 10 cm round the rim. With the wire completely off one side, the inner tube can now be taken out completely. Check round the inside of the cover with your fingers to see if there are any pieces of stone or metal embedded: if so, remove them. Pump some air into the inner tube and identify the location of the puncture. You may do this by listening for escaping air, or by immersing the tube in water and watching for a stream of bubbles. When found, mark the spot with the crayon supplied with the repair outfit. Dry the tube, and clean the area around the puncture with sandpaper, as supplied.

Select an appropriately sized patch to cover the puncture area. Squeeze a little rubber solution on to the tube and spread it thinly over and around the puncture. Red tubes need just one coat; black (butyl) tubes need two, allowing the first one to dry before applying the second. With the rubber solution dry, strip the foil (or plastic) from the adhesive side of the patch. Press the patch firmly down on the puncture, starting at the centre and working outwards with your fingers to remove any possibility of air bubbles.

On paper-backed patches, pinch the tube to crack the paper and peel off. Dust the patch and surrounding area with French chalk (if supplied) or talcum powder. Slightly inflate the tube and screw up the valve nut (on Presta valves). The tube is now ready to replace inside the cover, which should be patched on the inside with fabric if a large gash has been made in the tread. Put the valve into the rim hole before bedding down the tube inside the cover. Starting opposite the valve, push the cover wire back onto the rim with the thumbs, working round symmetrically towards the valve side.

You may be able to continue rolling the tyre on all the way, but if there is some tightness in the wire when it is stretched across the last section, then deflate the tube and bed the tyre more fully into the rim well. Then roll on the final section by the valve. Don't be tempted to use the tyre levers, as you are likely to pinch the inner tube and cause another puncture.

Finally, semi-inflate the tyre, screw on the valve locking ring and check that tyre is on symmetrically. If not, centre it up with your hands and fully inflate the tyre.

Tubular tyre

To locate the puncture, pump up the tubular and listen for signs of escaping air. If not obvious, immerse it in water, gradually working round the tyre. Mark the puncture when located.

With a fairly broad-bladed screwdriver, lift the two edges of the base tape adjacent to the puncture. Carefully work the screwdriver under the tape until you can grip it between finger and thumb. Pull away a section of base tape about 10 cm (4 in) each side of the puncture location. Using a scalpel or small pair of nail scissors, carefully snip away the stitching about 5 cm (2 in) each side of the puncture. Pull a short section of the inner tube out of the tyre, and slightly inflate it to determine the exact point of the puncture. Proceed with repairing the puncture with rubber solution and patch, as for the wired-on tyre. When the repair is effected, push the tube back inside the tyre cover. Lightly inflate it to seat it down correctly, then deflate again.

To restitch the section of tyre, you will need the sturdy needle supplied with the repair kit threaded with about 25 cm (10 in) of thread. Start stitching at one end, holding the tube down inside with the first finger of one hand as you work the needle through the old stitch holes. Start (and finish) this operation about 12 mm (½ in) beyond the gap left by the removed stitches. Use a simple, looping stitch, being careful not to pull the stitches too tight as this will cause an unwanted ridge to form. If you find it difficult to pull the needle through by hand, either push it with a metal thimble on your thumb or hold the two sides of the tyre together and push down over the needle, which should be supported by a piece of metal – not

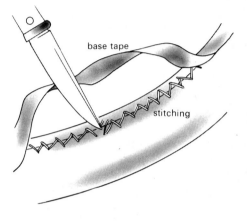

Cutting the stitching on a tubular.

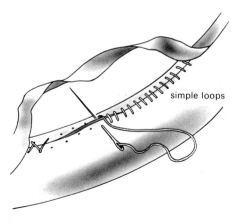

Use simple loops to restitch. Feed the needle and thread through the existing stitch holes.

on a piece of furniture such as the kitchen table!

When stitching is complete, take the needle back between two or three stitches before cutting the thread. Lightly inflate the tyre, checking that the stitching is even before pumping up to about half the normal pressure. Apply rubber solution over the new stitching and to the underside of the base tape. When the solution is dry, press the two sections together, deflating the tyre to complete the job. Finally, semi-inflate the tyre again and hang it in a dry, cool place to allow the adhesive to harden up.

A repaired tubular tyre should be carried as a spare, rather than being immediately stuck back on the rim. If you have a number of spares, it is advisable to store them, lightly inflated, on old rims.

Liberty-type tyre
This is a tubular tyre without the stitching, the cover being a complete cylindrical tube. When punctured, it is repaired without removing it from the rim, by inserting a special needle through the puncture and inserting a special quick-drying repair solution. Full instructions are supplied with the repair kit and these should be followed precisely.

One of the advantages of touring in a group is that there is always someone else to help mend a flat tyre. The problem here seems to be a spoke sticking too far through the wheel rim and causing the inner tube to puncture.

Valves

Three different types of valve will be encountered. These are the Woods' type on heavy roadster tyres; the Presta valve on lighter wired-on tyres and tubular tyres; and the Schraeder on most American clincher tyres and most children's bikes.

The Woods' valve has a short section of rubber tubing inside to effect a valve seal. When this becomes perished, the valve can be unscrewed and a new piece of tubing slipped over the end. These valve rubbers are supplied with some puncture repair outfits – check the contents before buying. Alternatively – and better – fit an 'Easipump' replacement: this is a pressure plunger which makes the tyre much easier to inflate.

There is no rubber in a Presta valve, which works on a plunger principle, the plunger being locked in place by the knurled nut at the end. This should require no maintenance, and if it becomes damaged it means replacing the valve or even the whole tube.

The Schraeder is also a plunger type valve, the plunger being sprung in this case. A normal service station air line can be used to inflate a Schraeder valve, but only the special adapter or connection supplied with the bicycle pump can be used on the Presta valve.

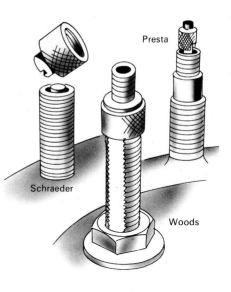

The three types of tyre valve.

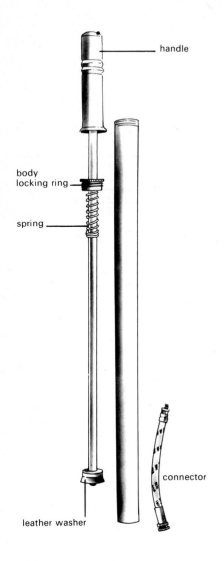

handle

body
locking ring

spring

connector

leather washer

Dismantled pump.

Emergency repairs

It sometimes happens that a crash or a sudden breakage puts your bike out of commission. Perhaps a friendly driver will give you a lift to the nearest bike shop, but it is more likely that you will have to effect an emergency repair to get you home.

The most likely damage is a buckled wheel. This may be rideable by slackening the brake quick-release so that the rim does not bang against the brake blocks. If the buckling is more severe the drastic course of action is to remove the wheel from the bike and to attempt to lever it back into shape with the wheel held in a drain or fence railings. If the wheel has dished symmetrically, it is possible to straighten it by placing it on the ground and standing astride the wheel on the two high points.

If your rear derailleur is broken or twisted, then remove the mechanism and shorten the chain so that it engages with one of the middle sprockets to give you a single, medium gear. A broken gear cable can be replaced if you have a spare; otherwise, screw in the gear adjusting screw so that the derailleur does not shift to top gear.

If the handlebar stem, front forks or rear stays fracture, then the bike is unrideable. It is also dangerous to attempt to ride a bike on which one of the main frame tubes has broken, although it is sometimes possible to scoot the bike when the seat tube breaks. But be very careful that you don't cause the rear wheel to jam solid when you have to stop.

If one side of the handlebars snaps off, it is possible to ride the bike, although difficult and probably illegal. A broken saddle means riding without one, but a snapped seat post or pillar can perhaps be pushed further into the frame to give a temporary saddle position.

If a pedal breaks, it may be possible to dismantle it and still leave the spindle giving a temporary support. Otherwise, one-leg riding is very arduous, unless you have a fixed-wheel bike.

A jammed freewheel means that you will have to keep pedalling continuously, otherwise the chain will wrap itself around the derailleur and cause you to crash. An alternative is to shorten the chain and to remove the derailleur. If the freewheel spins in both directions and cannot provide any drive, then you will have to be content with freewheeling down hills and scooting along the flat. But first try getting up speed down a hill, and you may find that the centrifugal force re-engages the pawls and ratchet – allowing you to pedal, although do not try to freewheel.

When touring and using a saddlebag it is possible to overload the bag support, which will start to push down on the rear mudguard or the wheel. At the first sign of such problems, you can pull the bag clear by means of a strap joined tightly between the saddle wires and the back of the bag; or, by raising the saddle two or three centimetres (about an inch) you may solve the problem until you can get a replacement carrier.

Remember, in all cases when the bike is being ridden with a defective part, take extra special care. Leave extra stopping distance, so that brakes can be applied very slowly. And do not attempt to ride fast. If you have any doubts, you can always walk or hitch a lift.

Accessories and lighting

The various accessories that are fixed to the bike – mudguards, (fenders), bottle cages, lamp brackets and generators – should be regularly cleaned and polished, and it is a good idea to check and retighten all their fixing bolts, screws and nuts at the same time.

One of the few items likely to require more attention is the pump. Its efficiency depends on a leather washer, which is screwed to the end of the plunger. This washer must be airtight and should be able to be pulled (and pushed) smoothly through the inside of the pump barrel. Replace worn out washers by unscrewing the top of the pump barrel, which releases the handle and plunger. Unscrew the end bolt to remove the washer. Fit the new one, making sure it has sufficient grease on its edges for it to slide smoothly through the barrel. Never use oil in a pump as it could vaporize and if blown inside the inner tube, will rot the rubber.

To be effective, mudguards are fitted with a flexible plastic flap at the base of the front 'guard. In time, this mudflap will become bent and possibly broken. It is possible to buy replacements or cut to size any suitable material (thick plastic, rubber or fabric-backed PVC). This can be fixed to the inside of the mudguard by removing the old rivets and bolting it in place through the same holes with new rivets or short nuts and bolts.

Tools

A Tour de France mechanic is likely to possess a hefty box of tools and a bulky bike stand costing more than the average bicycle, whereas a tourist on a short, one-day ride will probably carry little more than an adjustable spanner (wrench), a screwdriver, a puncture repair outfit and tyre levers.

Each is well equipped for his own purposes – but where does one draw the line in acquiring specialist tools? The answer is that there is a small number of essential tools required for everyday maintenance or roadside repairs, and that the specialist items should be bought only when you contemplate a major overhaul of a specific component.

<table>
<tr><td>

Tools you will need

For your everyday journey you will need to take the following items:
Essential – adjustable spanner (wrench), screwdriver and 6 mm Allen key, spare tubular tyre (for sprint rims), or inner tube, three tyre levers and puncture repair outfit (for high-pressure, wired-on tyres).
Preferable – special metric tool kit (with various sizes of spanners/wrenches and Allen keys), chain link remover and pliers. Piece of cloth and hand cleanser.

Specialist tools that will be needed when the occasion arises include – spoke key, cotterless crankset tool (spanner/wrench and extractor), freewheel removing tool plus long adjustable spanner (wrench), thin spanner (wrench) for adjusting hub cones, combined with peg fixture for adjusting bottom bracket cups.
Other tools you may consider buying for your workshop are a freewheel sprocket remover, bench vice, bike stand and foot pump (with pressure gauge).

</td></tr>
</table>

Following pages: A bunched group of riders on the Tour de France. The Tour, the world's most famous bicycle race, takes a slightly different route each year – but the hard physical challenge remains the same.

On The Road

6

Touring

Pedalling a bicycle silently through an unfamiliar landscape – hearing birdsong, smelling the aroma of spring flowers, feeling the brush of warm air against your cheeks – is one of cycling's greatest pleasures. There can be no precise definition of 'bicycle touring'. It is the term used to describe all forms of recreational, non-competitive cycling. There are no age limits. Most types of bike can be used. Any highway, back road or cross-country track can provide the setting. And no time or speed limits are imposed on the participant.

To the beginner, a 20 km (12.5 mile) ride through the countryside close to home may open up a whole new world. To the experienced tourist, technically and physically prepared, the ultimate challenge could be a 200 km (125 mile) day trip over high mountain passes. To both, the tour will be an adventure, perhaps educational as well as mentally and physically satisfying.

Bicycle touring has contributed in an inspirational sense to the arts. English composer Edward Elgar was an inveterate cyclist, and his rides around the Malvern Hills are reflected in many of his pastoral works. Irish playwright George Bernard Shaw was a lifelong member of the Cyclists' Touring Club. And Mexican-based philosopher Ivan Illich has drawn much of his writing from bicycle-inspired thinking.

Cycle touring is equally enjoyable on your own or in a group. The sharing of the pleasure of discovery can enhance the pleasure. Even pooling your inexperience can be fun! Experienced companions can help a beginner – an important part of the job of cycling clubs.

Your choice of company may be dictated by your decision to cycle as a family. But if you are making up a party for, say, a short tour, then a group of four or six is most convenient. On quiet roads it's pleasant to be able to ride alongside a companion, while it is as well to remember that the members of a small group can share the work of riding into a head wind. At the same time, you will be delayed longer by the small, inevitable mechanical mishaps that befall any group.

The touring bicycle

After your first few local rides, followed perhaps by some all day or weekend trips, you will find that a bicycle designed for the job will make touring an even more enjoyable experience. You will want a bike that is light, yet also reliable, comfortable and versatile. It may be possible to adapt your present machine by judicious choice of the more specialized touring accessories, but a purpose built bike will be the ultimate goal.

The essentials of the ideal touring bicycle are well-supported luggage, well-treaded tyres, mudguards, and lower gearing to enable you to climb hills with the fully laden bike. When ordering a frame tailored to you, specify lightweight butted tubing (but not the ultra-thin gauges such as Reynolds 753), wider clearances for the thicker tyres, mudguard-fixing eyes in front and rear fork ends, and preferably brazed-on fittings for a bottle cage (on the down tube), front lamp, rear brake cable and derailleur cables. Knowing the bike is for touring, the builder will fit the frame to your needs and measurements, probably choosing a longer wheel-base, longer fork rake and shallower angles than for a conventional model.

Find your ideal riding posture as detailed in Chapter 3, but remember that the handlebar stem should be at about the same height as the saddle. Fairly shallow drop handlebars are the most comfortable and most experienced tourists prefer leather saddles.

Most side- and centre-pull caliper brakes are less effective on a touring frame with broad wheel clearances. You could specify cantilever brakes, which operate efficiently irrespective of wheel clearance, but these require fixtures brazed on the front forks and seat stays. This results in a slight disadvantage in that you will never be able to use wheels of a different size. For instance, this means that you will not be able to change from standard 27-inch wheels to the increasingly popular 700C size, or to the smaller,

Left: The images of cycle touring can be just as strong on a short evening ride near home as on an extended tour in a foreign land. The end of the day can also provide the cycling amateur photographer with some of his best subject matter as this evocative picture graphically shows.

Autumn is perhaps the best season to take an extra week's cycling vacation. Roads and hotels are less crowded, the weather is often still mild enough for cycle touring and the countryside can be at its most colourful.

wider 650B that many European tourists prefer.

Wired-on tyres of moderate weight are most suitable for touring, particularly off paved roads, where there is a higher risk of punctures. Moreover, a replacement tubular tyre could pull round under a heavy touring load, and it would be inconvenient to repair such a tyre if you should exhaust your supply of spares.

It is more convenient to carry one or two spare inner tubes, which are less bulky than tubulars and allow a quicker on-the-spot solution. The rims should be of robust section, preferably of aluminium alloy but steel ones are better for really rough terrain. Small (low) flange hubs give the wheel added flexibility, while good quality quick-release hubs make puncture repairs even quicker.

To obtain those necessary low gears on a regular bike requires fitting a freewheel block (cluster) with the biggest available sprocket (one with 28 teeth probably). Such a bike will probably be fitted with chainwheels that are unnecessarily large for touring, for which most experienced riders use a top gear of between 6 and 7 m (about 75 to 90 in). Really low gears are essential on long mountain climbs as well as on shorter, steeper types of hill. Your cadence will be less when climbing, partly because the slower airflow over your body alters its cooling rate, but even so gears down to about 2.5 m (about 30 in) are often useful.

Most derailleur gears work best with the less extreme chainwheel and sprocket sizes, so choose an outer chainwheel of 50 teeth or smaller, and a top sprocket bigger than 14 teeth. It is convenient to have two separate sets of gears by specifying widely spaced chainwheels, one for use in gently rolling countryside, the other for hilly or mountainous terrain. A typical choice would be chainwheels of 44 and 30 teeth combined with a freewheel of 16-18-20-23-27. Most makes of freewheel allow such a range (although some only employ a 26 or 28 lowest sprocket), but such small chainwheels are only possible with three major manufacturers: the French Stronglight and TA, and the Japanese SR TG series.

To take up the extra chain length required for widely spaced gears such as these, demands rear derailleur mechanisms with longer roller cage extensions than normal and most derailleur manufacturers include special touring models in their ranges. Any of the modern parallelogram action front derailleurs will easily cope with the 14-tooth difference of the chainwheels. Properly fitted toeclips and straps make climbing much more efficient, but if any off-the-bike exploration is contemplated then shoeplates (cleats) can prove uncomfortable or slippery, particularly when walking over rocks.

Cycle touring is a pastime enjoyed by people of all ages. This enthusiastic American in his late sixties is pictured climbing one of the many mountain roads on the Trans-America trail that traces a scenic course from the Pacific to the Atlantic.

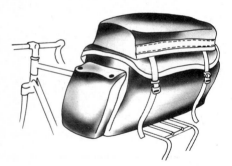

A 'karrimor' saddle bag.

Handlebar bag and support.

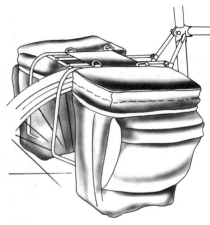

Rear panniers on their carrier.

Bags and clothes

For all but the shortest day trips, the bicycle tourist will need to carry many items, as suggested by the check list on page 157. There are four basic types of practical container: the saddlebag attached behind and under the saddle (the traditional British solution); the handlebar bag fitted just in front of the handlebars (standard among French tourists); panniers fitted on either side of a rear carrier (popular in the United States); and panniers fitted on either side of a carrier over the front wheel.

It will take a short time to get used to riding with luggage as all types of bag affect the handling of the bicycle. The weight of the actual bags has some significance and you should note that the more traditional thick canvas (so-called cotton duck) material weighs about twice as much as proofed nylon.

A saddlebag has the advantage of carrying a complete, comprehensive load – the biggest ones by British manufacturers Carradice and Karrimor hold about 15,000 cc (900 cu in). And, when firmly fixed to the bicycle and supported by a good carrier, they probably least affect the bike's handling. They are normally fixed by three straps, two of which fit to loops on the saddle and one to the seat post.

Handlebar bags are generally smaller, perhaps half the volume of a saddlebag. The extent to which they affect the steering depends on the frame's geometry, the front tyre pressure (the higher the pressure, the less the effect) and, above all, on the weight carried. They need some form of adaptor or fitting to keep them clear of the straight part of drop handlebars, otherwise they interfere with the variety of hand positions, and they also usually require a support beneath.

These two bags between them should carry all you need to take for tours longer than a week – unless you are camping. Camping means carrying a considerable bulk – although if properly chosen not a tremendous weight – and some type of pannier bag will be needed. American manufacturers, such as Eclipse, Kangaroo and Kirtland, as well as the British manufacturers Carradice and Karrimor, make both the normal rear and smaller front panniers. Typical capacities are 25,000 to 30,000 cc (1,500 to 1,800 cu in) for rear panniers and about half this for front ones. Because rear panniers have to be fitted well back to be missed by the heels when pedalling, they do considerably alter the feel of the bicycle. It is best to balance the load by using, if necessary, front panniers to complement rear ones or a saddlebag rather than to combine rear panniers with a saddlebag which overloads the rear wheel, possibly leading to spoke breakages.

A Tour of South-East England

A 600 km (350 mile) circular tour of an area rich in history and architecture with a wide range of lowland scenery – forest, heathland, orchards, meadows, riverside – with attractive country towns and villages, and three cathedrals. This is a comfortable one or two-week tour.

● Starting point: Hampton Court – with links to central London and London airports (Heathrow and Gatwick). As with any circular tour – start and finish at any point.

● Access: rail to London, (easy) rail links out of central London to larger towns (en route). Air to Heathrow and Gatwick. Sea to Dover, Folkestone, Newhaven, Portsmouth, Southampton.

● Maps: essential – either Bartholomew National Map 1:100,000 sheets 5 (New Forest and Isle of Wight), 6 (Sussex), 8 (Reading and Salisbury Plain), 9 (London and Surrey), 10 (Kent), or Ordnance Survey 1:250,000 Routemaster Sheet 9. Optional – Ordnance Survey 1:50,000 174, 175, 176, 179, 185, 186, 187, 188, 189, 195, 196, 197, 198, 199.

● Terrain and equipment: although the highest point, Leith Hill, is only 294 m (965 ft), some of the gradients can be very steep, though short – up to 20 per cent (1:5). Low gears advisable. Suggested routes outside London area are mostly narrow country lanes: there are many of these avoiding the main roads radiating from London which carry heavy traffic.

● Best season: April-June and September-November; possible all year.

● Overnight stops: hotels of all grades are plentiful in the moderate-sized towns, also some in remoter places. About 20 youth hostels nearby. Many camping possibilities.

● Further information: Tourist Boards – South-East, 4-6 Monson Rd, Tunbridge Wells, Kent; Southern, Old Town Hall, Leigh Rd, Eastleigh, Hants; Isle of Wight, 21 High St, Newport, IoW; Thames and Chilterns, 8 Market Pl, Abingdon, Oxon. Also: Cyclists' Touring Club and Youth Hostels Association (see Chapter 8).

● Hampton Court – palace of Henry VIII. From central London follow Fulham Road to Putney, cross Thames, turn immediate right on Lower Richmond Road, follow

Cycle camping in England's scenic New Forest.

signs into Richmond Park. Cross park south-west to Kingston, cross Thames to Hampton. From Gatwick airport see map.

● Windsor – royal Castle and Great Park. From Hampton via Sunbury, Shepperton and Chertsey to Virginia Water: entrance to Great Park, with car-free roads and superb panorama of Windsor Castle from horseback statue of George III. From Heathrow airport via Colnbrook and Datchet.

● Eton – prestigious school, Eton College, dating from 1443. From Windsor cross Thames by wheeling bicycle over bridge closed to motor traffic.

● Thames Valley. From centre of Eton to Dorney, Maidenhead, cross Thames again to Cookham, over Winter Hill to Marlow, another Thames bridge, Henley-on-Thames – scene of annual Royal Regatta in July. By minor roads from Henley to Pangbourne: cross Thames for the last time.

● Rural Berkshire. Minor roads by Bradfield to Woolhampton, and then cross historic Bath coach road, minor roads to Kingsclere.

● Hampshire Downs. Steady climb south over open chalk hills to Overton.

● River Test valley. Through attractive villages Freefolk, Whitchurch, Hurstbourne Priors, Longparish and Chilbolton.

● Winchester – mediaeval capital of England, in 9th century seat of King Alfred (statue in High Street); 900-year old cathedral – longest in Europe. Reached from Chilbolton by very undulating B3420 over open downland and woodland.

● New Forest – royal forest, now largely heathland, founded in 11th century by William the Conqueror; wild ponies. From Winchester follow Romsey road A3090 but re-enter lanes at Standon. Minor roads through Braishfield, Timsbury, Bramshaw, Stoney Cross to Lyndhurst. Open forest

141

road, B3056, to Beaulieu.

● Beaulieu – abbey incorporating car, motor-cycle and bicycle museum.

● Lymington – small Georgian town and ferry terminal for Isle of Wight.

● Isle of Wight. West from ferry terminal at Yarmouth to Alum Bay and the Needles: cliff scenery. Coast road through resorts of Ventnor, Shanklin, Sandown to Ryde – many by-road alternatives. Ryde is ferry terminal for Portsmouth; alternative, hovercraft to Southampton.

● Portsmouth – naval town, Admiral Lord Nelson's flagship *The Victory* preserved.

● Chichester – cathedral city, Roman palace site at Fishbourne. Little alternative from Portsmouth to main A27 route.

● South Coast resorts: Bognor Regis, Littlehampton, Worthing and Brighton. Busy seaside resorts with main road links – alternative minor roads possible but complex. Brighton – famous Regency resort, with notable and eccentric Pavilion.

● If time is short, ride directly via Cuckfield

and Balcombe to Gatwick Airport or via Lingfield to London.

● South Downs. Chalky uplands – minor road from Brighton over Ditchling Beacon, 248 m (813 ft), Wivelsfield to Sheffield Park – Bluebell Steam Railway.

● The Weald. The still-wooded remnant of the primaeval forest. Eastwards from Sheffield Park by Fletching, Uckfield, Blackboys and Heathfield to Burwash (home of author Rudyard Kipling, Bateman's, open to public) and Bodiam – a 14th century castle.

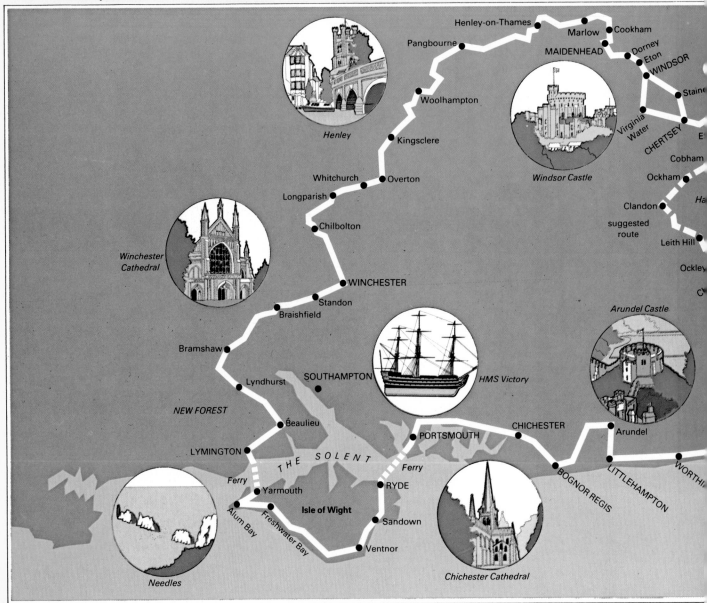

Henley

Winchester Cathedral

Windsor Castle

HMS Victory

Arundel Castle

Needles

Chichester Cathedral

142

- Cinque Ports – once seagirt, now left inland by sea's retreat, formerly England's front line defence against France. Winchelsea, south-east from Bodiam by minor roads, and Rye – steep, cobbled Mermaid Street with 15th and 16th century houses.
- Romney Marsh – impressively dead flat area, leading to Hythe – miniature railway leading to shingle headland, Dungeness.
- Canterbury – walled inner city with cathedral dating from 597, seat of Archbishop of Canterbury, 'primate of all England'. From Hythe, minor roads north through Lyminge and Bossingham.
- Garden of England – the Weald of Kent, with the apple orchards and hopfields which justify the name. Avoid A2 and A20 trunk roads with heavy coastal traffic: suggested route is via typical villages Chilham, Charing, Biddenden and Goudhurst to Tunbridge Wells – Regency spa town. Continue through Speldhurst, Penshurst and Chiddingstone to Chartwell – former home of Sir Winston Churchill, now museum.

Gatwick airport is 20 km south-west via Edenbridge and Lingfield. London can be reached via Westerham and Bromley.
- Surrey summits. Through Charlwood to Newdigate and Ockley, steep climb up flank of Leith Hill, 294 m (965 ft), in pine forest. Then via Abinger and Gomshall, over North Downs to Clandon, Ockham, Cobham and Esher. Cross Thames at East Molesey to reach Hampton Court. Heathrow airport can be reached via Shepperton and Staines.

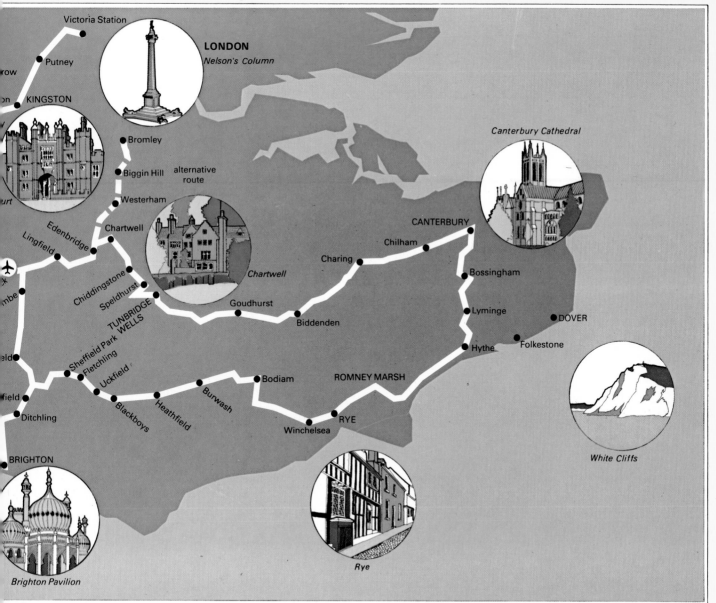

Victoria Station

LONDON
Nelson's Column

Putney

KINGSTON

Bromley

Biggin Hill · alternative route

Westerham

Edenbridge · Chartwell

Lingfield

Chiddingstone

Speldhurst

Chartwell

TUNBRIDGE WELLS

Sheffield Park · Fletchling

Uckfield

Blackboys · Heathfield

Ditchling

BRIGHTON

Brighton Pavilion

Burwash

Bodiam

Winchelsea

RYE

ROMNEY MARSH

Rye

Goudhurst

Biddenden

Charing

Chilham

Canterbury Cathedral

CANTERBURY

Bossingham

Lyminge

Hythe

DOVER

Folkestone

White Cliffs

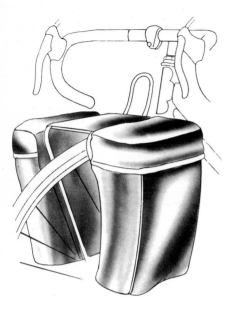

Front panniers on their carrier.

All bags require an appropriate support. The most effective rear (or front) carrier is made of steel, is triangular-shaped and bolted at its lowest point to the mudguard eyes incorporated into the fork ends. The type which attaches to the brake bolt at the top is adequate for saddlebags and light front panniers; but for heavier rear loads the carrier should have two separate top fittings, one to each seat stay. Plastic-coated carriers are more durable than chromed, as they are less susceptible to rust. Avoid the type of carrier which relies for its lower fixture on clips round the front forks or the bottom of the seat stays.

Chapter 4 outlines the types of clothing available and suitable for cycling, but personal taste will affect your choice. When touring, you should carry enough clothes to keep you warm in all outdoor conditions, together with a dry change of indoor clothing if your day's ride does not end at home. Also leave baggage space for clothing removed in hot weather. It is useful to take some fabric-covered elasticated, hooked straps to fix light and bulky items such as spare pullovers on top of a bag or carrier.

Waterproof clothing is a necessity for all but the shortest of trips – however fervently you hope not to need it. Remember that the body maintains its temperature during exercise by evaporating sweat from the skin into the airstream over it, and most types of proofed material cut off the bulk of this airflow, so that sweat condenses on the inside of the waterproof surface and you get both hot and wet. With only a moderate effort a cyclist can sweat remarkably heavily. To counteract this phenomenon, some wet-weather clothing exploits synthetic microporous materials which have porosity built into the material to allow out the passage of water vapour molecules, but which are too fine to allow in liquid water molecule groups.

Meanwhile, the choice is between the all-enveloping cape (poncho) and various, closer fitting proofed or impervious jackets. The cape allows some airflow round the body – although it can still be uncomfortably warm uphill – and effectively covers the hands and, to some extent, the lower half of your body. Arguments against it are the restriction on movement – hand signals require practice, for example – and its near unmanageability in the strong winds which often accompany rain. In contrast, the various nylon jackets and racing capes (which cover the top part of the body only) and waterproof leggings are no problem in the wind but are uncomfortably sticky after only the shortest of journeys. You will have to accept that, to some degree, wet weather means getting wet, although it's not always unenjoyable. You should be more concerned at keeping warm, particularly after removing waterproofs outdoors,

Discovering a new landscape with the aid of bicycle and map is a challenge, especially in the depths of winter. When snow covers the unfrequented trail, things can get even trickier!

as in showery weather.

Another occasion when you need some protective clothing is in the cold. Windproof gloves which allow some 'breathing' (such as ski mitts) are good, and a cap or woollen hat can protect the forehead and ears. You may feel particularly cold when no longer active after a strenuous effort, such as when waiting for companions at the top of a hill or when freewheeling down the other side, or at any moderate altitude, even in summer.

Maps and routes

When you start touring, it is possible to jump in at the deep end by joining a club and enlisting for, say, a week's tour organized by one of the major touring bodies. But it is advisable to start with short, local trips. Buy a large-scale road map of your area – probably a 1:50,000 (1 cm to 500 m) Ordnance Survey map in Britain or the 7½-minute series (1 cm to 240 m) US Geological Survey in the States. Such maps show a wealth of topographical and general detail, as well as the back roads, so vital to the bicycle tourist.

If you live in the middle of a big city, your choice of route may be limited to park roads or perhaps a canal tow path. But weekend trips can be made into the countryside, perhaps using the train or car to transport you and your bike to a suitable starting point. Initial trips should be closely planned beforehand on your map,

A Tour of the French Alps

A one-way tour of medium difficulty, linking Lyon in France with Geneva in Switzerland. The suggested route takes in a range of valley, vineyard, gorge and mountain roads to a total 700 km (435 miles), comfortably ridden in 7-10 days.

● Starting point: Lyon.

● Access: air from Paris, London and other European centres; rail from Calais, Paris, Marseille; road by Autoroute A7 from north or south.

● Maps: Michelin 1:200,000 sheets 74 (Lyon-Genève) and 77 (Valence-Grenoble) or IGN 1:250,000 (Savoie-Dauphiné) or IGN 1:100,000 sheets 45, 51, 52, 53, 54.

● Terrain and equipment: followed in the direction given this tour builds up from lower hills to the higher mountain passes, up to 2,800 m (9,100 ft) high. Low gears (2.4 m) are essential: climb steadily at your own pace, do not try to keep up with companions while riding but arrange to regroup at the summits. Have warm clothing ready for waits and descents. In going down long passes, use both brakes – generally means more pressure on rear brake than usual – to avoid overheating rims which could lead to tyre failure or even blowouts: if necessary stop to let rims cool. If you seem to be running out of road at a hairpin bend concentrate on stopping in as nearly as possible a straight line rather than try to take the corner too fast. Not necessary to carry midday food but this offers most flexibility. Note that British- and US-fitting cycle spares are not available.

● Best season: high passes open from mid-June –from then to early July or September are best; August is possible but crowded.

● Overnight stops: hotels of all classes plentiful, about a dozen youth hostels on or near the route, campsites of all grades. Little accommodation at or near tops of passes.

● Further information: Fédération Française de Cyclotourisme (see Chapter 8), Fédération Unie des Auberges de Jeunesse, French National Tourist Office, local *syndicats d'initiative*.

● Lyon – large industrial city, originally textiles but now diversified, at confluence of major rivers Saône and Rhône. From Lyon-Perrache rail station follow west bank of Rhône, crossing river at Givors to Vienne; from Lyon-Satolas airport direct by minor roads to Vienne.

● Vienne to Romans. From Vienne – Roman temple – south by undulating minor road D46 to Jarcieux, cross into *département* of Drôme: note that D-road numbers change at *département* border. Follow D53 by Châteauneuf-de-Galaure and St Donat-sur-l'Herbasse to Romans-sur-Isère.

● Vercors – Regional Natural Park. Cross River Isère and follow N531 through St Nazaire and Pont-en-Royans to climb Gorges de la Bourne – spectacular shelf road in limestone gorge. At top, right on D103, then D518 through la Chapelle-en-Vercors – Résistance memorial – to climb Col de Rousset (1,367 m, 4,483 ft) – spectacular limestone scenery. Rapid hairpinned descent to Die – centre of small wine-growing area.

● Die to Mens. Follow River Drôme valley on D93 to Pont-de-Quart, left on D539 to Chatillon, then D120 to climb Col de Menée (tunnel, 1,402 m, 4,599 ft) winding road, now D7, to Clelles, then D526 to Mens.

● Mens to Bourg d'Oisans. Gentle climb to Col Accarias (892 m, 2,926 ft) – extensive views to south – then undulating road to join N85 – 'Route Napoléon'. Right and after 2 km left once more on D526 through Valbonnais to climb Col d'Ornon (1,367 m, 4,483 ft) – upland Alpine meadows, then descent to Bourg d'Oisans - spectacular rock folding and colouring.

● Three cols (mountain passes) – all three are on the same road and, the Galibier particularly, have often been the decisive points of the Tour de France. Main road climb on N91 with lake and waterfall scenery to la Grave – spectacular views to south of la Meije peak (3,983 m, 13,064 ft) with glaciers. Upland Alpine and meadow scenery to Col de Lautaret (2,058 m, 6,750 ft) – Alpine Garden with collection of rare Alpine flowers. Left on stiff climb of Col du Galibier (2,645 m, 8,675 ft) passing memorial to Henri Desgrange, founder of Tour de France. Steep winding descent to Valloire, then relatively short climb of Col du Télégraphe (1,570 m, 5,150 ft), followed by fast, winding descent to St Michel-de-Maurienne.

● Roof of the Alps. Right on N6, main road up valley of River Arc unavoidable for 17 km to Modane, then hilly alternative on D215 and D83 on north of valley to Sollières-Sardières. Rejoin main road to Lanslebourg then ahead on N202 up narrowing valley for major climb of Col de l'Iseran (2,770 m, 9,086 ft) – second highest road in France, with spectacular views to south. Climb is often through high banks of snow even in late June and July. Long descent (44 km) through Val d'Isère with grandiose mountain, lake and forest scenery – tunnels on road, to Séez and Bourg St Maurice.

● Bourg St Maurice to la Clusaz. Initially wooded climb on D902 up Vallée des Chapieux to Cormet de Roselend (1,922 m, 6,304 ft) – artificial lake. Very winding forest descent to junction with D70, right to Hauteluce, then D218 to climb Col des Saisies (1,633 m, 5,356 ft). Descent either on D218 or left on forest road to Gorges de l'Arly at Flumet. Climb Gorges de l'Arondine on D909 to Col des Aravis, last major col, (1,498 m, 4,913 ft). 3 km out-and-home detour to south of col on steep minor road leads to viewpoint giving panorama of Mont Blanc range (Mont Blanc is highest European peak, 4,810 m, 15,782 ft).

● la Clusaz to Geneva. Long descent on D12 through St Jean de Sixt to St Pierre-de-Rumilly. Left on D19c then D19 and D2 to Geneva or right into Bonneville, then choice of minor roads to Excenevex on southern shore of Lake Geneva (Lac Léman). The shore road D25 through Yvoire (castle) and across Swiss border to Geneva.

● Geneva - major Swiss and international city, literary and ceramic museums, lake voyages. Access: air– Geneva-Cointrin airport to all major international destinations; rail to Paris and Calais and other European centres; road – Dijon then Autoroute to Paris, links to German Autobahn system, direct Autoroute to Lyon and south.

A snow tunnel in early June near Bourg d'Oisans.

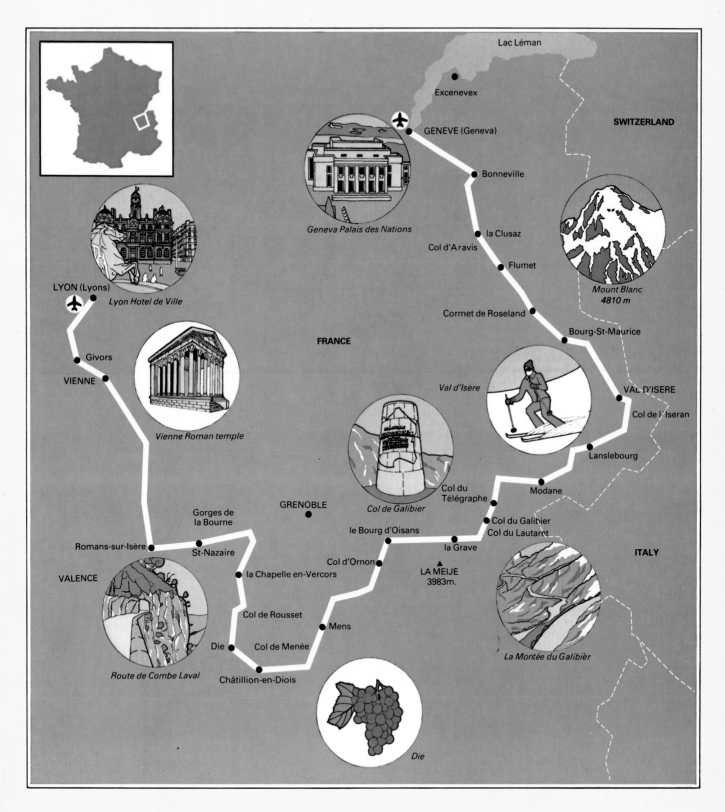

Lac Léman

Excenevex

SWITZERLAND

✈ GENEVE (Geneva)

Geneva Palais des Nations

Bonneville

la Clusaz

Col d'Aravis

Flumet

Mount Blanc
4810 m

Cormet de Roseland

Bourg-St-Maurice

FRANCE

LYON (Lyons)

Lyon Hotel de Ville

✈

Givors

VIENNE

Val d'Isère

VAL D'ISERE

Col de l'Iseran

Vienne Roman temple

Lanslebourg

Col du
Télégraphe

Modane

Col de Galibier

GRENOBLE

Col du Galibier

Col du Lautaret

Gorges de
la Bourne

le Bourg d'Oisans

la Grave

ITALY

Romans-sur-Isère

St-Nazaire

Col d'Ornon

▲ LA MEIJE
3983m.

VALENCE

la Chapelle en-Vercors

Col de Rousset

Mens

La Montée du Galibièr

Die

Col de Menée

Route de Combe Laval

Châtillon-en-Diois

Die

147

perhaps leaving some alternatives to allow on-the-spot choices of route as the ride develops. Make each 'tour' a ride of discovery so that you gradually improve your knowledge of the district.

Map reading is an art that will improve with practice. You will learn to avoid the main highways and choose the back roads. Don't be discouraged by roads that, on the map, appear to seek out the highest terrain. Some of your best touring experiences will be gained when riding along a hilltop road that provides extensive views and exciting swoops back to the valley.

For planning longer trips, which may take you up to 150 km (about 90 miles) away from home, the best scale of map is 1:250,000 (1 cm to 2.5 km). Both the British Ordnance Survey and the US Geological Survey produce excellent maps to this scale, while much of continental Europe is covered by the Michelin 1:200,000 series. An intermediate scale that can be useful for both detailed touring and long distance riding is 1:100,000 (1 cm to 1 km). Most countries offer such maps, the Bartholomew series in Britain being a good example because it shows all the important back roads as well as the topography (denoted by shading of 'green' valleys up to 'dark brown' hills). Other examples are the comprehensive IGN series in France and the exquisitely detailed Swiss national survey. In the United States, the USGS 15-minute series (1 cm to 480 m) is the main choice, but these maps are usually printed on unfolded art paper and are becoming replaced by the larger 7½-minute scale.

Many tourists carry their current map folded in a clear plastic pocket on the handlebar bag. This protects the map from the elements, gives you an instant display of the area and avoids troublesome refolding of the map in windy conditions.

Do not be overcome by ambition when planning tours. Record breakers may be able to average 300 km (nearly 200 miles) a day on their way from Los Angeles to New York, but 10 to 20 per cent of that daily distance would be more appropriate for a novice. Cycling pleasure is not directly proportional to the distance covered; it's how and where you go that matters. A comfortable riding speed will be about 20 km/hour (12.5 mph). But with stops for sightseeing and food your average may be half this, so that a gentle trip of about 50 km (30 miles) could last five hours. In mountainous areas, you will probably need to add an hour to your estimated time for each 300 m (1,000 ft) of climbing.

Where to stay

If you are going to ride in one direction for more than a few hours you will need somewhere to stay. Traditionally, touring cyclists have tended to move on from day to day and it was one of the first functions of the early touring organizations to collate members' recommendations of overnight accommodation. Nowadays travel is more general and there is a much wider choice.

Hotels and motels are the most expensive choice, but also the most flexible. You will probably be able to stay just one or two nights, particularly in the busier seasons. Most accommodation is in double rooms and the lone traveller may have to pay proportionately more than two people prepared to share one room. Most national, state, regional or city tourist boards are able to supply lists of accommodation, while national motoring organizations are also good sources.

Next down in cost come guest houses, *pensions* (small hotels, without restaurants) and, in Britain, 'Bed and Breakfast' establishments. Both the Cyclists' Touring Club and the British Cycling Federation publish annual handbooks listing such accommodation in Britain. These establishments also figure on local tourist authority lists. At busy times, it's usually worth reserving beds by telephone once it becomes clear where you're likely to finish the day's ride.

Less expensive, particularly if you prepare your own food, are youth hostels, YMCAs and YWCAs. And most countries have youth hostel organizations. To use them you have to be a member of the association of your own country or hold the rather more expensive international card. Rules vary slightly from country to country, but basically all youth hostels aim to provide simple accommodation in multiple-bedded dormitories (segregated by sex in some countries, including the British Isles). Blankets or duvets are provided, but the hosteller has to bring a sheet sleeping bag to protect the bedding. Some hostels provide meals and most (except one or two temporary holiday ones) have a kitchen where members can cook their own food.

In addition to breakfast and dinner you'll need food during the day. It is usually straightforward to find a convenient restaurant in popular areas but you will need to carry a picnic lunch (and/or emergency rations) in remote places. It's desirable to carry a sharp knife for slicing and another for spreading, since it's frequently best to buy food at a local shop or store and carry out the minimal preparations when you stop. This can be quite a social affair in, for example, France where visits to the *boulangerie, épicerie* and the market fruit stall can be followed by a leisurely picnic accompanied by a *vin du pays* – dining like a prince for a pittance. In remote country, check where the next shop is to be found before you pass what might be the only one that morning.

Another form of vacation is 'centre-touring' which comprises staying for a period – say a week – at a fixed centre and riding out

A WARNING TO ENTHUSIASTS.

A warning to the Ordinary or 'high wheeler' rider from Punch *magazine in 1889.*

The rugged mountains dwarf the small group of cyclists on this early section of a pass through France's Massif Central. Ultra-low gears are the best insurance of successfully negotiating the climbs that can sometimes extend for 40 km (25 miles).

into the surrounding area each day. Pick an interesting centre, and not necessarily one on the coast (which is likely to reduce by half the directions in which you can go).

Cycle camping

Cycle camping with well-chosen equipment offers the ultimate in cheap, versatile and independent travel, but naturally needs some extra purchases. The obvious requirements are a tent and sleeping bag, but you will also need some degree of independence as regards food (including its preparation and cooking) and water.

There are many tents on the market in the right weight range for the cycle camper – about 2 kg (around 4 lb). Price can be a fair indication of quality, but the only type worth considering is double-skinned with a sewn-in groundsheet. The outer skin is usually of synthetic waterproof material and the separate spaced inner skin of light cotton or porous fabric to avoid condensation. The outer skin (or flysheet) should come right down to ground level to provide a certain amount of undercover storage space. Many experienced cycle campers use a so-called 'two-man' tent for one person: the weight and bulk are by no means double, and the higher price is offset by extra storage and moving space. The tent may be rolled up to fit in a 'stuff sack' about 20-25 cm (8-10 in) in diameter and 40-50 cm (16-20 in) long. Alternatively, the poles, inner tent and flysheet can be distributed in separate bags for carrying on your bicycle.

The best sleeping bags weigh a little over 1 kg (about 2.2 lb). They can be filled with natural down or synthetic fibre (which is a little heavier and bulkier, but substantially cheaper). They compress into a roll about 20 cm (8 in) in diameter and 25 cm (10 in) long. Most of these light bags are sold as 'three-season' types (i.e. not for winter or high mountain use) and have polyurethane or polyamide covering. A youth-hostel type sheet sleeping bag is best used as a liner to keep them clean and to avoid condensation.

Opinions differ wildly on what degree of independence is necessary, particularly as regards cooking. Some campers prefer to travel as light as possible, perhaps using the overnight accommodation cost saved to treat themselves to restaurant meals, while others carry quite elaborate cooking equipment. If you're going to make the best use of the independence, you will need some sort of stove for heating water. The choices are: the traditional paraffin (kerosene) pressure stove (expensive to buy, and slow to start, but long-lasting, cheap to run and efficient); the petrol (gasolene) pressure stove (slightly cheaper to buy and a bit easier to start, but really requires non-leaded fuel and has the same problems of carrying a smelly liquid); and the gas (butane) cartridge stove (cheap to buy and very easy to start, but relatively expensive to run and with some loss of efficiency in cold weather when the gas is less inclined to vaporise). All are of about the same bulk, say $10 \times 10 \times 20$ cm ($4 \times 4 \times 8$ in) and weigh about 500 g (a little over 1 lb). You will also need lightweight aluminium cooking pots (the 'nesting' type fit inside each other and you can carry food in them as well) and the appropriate items of cutlery. For carrying water, some form of collapsible container of low bulk but holding 2-4 litres (3.5-7 Imperial pints, 4-8 US pints) is desirable.

If you're thinking of camping in even moderately hilly country, both your daily mileage and your gears will have to be lowered. Bottom gears as low as 2 m (about 27 in) using perhaps a 28-tooth inner chainring and a 28-tooth rear sprocket, are by no means excessively low. Unless your load is well distributed, however, the bicycle's front wheel can tend to lift under effort on such low gears.

Getting there

In most countries bicycles may be carried by train although costs and practices vary widely. To travel long distances or abroad, you may have to register your bicycle as luggage. It might go by the same service as you do, but don't bank on it. If possible send it a few days in advance and always remove loose items such as pumps, bottles, bags and lamps. It's also not a bad idea to wrap something round the frame tubes; the foam plastic used in the home for insulating water pipes is excellent and subsequently packs away to almost nothing in the bottom of a bag. Customs formalities may have to be gone through at your destination so you should register your bike to places only where customs facilities exist.

If travelling by sea, you will find that few boats do not carry bicycles though once more costs vary from free to quite expensive, sometimes more than the passenger fare. For sea travel, the most convenient boats are roll-on/roll-off car ferries on which the cyclist can ride or wheel his bike aboard and ride off at the other end. On some passenger ferries you may have to carry your machine aboard or even see it suffer the indignity of being hoisted aboard by crane.

Bikes can generally be carried by scheduled air services, often free if they come within the baggage allowance which is normally 15 kg (33 lb) for internal flights and 20 kg (44 lb) for international flights. Some airlines charge per piece and size of baggage, counting the bicycle as one. There is usually a limit to the number of bikes that can be taken on any one flight and you may be asked to place it in a special container or to 'streamline' the bike by removing the wheels and strapping them to the frame, turning handlebars so they take up less space, and removing or reversing pedals so that they face inwards. Most modern planes have loading hatches large enough to limit these operations to only reversing the pedals.

Carrying bicycles by car to a centre is most economical if a small group is travelling together. Most estate cars (station wagons) can hold at least two bikes with front wheels removed. Or roof racks (car-top carriers) are available with special fittings (to which the bike's front forks can be bolted) and cradles (for the rear wheels). About four bikes per car is the limit – although some roof racks can accommodate as many as nine machines with associated wheels. Check that the bikes and the rack are securely fixed and are not overloading the car. Measure the car and bikes' combined height in case you meet limits in car parks, at low bridges or if taking the car and bikes on a car ferry.

In some countries, particularly in more remote areas, buses will carry bicycles, perhaps piled with other luggage on a roof rack. Some long-distance buses and coaches also accept a bicycle if it is packaged to fit in with and not damage other luggage. You will have to check with tourist offices and individual tour operators to find out if this is a possibility on your intended route.

Where to go

Now that you are well informed on touring equipment, clothing, accommodation and transport, your next question is likely to be 'Where do I go?' The short answer is 'Anywhere', but your choice will be limited by the time available and by how much money you want to spend. Travel books are good sources of ideas, as are the tour suggestions provided by touring organizations such as American Youth Hostels, Bikecentennial or the Cyclists' Touring Club. To illustrate the planning and preparation necessary, we have included in this chapter three very different types of tour in different parts of the world. All three examples, however, have been approached in the same manner to show how you can make the most of the time available.

Do not be afraid of tackling any type of terrain. Even mountain passes can be tackled by making use of your knowledge of gearing and pedalling rates. Flat country also has its attractions – a broad openness, the great dome of the changing sky – but broad horizons can take a long time to reach. There can be few countries to which cycle tourists have not travelled in the past century. One, Englishman Ian Hibell, has even travelled (almost like a Victorian explorer) the length of the world's longest land masses – from southern Chile to northern Alaska in the Americas, and from North Cape in Scandinavia down to the Cape of Good Hope at the tip of South Africa.

This tourist has made his bike more compact for transportation by strapping the front wheel and mudguard (fender) to the frame and reversing the right-hand pedal so that there are no unwanted protrusions.

153

A Tour of the American Continental Divide

A long-distance, one-way tour to explore some of North America's most spectacular natural beauty. The route roughly follows the Continental Divide through the mountain states of Montana, Wyoming and Colorado. Total distance is about 2,400 km (1,500 miles), linking four National Parks, and will take three weeks or more.

● Starting point: Missoula, Montana.
● Access: air, Amtrak rail, Greyhound bus, road by Interstate 10.
● Finishing point: Denver, Colorado.
● Alternative intermediate finishing points: Missoula; Jackson, Wyoming.
● Maps: US Geological Survey 1:500,000 sheets of Montana, Wyoming and Colorado; 1:125,000 sheets of Yellowstone and Rocky Mountain National Parks; or Rand McNally state maps, approx 1:1,500,000, Idaho/Montana, Wyoming/Utah, and Colorado.
● Terrain and equipment: This is a trip for the experienced rider, involving passes 3,000 m (10,000 ft) up. The scenery is spectacular. A feature of touring in the US is the relative isolation of each community, with much greater distances between towns than in Europe – even in the two most populous states, California and New York. This means that the touring cyclist should be fully equipped for emergencies, with extra food, water, clothing and bike spares. A lightweight tent would be useful on some stretches: indeed, this would make an ideal cycle camping tour. Special attention should be paid to prevailing weather conditions and forecasts, particularly in desert and mountain areas where shelter is rare. For hints on mountain riding see the details in **A Tour of the French Alps**.
● Best season: early June or late September to avoid traffic and excessive temperatures.
● Overnight stops: possibilities indicated.
● Further information: Bikecentennial, League of American Wheelmen, American Youth Hostels Inc (see Chapter 8); National Park Service, US Dept of the Interior, Washington, DC 20009.
● Missoula to Glacier National Park (about 235 km, 150 miles). North through Mission Valley, Ravalli – National Bison Range with other protected animals too – Flathead Indian Reservation, Polson, Flathead Lake. Kalispell, then US 2 to Hungry Horse (overnight). Climb Middle Fork valley to

first crossing of Divide, Marias Pass (1,596 m, 5,236 ft), 90 km after Hungry Horse.
● Glacier National Park. Fast descent to East Glacier, left off US 2 to Kiowa and St Mary (overnight). 'Going-to-the-Sun' Road: breathtaking shelf road climb to Logan Pass (2,031 m, 6,664 ft) after following north shore of St Mary Lake; spectacular vistas at summit. Long hairpinned descent to Lake McDonald: overnight – Avalanche camping ground (3 km detour to Avalanche Basin, natural amphitheatre,

falls). Possible overnights in Glacier Park lodges (open from June 15). Retrace along US 2 to south of West Glacier.
● Back to Missoula. Follow State 35 through Creston to Bigfork, left to Swan Lake (overnight). Through wooded country to Seeley Lake (overnight). From this point direct return to Missoula if required, otherwise continue towards Yellowstone.
● Missoula to Yellowstone (about 460 km, 290 miles). South-east on US 10 to Drummond; or direct from Seeley Lake via Gar-

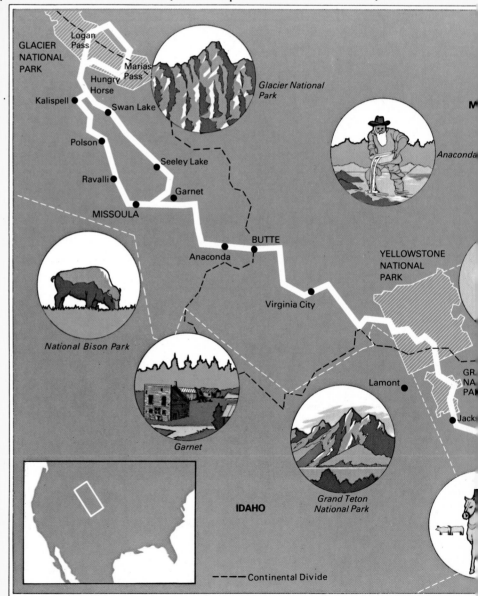

Glacier National Park

Anaconda

National Bison Park

Garnet

Grand Teton National Park

YELLOWSTONE NATIONAL PARK

GLACIER NATIONAL PARK

Logan Pass

Marias Pass

Hungry Horse

Kalispell

Swan Lake

Polson

Seeley Lake

Ravalli

Garnet

MISSOULA

BUTTE

Anaconda

Virginia City

Lamont

IDAHO

- - - - Continental Divide

net (ghost town). US 10A to Philipsburg (overnight) on edge of Lolo and Deerlodge National Forests. Anaconda and Butte – historic mining area: world's largest gold nugget came from near Anaconda; true ghost towns can be explored; Butte has mining museum. Follow US 10 to Pipestone Pass on the Divide, then easy climb up Jefferson and Ruby valleys to Virginia City (overnight) – gold boom town now restored. Up narrowing Madison valley, through forests to Earthquake Lake, past Hebgen Dam and Lake to West Yellowstone (overnight).

● Yellowstone National Park – 9,000 sq km of scenic wonders, world's first National Park, created in 1872. After Madison Junction (22 km) choice of routes: (1) ahead through Norris, climb then descend to Canyon Village and Inspiration Point – one of Park's greatest sights: 400 m Lower Falls of the Yellowstone River, gorge of vivid yellow and red rocks in brilliantly green forest. Then up Hayden Valley to Yellowstone Lake, round lake to West Thumb and Grant Village. Alternative: (2) right at Madison Junction over Craig Pass on the Divide (2,518 m, 8,262 ft), passing geysers including regular Old Faithful, (Visitor Center with information), then recross divide to Grant Village (overnight).

● Grand Teton National Park – jagged mountain range including Grand Teton (4,197 m, 13,766 ft). Route US 89 from Yellowstone involves one more crossing of Divide and follows shore of Jackson and Jenny Lakes at about 2,000 m (6,500 ft), US 187 to Jackson.

● Jackson, Wyoming (about 665 km, 414 miles from Missoula). Overnight: Jackson Hole hostel. Access: air, or road from Interstate Highway 15 at Idaho Falls (150 km).

● Jackson to Rawlins (about 480 km, 300 miles). This stretch includes some of the United States' loneliest country outside Alaska. The lightweight tent could be very useful and emergency extra food is essential as the route crosses the Divide and the 'desert' of the Great Divide Basin. Two alternative routes: (1) north, then east on US 26 through Bridger and Shoshone National Forests, over Togwater Pass (2,944 m, 9,658 ft) to Dubois and Lander; (2) longer route south on US 189 and east on US 187 through Pinedale (cattle country) over South Pass (2,301 m, 7,550 ft) to South Pass City and Atlantic City – restored twin ghost towns. Routes reunite south of Lander, through Jeffrey City on US 287 and Lamont – only communities with more than 100 inhabitants in 200 km! – to Rawlins.

● Rawlins to Granby (about 270 km, 170 miles). Greener scenery again following North Platte River through Medicine Bow National Forest, camping overnight probably necessary, crossing Divide again at Willow Creek Pass, to southern entry to Rocky Mountain National Park at Granby.

● Rocky Mountain National Park – highest mountains and passes of tour: main mountain summit is Longs Peak (4,346 m, 14,255 ft). North by Lake Granby to culmination of tour in Milner Pass (3,279 m, 10,758 ft) and Fall River Pass (3,595 m, 11,796 ft). Trail Ridge Road climbs above treeline, skirts chasms and offers tremendous mountain panoramas. Descent to Estes Park.

● Denver, Colorado (about 930 km 580 miles from Jackson). Reached by long descent through Boulder, then US 36. Access: air, Amtrak rail and road.

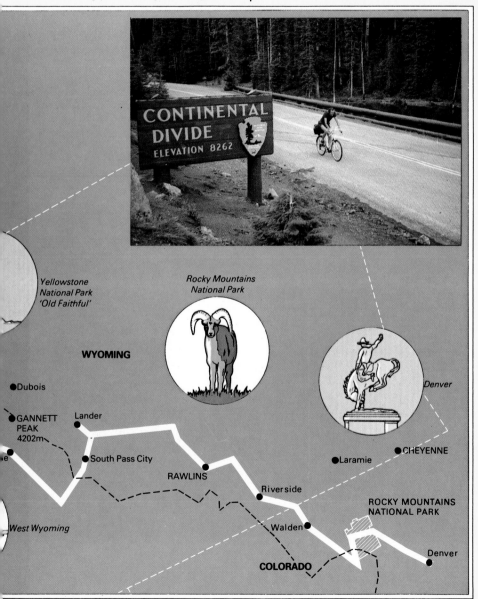

CONTINENTAL DIVIDE ELEVATION 8262

Yellowstone National Park 'Old Faithful'

Rocky Mountains National Park

WYOMING

● Dubois

● GANNETT PEAK 4202m

Lander

South Pass City

RAWLINS

Riverside

West Wyoming

Walden

COLORADO

Denver

● Laramie

● CHEYENNE

ROCKY MOUNTAINS NATIONAL PARK

Denver

The Americas

There is a great tradition of bicycle touring in North America and the pioneer spirit that helped open up the varied and inspiring landscape is today reflected in the wide variety of tours available. Each of the 50 United States offers contrasting opportunities, varying from the intimate, green countryside of New England to the lonely deserts of the West; and Canada offers no less exciting prospects.

Interest in touring increased rapidly through the 1970s and a comprehensive programme of annual events (mass rides, escorted tours, century runs, area rallies) has been developed. New bikeways and posted bike trails are continually being added to a system of touring routes that is unique in North America. Not all of the bikeways are well planned, especially when they form short lengths of a discontinuous network. But they can be useful for riding out from cities such as Washington DC, which has developed many commuter bikeways. The first official bikeway was designated at Homestead, Florida in 1962; while the longest continuous bikeway, part of it along the route of an abandoned railroad, is 534 km (332 miles) across Wisconsin state from Kenosha to La Crosse. Most long distance trails – like those listed in the American Youth Hostels' invaluable North America Bicycle Atlas – are routes that comprise lightly trafficked back roads. The longest posted route is the 6,840 km (4,250 mile) TransAmerica trail from Oregon to Virginia, which was first researched by the Bikecentennial organization in 1975.

Well equipped, experienced bicycle tourists will certainly enjoy the widely contrasting conditions encountered in Mexico, and perhaps neighbouring Guatemala. To be avoided are the heavily trafficked main highways across the US/Mexico border and around the main industrial areas of Guadalajara, Monterrey and Mexico City. Imaginative tours can be enjoyed along the exotic Pacific coast, in the central mountains between Guadalajara and Veracruz, or around the Yucatan peninsula.

Similar touring – although wilder and more adventurous – can be found in South America. The safest destinations may be tropical Colombia and Venezuela; Brazil's coastal region near Rio de Janeiro; or central Chile.

Europe

Despite its modest size – only 2,500 km (1,500 miles) from the Atlantic coast to the Black Sea – Europe contains a wealth of countryside of great interest to the bicycle tourist. It is something of a paradise to visiting American cyclists, who find an intricate network of paved back roads, hotels and hostels sympathetic to the tourist's needs, and ancient towns that are never too far away.

The continent is divided into north and south by the great mountain chains of the Pyrenees and the Alps (and their eastern extensions). The areas to the north (most of France, Belgium, the Netherlands, most of Germany, Poland, Denmark and southern Sweden) are gently contoured, generally quite varied, with much of historic and architectural interest. Comprehensive systems of bike paths exist in Denmark and the Netherlands, and it is the bicycle's widespread use here that probably led to the myth that flat places are best for cycling. Note that in many countries (including Belgium) the use is compulsory of bike paths that run alongside highways. The standard sign is a white bicycle on a blue, circular background.

Northern Sweden and most of Norway is wilder and much more mountainous than the rest of Scandinavia, with spectacular fjord scenery along the Atlantic coast providing arduous but well rewarded touring. Most roads in southern Sweden are adequately paved; elsewhere, oil-bound or unpaved roads are the rule – dusty in summer, muddy when wet. But such conditions are rarely met in the rest of Europe.

France offers the bicycle tourist the greatest variety within any single continental European country. Every type of upland scenery and quiet back roads are found in Pyrenees, Alps, Massif Central, Jura and Vosges mountains. The other main touring areas are the Brittany coast, the castle strewn Loire Valley, the Burgundy and Champagne wine country and sunny Provence.

Switzerland and Austria, with the adjoining parts of Germany, Italy and Yugoslavia, encompass the major portion of the Alps. Roads are generally confined to river valleys and the spectacular mountain passes, most of which are blocked by snow until late June or July. As the mountains descend eastwards into Austria there are more back roads. Accommodation is plentiful as these countries – together with the mountain parts of France – have a well developed winter sports industry, with most resorts staying open through the summer and autumn (fall).

Before tackling a rugged Alpine tour it is possible to gain valuable experience of climbing the shorter, yet still demanding pass roads that abound in the Ardennes forest of Belgium and Luxembourg, and the popular West German areas of Bavaria, the Eifel mountains and the Black Forest.

The European countries around the Mediterranean Sea enjoy mild winters and sometimes unbearably hot summers. There is a different mood from that of northern Europe. Except in the more

---

Check List 2

For a longer tour:

Clothing according to season: spare underwear, handkerchiefs, shirts, T-shirts, shorts and ankle socks, 'plus-ones' or training trousers/slacks and long socks, lightweight trousers/slacks/skirt for evening, light sandals or shoes. Overnight: soap, towel (two small ones are better than one large), razor, toothbrush, toothpaste, petroleum-based grease-removing jelly in small tin, sleeping bag, sleeping wear.

Sundries: first-aid kit, needle and strong thread, scissors, safety pins, 'stuff sacks', elastic straps, extra toestraps, plastic insulating tape, small shoulder bag, money, cheque book and credit cards, travellers' cheques, membership cards (YHA, CTC etc), camera and films, maps, handbooks, address book, coins for phone calls.

Eating: cutlery including sharp knife, can and bottle openers.

Tools: spanners (wrenches) and Allen keys to fit every nut on the bike, chain rivet extractor, spoke key, pliers. For long journeys or just after servicing: cotterless crankset tools (spanner & extractor), freewheel remover to fit *your* freewheel.

Spares: extra spare inner tube, rear brake and gear cables (can be used on front in emergency), spokes, cotter pin (for cottered crankset), lamp bulbs. For long journeys: brake blocks, spare nuts and bolts, freewheel pawl springs, spare outer tyre if journey is longer than 2,000 km (assuming new one at start).

The rocky landscape of Yellowstone National Park is one of the highlights of the American Continental Divide tour. A choice of routes through the park can mean a visit to the Old Faithful geyser or a trip to Inspiration Point in the Yellowstone River gorge.

fertile valleys, agriculture is hard and is generally devoted to growing vines and raising sheep. These are countries for relaxation, for more leisurely touring, where the siesta is a necessity to escape the midday sun. Don't forget to buy your day's provisions before the banks and shops close at noon.

Britain and Ireland

You should not be deceived by the comparative smallness of Britain – which is but 1,400 km (about 870 miles) between its south-western and north-eastern extremities, while highest mountain Ben Nevis is only 1,343 m (4,406 ft) above sea-level. Britain contains everything for the cycle tourist.

English, Welsh and Scottish tourists have been exploring and describing their country since before the Cyclists' Touring Club became the world's first ever touring body in 1878. Charming countryside lies close to all the major urban areas. Further afield, the most popular holiday centres are Devon and Cornwall (steep hills, with wonderful scenery), East Anglia (flat, but full of historic associations), the Cotswold Hills (picturesque villages, upland views), the Welsh mountains (lonely, open country, with many grassgrown trails), the Peak District and Yorkshire Dales (wildly spectacular moorland, steep-sided valleys), the Lake District (compact, but Britains's loveliest lake-and-mountain scenery), the Border country (from Northumberland's green hills to the Galloway coast), and the Scottish Highlands (rugged mountain scenery on a scale approaching that of continental Europe).

Most of southern and eastern England has an abundance of those back roads and lanes which make for enjoyable cycling. This makes the region ideal for centre-touring or long weekend trips from the urban areas. Equally satisfying is coastal touring, especially in the south-west, where the many sandy beaches will prove popular on a family vacation. But this can involve a considerable amount of retracing your route since there is rarely a continuous coastal road. Combined with the frequent climbing back from sea-level, this should limit your ambitions to perhaps less than 50 km (30 miles) a day on this type of tour.

Many of the youth hostels in Britain are in isolated country, which may encourage you to explore some of the less frequented, unpaved tracks that abound in the mountains of central Wales, the northern Pennines and the Grampians. If you are seeking solitude without the loneliness of these wilderness areas, then perhaps the relatively traffic-free roads of Ireland are the answer.

The nearness of the ocean and the admittedly high rainfall give the Emerald Isle both its famed greenness and a haunting, azure clarity to its landscape. The touring cyclist will find a ready welcome in the often isolated communities, especially in the island's south and west. Roads are generally well paved, although perhaps a little bumpier and more sinuous than those in mainland Britain.

Rest of the world

From its well established origins in Britain, Europe and North America, bicycle touring has gradually spread throughout the world. Recognition of this came in 1980, when the Alliance Internationale de Tourisme (AIT) held one of its annual bicycle rallies in Japan, the first ever in the Eastern Hemisphere. Japanese cycle tourists are frequent visitors to Europe and America, and it is no surprise to find European-style hostels a dominant feature of touring in Japan. Also conducive to bicycle touring are the climate, the scenery, the high quality roads and the country's compactness.

In Australia, only parts of New South Wales, Victoria and Tasmania are popular cycling areas, but even here roads are often unpaved once the densely populated urban areas are left behind. New Zealand is more suited, with its spectacular coastal and mountain scenery and its mild climate. Elsewhere, the conventional cyclist would most feel at home in South Africa, Israel, Turkey and parts of North Africa (in the winter).

India is off the beaten track for most cycle tourists. But bicycles – and their uses – abound in a country which ranks among the top six nations in the number of cycles manufactured.

7

Racing

Few sports offer as many challenges to competitors as does bicycle racing. Since Englishman James Moore sped through a Paris park on his 40 kg (88 lb) boneshaker in 1868 to win the first ever cycle race, every conceivable type of competition on wheels seems to have been invented. Races vary in length from the 11-second sprint at the end of a 1,000 m (1,093 yd) scratch race on a banked track, where only the final 200 m (218 yd) are timed, to the 4,000 km (2,500 mile) Tour de France, with its five or six hours of racing every day for three weeks. Competition can be decidedly amateur, such as the road time trials contested by club cyclists in Britain; or very professional, such as the gambling-based Keirin races in Japan contested by highly paid and disciplined track racers. But whatever the rewards and whatever the challenge, it takes skill, speed and stamina to succeed.

Cycling is a flourishing, highly organized Olympic sport that has spread to every part of the world from its origins in Western Europe. Its development has varied greatly from country to country, but a better understanding of the sport can be gained by studying the three main streams of its evolution: in Great Britain, Europe and the United States.

Racing in Britain
The British were the first to develop an organized system of cycle racing, its progress closely following the history of the bicycle itself. When, in 1870, war broke out in France, James Moore returned to England and dominated the velocipede races of the early 1870s. Competing on the unpaved roads – rutted and dusty in summer, muddy in winter – was virtually impossible, so the early races took place on closed circuits, or tracks. At first these were unbanked and made of cinders or grass, but later were built of hard surfaces of concrete or timber. Long distance track and road races were invariably paced events, teams of riders on other machines taking turns to provide pace and slip-stream shelter for each competitor.

As the Ordinary (penny-farthing) bicycle became faster, so complaints from coach drivers and horse riders increased until the roads were left to cycle tourists and racers concentrated on the track.

At the end of 1878, the first ever indoor six-day race was contested. Reports vary on the results of the event, but there must have been more than one race because some records show F. Smythe as the winner, covering 1,800 km (1,118 miles), while others indicate that a Yorkshireman named Carns won, riding 1,705 km (1,060 miles). The races were non-stop according to most records, but others say that six hours rest was allowed in each 24-hour period. In 1881, all four British track championships – 1, 5, 25 and

COLLECTION FÉLIX POTIN

ZIMMERMANN

50 miles (1.6, 8.0, 40.2 and 80.5 km) – were won by G. Lacy-Hillier. And the following year, the 20 miles-in-the-hour barrier was broken by H.L. Cortis, paced by teams in the usual manner.

To cater for Britain's growing interest in road riding, the Road Records Association (RRA) was formed in 1888. This body was formed to officiate at and qualify any road record attempt such as the 1,400 km (870 mile) Land's End to John O'Groats. Clubs such as the North Road Club and Bath Road Club were formed to organize races on these specific roads – one leading north from London, the other to the west. The famous Bath Road 100 mile (161 km) race was first run in 1890, but the huge increase in cycling during the early 1890s contributed to the roads becoming too congested for the police to allow road racing to continue, and even the Bath Road '100' moved to the track.

Road racers did not like the decision, particularly at a time when massed-start, city-to-city races were booming on the continent of Europe. A partial solution came in 1895 when F.T. Bidlake, holder of a number of RRA records, organized the world's first road time trial, the North Road '50' (80.5 km). In this, riders started off at one-minute intervals, riding alone and unpaced over the 50 miles, with each man's finishing time being recorded. The winner was the one with the shortest time. Time trials remained the only form of road racing until World War II; and more amateurs still compete in road time trials in Britain than in true road races.

Above: *A major skill in road racing is to be able to raise a rapid sprint at the end of perhaps seven hours of continuous racing. Pictured here is a typical finish to the Milan-San Remo classic in Italy, won here by a youthful Eddy Merckx, who was to win this particular event seven times – a record.*

Left: *One of the first ever world champions was American track sprinter Arthur Zimmerman, who was noted for his elegance and smooth pedalling style. He was also one of the first professional racers to be sponsored by the Raleigh Cycle Company.*

There were no such restrictions on the development of track racing in Britain, and British cyclists were a dominant force in world championships until World War I. The first world title for Britain was won in 1895 by 18-year-old Welshman Jimmy Michael. This was the professional paced 100 km (62 mile) event, with the pace being provided by triplets and quads (three- and four-man bicycles). Motor bikes replaced the human powered pace machines by the early 1900s, and it was with mechanical pacing that one of Britain's greatest ever cyclists, Leon Meredith, won seven world championships in amateur paced events between 1904 and 1913.

Similar success was not repeated until after World War II, when Reg Harris won five world sprint championships (one amateur, four professional) between 1947 and 1954. Four world titles (in the professional 5 km pursuit) were won by Hugh Porter between 1968

Road racing is Europe's most popular summer sport, with the major events attracting crowds of up to 200,000 spectators. This picture shows the famous Mur de Grammont Hill in southern Belgium, scene of action in classic races such as the Tour of Flanders.

and 1973; and after the introduction of women's championships, Beryl Burton won seven titles in the period 1959-1967.

Entering the 1980s, Great Britain was re-emerging as a force in world cycling. Bunched road racing has been successfully revived in Britain, although the numbers of riders in each race are still strictly controlled by the police, with major events restricted to a maximum of 60 riders. The most successful races established through the 1960s and 1970s were the Tour of Britain (the Milk Race), a two-week, 1,610 km (1,000 mile) stage race for leading amateur internationals; the five-day Sealink International, also for amateur internationals; and the Empire Stores Marathon, a 400 km (250 mile) one-day race for· professionals, usually held from London to Bradford, Yorkshire.

A large number of amateurs still compete each week in road time

Time trials are individual contests of speed over a set distance, with each competitor starting at one-minute intervals and racing completely alone. In some events, especially in Europe, each rider is followed by a service vehicle to give the rider any necessary mechanical assistance.

Widely recognized as the most arduous and most prestigious of one-day classic races is Paris-Roubaix, a 260 km (161 mile) race that passes over farm tracks and neglected cobbled streets on its intricate journey from the French capital to Roubaix on the Belgian border. The roads used are muddy and slippery when wet, bumpy and dusty when dry. Despite these conditions, Europe's top professionals still average more than 40 km/hour (25 mph) in their efforts to be the winner at the Roubaix finish.

trials, however, partly because up to 150 starters are allowed, compared with the normal 40 or 50 in massed start road races. Winning times in time trial events have reduced tremendously with improvements in road surfaces, the greater efficiency of bikes, the increase in motor traffic (a mixed blessing, but it can provide artificial wind assistance) and modern methods of physical training. A mark of the progress is the classic distance 25 mile (40.2 km) competition record, which stood at 59 min 29 sec in 1939, and 40 years later had been reduced by 10 minutes. Other standard distances under regulations of the Road Time Trials Council (RTTC) are 10, 30, 50 and 100 miles (16, 48, 80.5 and 161 km) and 12 and 24 hours (in which the rider covering the greatest distance is the winner). Separate events are held for juveniles (under 16 years old), juniors (under 18), men, women and veterans (over 40). Time trials are also sometimes held as stages of multi-day road races. Track racing also thrives, with the annual professional six-day race in London, various international meetings and national championships.

North America

A measure of the high early status of American cycling is that the first world championships were held in Chicago in 1893 (followed by Montreal in 1899 and Newark, New Jersey, in 1912), and that the two-man formula for six-day racing first evolved at Madison Square Garden, New York in 1898.

There was massive public interest in the six-day 'race to nowhere' throughout North America in the first half of this century. It was at its height of popularity in the 1930s, a decade in which 20 American and four Canadian cities hosted their own events. This was the period when the Canadian William ('Torchy') Peden accumulated a world record 38 six-day victories, a total since beaten by only four men – Belgians Patrick Sercu and Rik Van Steenbergen, and Dutchmen Peter Post and Rene Pijnen.

Interest waned sharply after World War II, and Montreal was the only city to regularly run a six-day (mostly contested by European professionals) in the 1960s and 1970s, following the final New York six-day in 1961. The progress of track racing in the United States largely reflected that of the six-day event.

Road racing had never become established, partly due to the long distances between towns and to the early evolution of long distance tourist trials – such as the 100 mile (161 km) 'century' runs organized by the League of American Wheelmen. The sport therefore lay practically dormant until the bicycle revival of the late 1960s and early 1970s.

Unprecedented sales of bicycles and closer communications with Europe then saw both the development of road racing and a revived interest in track racing in the US. The first evidence of this upsurge was the shock win in the 1969 Women's World Road Race Championship at Brno, Czechoslovakia by the slim Californian, Audrey McElmury. She was the first American to win a cycling world title for more than 50 years. Her feat was followed by sprinters Sheila Young (1973) and Sue Novarra (1975 and 1976).

Many new banked tracks were built through the 1970s, with the one at Trexlertown, Pennsylvania hosting the world junior championships in 1978. The sport was becoming Europeanized, with the old-fashioned Amateur Bicycle League of America significantly changing its name to the United States Cycling Federation, catering for professionals and amateurs. Encouragement was gained from successes in Pan-American Games, and victories obtained by amateur American road racers in major international events in Great Britain, France and Italy during the late 1970s. In the US, the majority of road races are of the so-called criterium type – events of less than 100 km (62 miles) on short circuits closed to

---

Road Racing 1

Road races are contested by a group of 20-200 riders, all starting together.

Criterium A race of up to 100 km (62 miles) contested on a circuit 1–3 km (0.6–1.8 miles) round.

Kermesse A race of up to 161 km (100 miles) contested on one or more circuits, each 5–20 km (3–12 miles) round.

Circuit race A race of up to 290 km (180 miles) for professionals, 200 km (124 miles) for amateurs, 120 km (75 miles) for juniors, 75 km (47 miles) for women, and 60 km (37 miles) for under 16s; contested on one circuit, normally 10–25 km (6–15 miles) round, but sometimes as long as 40 km (25 miles).

Place-to-place A race of up to 670 km (416 miles) for professionals, 240 km (150 miles) for amateurs, and 130 km (81 miles) for juniors, contested between two different places, sometimes finishing with a few laps of a small circuit 3–15 km (1.8–9.3 miles) round, on a velodrome track, in a town centre, or at the top of a long hill.

Road Racing 2

Stage race (or tour) **A race comprising 2–24 separate stages, each stage normally being place-to-place; contested by 40–150 riders, all of whom must have finished the previous stage. Stages can also be circuit races, criteriums, individual or team time trials, or hill climbs. The winner is the rider with the lowest aggregate time, calculated by accumulation of the riders' individual times for each stage.**

Note: The Olympic road race of 175–200 km (109–124 miles) is held on a circuit of 13-25 km (8-15 miles). Annual world championship road races are held for professionals at 240–290 km (150–180 miles), amateurs at 175–200 km (109–124 miles), juniors at 110–130 km (68–81 miles) and women at 45–65 km (28–40 miles) on a circuit of 12–25 km (7.5–15 miles).

Right: *The most successful professional racing cyclist in history is Belgian Eddy Merckx, seen here climbing a mountain pass in the Tour de France, a race he won five times. He is wearing the so-called rainbow jersey, awarded to each world champion. Merckx won four official world road race championships, as an amateur in 1964 and professional in 1967, 1971 and 1976.*

Right (inset): *Most bike races in the United States are held on short, closed circuits in downtown areas. Shown here is the annual 50-lap Tour of Somerville, New Jersey.*

other traffic. But some true road races have evolved, including the Red Zinger international stage race held annually in the mountains of Colorado, and other European-type races and British-type road time trials have become established.

Europe

The traditional strongholds of European racing are France, Belgium and Italy, where the sport evolved in a manner completely different from that in Britain and North America. After the initial pattern of short distance road races and meetings on closed circuits through the 1870s and 1880s, the first really long distance events were organized in the 1890s. By then, main roads had improved from the former dirt and gravel tracks, and bicycles were of the modern safety type, equipped with pneumatic tyres.

Rival sports newspapers seeking enlarged readerships were responsible for organizing the first classic races, each trying to outdo the other with longer or more arduous events to capture the public's imagination. The 572 km (355 mile) Bordeaux-Paris, won by G. P. Mills in 1891, was followed in the same year by the even longer Paris-Brest-Paris (1,200 km, 745 miles), which was won by the extraordinary Charles Terront, who had already collected victories in several one-man, six-day races.

These races were followed by various one-day classics with varying degrees of success, but their popularity was nothing when compared with the enormous interest shown in the first ever Tour de France in 1903. Organized by former racer and then editor of the sports paper *l'Auto*, Henri Desgrange, this was a race of six stages, starting with Paris to Lyon (467 km, 290 miles) and encircling the country for its total of 2,428 km (1,508 miles). Winner by an accumulated margin of 2 hr 49 min was Frenchman Maurice Garin, one of 20 finishers from 60 starters.

The Tour de France has been held every year since 1903 (except for breaks for the two World Wars), attaining its longest duration in 1926 (5,795 km, 3,601 miles) and largest participation in 1928 (162 starters). The fastest Tour was in 1962 when Frenchman Jacques Anquetil averaged 37.3 km/hour (23.2 mph) for the 4,274 km (2,344 miles).

Other countries followed France's example and, in order of prestige, the leading national stage races are the Tour of Italy (founded 1909), Tour of Spain (1935), Tour of Switzerland (1933), Tour of Belgium (1908), Tour of Holland (1909), Tour of (West) Germany (1911) and the Tour of Luxembourg (1935). All these races are for professionals, all of whom compete for sponsored teams based in Belgium, France, Holland, Italy, Spain, Switzerland

Time Trials

Contested by individuals or teams, starting separately at strictly timed intervals of 1–4 minutes

Individual Normally on out-and-back basis, each rider covering a set route completely alone and unassisted, with the winner being the rider with the shortest time. Standard distances in UK and USA are 16, 40, 48, 80.5 and 161 km (10, 25, 30, 50 and 100 miles), or the greatest distance in 12 or 24 hours. Non-standard distances are 5–150 km (3–93 miles) on a circuit or place-to-place, often part of a stage race.

Team Contested by teams of 2–10 riders, each team riding completely separately. The course could be one or more laps of a circuit, place-to-place or out-and-back. Distances: up to 110 km (68 miles) for 2-, 3- or 4-man teams, or up to 161 km (100 miles) for 5-10 man teams. Note: The Olympic team time trial is 100–110 km (62–68 miles) for teams of four (the time of the third man across the finish line is recorded). The annual world championships are also for 4-man teams, distances being 95–110 km (59–68 miles) for amateurs and 60–75 km (37–46 miles) for juniors.

Hill climb This is an individual time trial of up to 15 km (9 miles), finishing at the top of a hill.

or West Germany and who race throughout Europe.

In the early part of this century, sponsorship money was provided by bicycle manufacturers alone; but most commercial organizations are now eligible to sponsor their own team, a typical annual budget in 1980 being between £200,000 to £500,000 (US $400,000 to $1 million). This budget provides for about 12 to 15 professionals to be paid monthly retainers plus winning bonuses to race from February to October in the major events all over Western Europe. These include the major national stage races, other regional stage races and one-day classics and national events.

Riders who distinguish themselves in the major classics and national tours augment their incomes with contract fees paid them to start in the hundreds of small town races (or criteriums) that take place towards the end of the season. Such events are rarely more than 100 km (62 miles) in length, compared with the 220 to 300 km (137 to 186 miles) of the one-day classics. Most successful amateurs in Western Europe turn professional in their early 20s, then race for 10 to 15 years before retiring, or reverting to amateur status. This is in contrast to the state sponsored East European racing cyclists, who remain amateur and usually attain their peak in their late 20s.

The most prestigious event held anywhere for amateurs is the 14-stage, 2,200 km (1,367 mile) Peace Race, first held in 1948 to commemorate the return of peace to Eastern Europe. It varies between starting at Berlin (East Germany), Prague (Czechoslovakia) and Warsaw (Poland) and traces its course between these three capital cities.

A limited number of races are given special permits to allow professionals and amateurs to compete together, while most important track meetings allow similar open competition. However, the annual World Championships have strict separation of categories – professionals, amateurs, women and juniors (under 19s). These championships are normally held in late August or early September, and the programme of European track meetings is structured to build up to this climax in the season. In Olympic years, world championships are held for only those events not contested at the Olympic Games.

Rest of the world

Besides the main centres of cycle racing, the sport has progressed considerably in the rest of the world since World War II. The World Championships had been held exclusively in Europe for more than 50 years before they were hosted by Montevideo, Uruguay (1968), Montreal, Canada (1974) and San Cristobal, Venezuela

(1977). Latin America has produced some outstanding cyclists, particularly in road racing, products of the many national stage races that take place in Brazil, Chile, Colombia, Costa Rica, Cuba, Guadeloupe, Mexico, Uruguay and Venezuela.

Among non-Europeans to have won world championships since World War II are Australians Graham French (1956), Jack Hoobin (1950), Gordon Johnson (1970), John Nicholson (1975 and 1976) and Sid Patterson (1949, 1950, 1952 and 1953) and the Japanese sprinter Koichi Nakano (1977, 1978 and 1979). It is significant that the sport is highly developed in both these countries, although the types of racing in Australia and Japan are considerably different from those in Europe.

In Australia, there is racing all the year round, with track racing in the summer and road racing in winter. Sydney and Melbourne are the centres for track racing, which is mostly contested by professionals, with emphasis on handicap races. There have also been a number of six-day races.

Most road races are also held on a handicap basis, with novices being given up to an hour's start on the leading men in a 100 mile (161 km) race. Country roads are often unpaved, but this has not deterred the Australians from organizing a nine-day stage race in Victoria, the Sun Tour, first held in 1952, and a similar event in Tasmania.

Japanese racing is virtually confined to velodromes, of which there are more than 50 in the country, attracting over 40 million spectators each year to the Keirin ('wheel-race') meetings. The crowds place bets on riders in each race, much like horse racing in Europe and America. Races are normally over set distances of 2, 4 and sometimes 6 km (1.2, 2.5 and 3.7 miles). Riders start from fixed starting gates, with probably ten men in each event.

The whole Keirin organization is run by the state, with the annual receipts of about £1,500 million (US $3 billion) being re-invested in the sport or financing major projects, such as the Sapporo Winter Olympics. The near 4,000 professional racers who take part all earn a good income, with top stars such as Nakano becoming millionaires.

Organization

More than 100 national federations are affiliated to the world controlling body, the UCI (Union Cycliste Internationale), making cycling one of the most widely practised sports in the world.

The actual control of international events is in the hands of UCI-approved commissaires (for road races) and judges (track). These officials act as independent referees, seeing that UCI rules are observed and that races are conducted in a safe and correct manner.

Cyclo-cross is an exhausting combination of cycle racing across fields and cross-country running, carrying the bike up the steeper climbs and over hurdles. Pictured here is many times British champion Chris Wreghitt.

Cyclo-cross

This is a winter form of racing contested by a group of 30–100 riders, who ride, push or carry bicycles around a cross-country circuit, normally of 1–3 km (0.6–1.9 miles) for a distance of up to 30 km (19 miles) for professionals, 25 km (16 miles) for amateurs and 20 km (12 miles) for juniors.

Officials also conduct random analytical tests for banned drugs. For administrative purposes, the UCI is composed of two parts, the FIAC (Fédération Internationale Amateur du Cyclisme) and the FICP (Fédération Internationale du Cyclisme Professionel).

Each national federation is responsible for framing its own national rules and controlling the sport in the UCI-approved manner. In turn, riders belong to clubs which are affiliated to the national federation, which has to approve the organization of each race and provide appropriate officials.

How to take up racing

There are various ways of starting in the sport, but the most usual is by joining a local cycling club and being introduced to racing after a period of general instruction and regular club training rides.

It is advisable to read about the sport as much as you can in books, specialist magazines and newspapers, so that you are in a position to ask questions about training, racing and equipment. It is important, before deciding the type of racing in which to specialize, to watch as many different races as possible. You should also try to seek out a coach to gain further knowledge, and attend any coaching course that is made available to you.

It is normal to begin racing in the under-16 category, for which special races are held both on road and track, with distances rarely longer than 25 km (15 miles). The maximum distance for juniors (16, 17 and 18 years old) is usually 100 km (62 miles); for women, 65 km (40 miles); for amateurs, 200 km (125 miles); and for professionals, 300 km (186 miles).

Acknowledged as the toughest track event is the individual pursuit. Competitors need to average about 50 km/hour (more than 30 mph) in top international meets.

Bicycle polo is played under similar rules to horse-mounted polo. But negotiation of polo moves is more difficult on the low, fixed-gear bicycles, as found here by Britain's Prince Philip.

Track Racing 2

Team pursuit Two teams, of four riders each, start on opposite sides of the track with the same rules as for an individual pursuit. The time of the third rider in each team is recorded. Distance is 4 km (2.5 miles) for amateurs and juniors.

Italian pursuit Similar to a team pursuit, but normally involves teams of five, with one rider dropping out from each team at the completion of each lap, with only one rider remaining on the track to contest the finish.

Scratch race Contested by a group of riders starting together, completing a set distance of 8, 15 or 20 km (5, 9 or 12 miles).

Points race This is contested by a group of riders starting together, normally over a distance of 50 km (31 miles) for amateurs or 30 km (19 miles) for juniors, with the winner being the rider who scores most points in intermediate sprints. Points are awarded at the completion of certain laps (say, every 5th or 10th lap), with double points on the final lap.

Devil-take-the-hindmost (or elimination) This is contested by a group of riders starting together, with the rider who is last over the finish line on each lap being eliminated, until two (or three) riders are left to contest the final sprint.

Techniques and training

Most clubs have a racing secretary and/or coach, whose job is to prepare racing members for their chosen type of event. This usually means forming teams of three or four to enter different races – juvenile, junior and senior road races; short or long distance time trials; track meetings; or, in the winter, cyclo-cross events. Some highly organized clubs also provide transport, mechanics and masseurs to provide the riders with the necessary back-up at major races.

Whatever type of cycling competition attracts you, the basic preparation is the same. You must pursue a general fitness programme before embarking on a specialized routine for your particular discipline. It is, of course, possible to become competent at several types of racing – as was so well illustrated by Belgian Eddy Merckx, perhaps the greatest ever cycling champion – and at the amateur level it is not unusual for club riders to compete in all branches of the sport in the same year – including road races, time trials, track races, hill climbs, cyclo-cross and tourist trials. But if you are aiming for international selection or professionalism, then some degree of specialization is necessary.

A general fitness programme generally begins in early winter, with daily exercises, weight training and specific alternative activi-

Paced race Contested by a group of 4–10 riders, starting together, with each rider paced individually by a specially adapted motor-bike for one hour for professionals* or 50 km (31 miles) for amateurs. Alternatively, a derny (a specially built moped) or teams of tandem riders provide the pace.

Madison (or American) A points race – usually over a set distance of 50, 80 or 100 km (31, 50 or 62 miles) contested by teams of two riders, one of whom is in the race at any time. Riders relay each other every few laps by means of one pushing the other's lower back or by a linked hand sling. The winners are the team that covers the most laps in the set period and/or has accumulated the highest total of points.

Six-day Race for 10–12 teams of two, with the overall result dependent on laps covered in each session of madison racing (normally three or four madisons in each 'day', starting in early afternoon and finishing around midnight). Other events (such as sprints, devil's and derny-paced races) contribute to the points total. It is usually contested on a steeply banked indoor track of less than 200 m (219 yd) inner circumference.

Note: Events marked with * are contested in the World Championships and/or the Olympic Games.

ties. Depending on where you live, these activities could be cross-country skiing (which many European professionals find beneficial), speed skating, jogging or work in the gymnasium (such as basketball or circuit training). Weight training should be done under the supervision of an experienced cycling coach and should be used to develop those muscles (arms, chest and back) which are not developed specifically by cycling. Similar results can be gained from a routine of daily exercises – such as sit-ups (for stomach and back), press-ups (for shoulders and arms), chin-ups (for wrists and arms) and bench steps (for legs and breathing).

Cycling training should begin about ten weeks before you plan to compete in your first race of the season. As the time approaches, step up the aerobic exercises (such as cross-country skiing) and decrease the strength-type conditioning. During the ten weeks of specific training, you should ride at least five days a week, preferably following a fairly strict programme, gradually increasing the distance of rides as well as the size of your gears. This should bring you to a smooth change-over from training to racing.

It is preferable to train with others of a similar or higher ability so that you can simulate racing conditions. Always keep gears lower than would be used for racing as this will improve your cadence (see Chapter 4) and enhance the suppleness of your muscles. It is also advisable to mix the type of training with long, slowish rides (say 25-30 km/hour, 15-18 mph) and short, faster rides (30-35 km/hour, 18-21 mph). Also practise some of the manoeuvres found in racing: attacking on hills, 'slip-streaming' behind other riders, forming echelons (step-like formations) into cross-winds, and sprinting out of tight turns.

Your physical fitness also depends upon your diet and how you take care of your body. Smoking and excessive drinking are certainly not recommended for a potential athlete, while sensible eating habits should be adopted. Avoid all processed foods and sweet confectioneries. Eat plenty of natural wholefoods, and avoid fatty foods as much as possible.

Special attention should also be paid to your clothing and cycle equipment. Keep both spotlessly clean and in good repair. For racing, you will need racing shoes, black shorts (with chamois-leather seat lining), white ankle socks, a long undervest, braces (suspenders), a racing jersey (wool for road, silk for track), a racing helmet (or crash hat) and racing mitts. A recent, expensive innovation is the so-called cat-suit: combined shorts and vest that cling to the body to reduce air resistance.

Actual racing tactics can only be learnt by experience in competition but the fundamental principle in all types of cycle racing is to conserve energy until the time you feel capable of making a winning effort. This could mean sprinting for an intermediate lap prize in a local road race or track meet, or perhaps attacking on a steep hill to join a breakaway in a long distance classic or stage race. It is easier to ride in the shelter of others, particularly if there is a head- or cross-wind. At speeds in excess of 40 km/hour (25 mph), for instance, more than half your effort goes into overcoming air resistance. So when you do go to the front of a group, stay there for as short a time as possible, unless you are on the attack. In time trials, where there are no other riders to shelter behind, take note of road-side objects – ride close to a wall or hedge if this will provide some sort of protection from the wind.

As in all athletic competition, there can be great pleasure in simply taking part. But there is even greater satisfaction in winning and, perhaps in cycling more than any other sport, any success depends on your individual attitude to the sport – from thorough preparation through to skilful use of tactics.

TYPICAL PRE-SEASON TRAINING SCHEDULE FOR A NOVICE RACING CYCLIST									
Week	Gears	Mon	Tues	Wed	Thurs	Fri	Sat	Sun	Distance
1.	less than 5.5 m (69 in)	30 km S	15 km F	50 km G	15 km G	30 km S	50 km S	80 km G	270 km
2.		30 km S	25 km F	50 km G	15 km F	30 km S	50 km S	80 km G	280 km
3.		30 km S	25 km F	50 km G	25 km F	30 km S	50 km S	80 km G	290 km
4.	less than 6.0 m (76 in)	30 km S	30 km F	30 km G	25 km F	30 km S	50 km S	100 km G	295 km
5.		30 km S	30 km F	50 km G	25 km F	30 km S	50 km S	100 km G	315 km
6.		30 km S	30 km F	50 km G	30 km F	30 km S	50 km S	100 km G	320 km
7.	less than 6.5 m (81 in)	30 km S	30 km F	50 km G	30 km F	50 km G	50 km G	100 km G	340 km
8.		30 km S	30 km F	50 km G	30 km F	50 km G	50 km S	115 km G	355 km
9.		30 km S	30 km F	50 km G	30 km F	50 km G	50 km S	115 km G	355 km
10.	less than 7.0 m (88 in)	30 km S	30 km F	50 km G	30 km F	50 km G	30 km S	Race (80 km)	300 km
11.		30 km S	30 km F	50 km G	30 km F	50 km G	15 km S	Race(100km)	305 km
S: Steady riding at about 29–32 km/hour (18–20 mph).								Total	3,425 km

F: Fast training, riding as hard as possible.

G: Group training, changing every 200–300 metres. Sunday group training should be done as a steady, non-stop ride carrying any food and drink that may be required.

Note: 1.6 km=1 mile (approx).

Glossary

Allen key: Patent hexagonal shaped tool that either fits into a hexagonal recess to turn bolt or fits over hexagonal nut.

American (or Américaine): Term used in Continental Europe to describe the two-man form of track racing otherwise known as *Madison* racing.

Ankling: Method of pedalling whereby ankles are dropped below level of toes at top of pedal stroke.

Balai: French term for *broom* (or *sag*) *wagon* that follows last rider in a road road.

Balloon: Wide section tyre (tire) that resembles a balloon in cross-section.

Ball race: Metal ring into which fit ball bearings for turning of bottom bracket, headset or pedals.

Barrow: Familiar term for an adult's tricycle.

Bickerton: Patented folding, small-wheel bicycle made largely from light aluminium alloy.

Bidon: Widely used French term for a cyclist's plastic drinking bottle.

Bikeway: Special path or separate section of roadway for exclusive use of cyclists.

Bit-and-bit: English term for shared pace-making by a group of not less that two cyclists.

Block: English term of the set of sprockets fitted to a freewheel for use with derailleur gears. US term: *cluster*.

Boneshaker: Familiar term for the wooden-wheeled Michaux velocipede of the 1860s.

Bonk: Familiar English term for fatigue due to not eating sufficient food during a long cycle ride or race.

Boss: Metal fixture brazed on bicycle frame to which are fitted items such as gear levers and drinking bottle cages.

Bottom bracket (assembly): Unit comprising metal cups, ball bearings and axle to which are fitted the two crank arms.

Brazing: Method of connecting different parts of a bicycle frame by application of a flame to a, usually, silver-based metal brazing mixture placed in the joint.

Break (or breakaway): Term in racing for one (or more) riders who accelerate away from the main group of cyclists.

Broom wagon: see *Balai*.

Bunch: Main group of riders in a road or track race, also called the *pack* (in America) and the *peloton* (in France).

Butted: Metal frame tubing that is thickened at end for added strength at frame joints. Double butted tubing is thickened at both ends. Spokes thickened at ends are also 'butted'.

Cadence: The rhythmic turning of the pedals at an even rate, usually measured in revolutions per minute (rpm).

Caliper brakes: Hand operated U-shaped rim brakes that operate on the principle of a pair of scissors.

Cantilever brakes: Hand operated rim brakes comprising two arms, each bolted to a boss on the frame and operated by a cable attached to outer end of pivoted arm.

Casquette: French term for peaked, cotton hat used by cyclists.

Centre-pull brakes: Caliper brakes that are operated by a central cable pulling up on short section of cable looped between two brake arms.

Chainstay: Oval-section frame tube connecting bottom bracket and rear drop-out.

Chainwheel: Toothed metal ring that fits to right-hand crank arm and on which chain runs.

Cleat: American term for slotted metal plate that is fixed to sole of cycling shoe to engage with back plate of pedal. UK term: *shoe-plate*.

Clinchers: American term for tyres (tires) that require a separate inner tube. See *wired-on*.

Cluster: See *Block*.

Close ratio: Gear combination in which there is usually just one tooth difference between the block's adjacent sprockets.

Coaster brake: Internal hub brake operated by pedalling backwards.

Col: French term for a mountain pass.

Commissaire: Internationally recognized name for an official appointed to control road or track racing.

Cone: Tapered piece of metal that screws on to axle of hub or pedal to locate ball bearings.

Contre la montre: French term for a time trial.

Cotterless crank: A pedal crank arm that is bolted directly to the bottom bracket axle.

Cotter pin: Cylindrical piece of metal with one flat, tapered edge that slots into eccentric hole of conventional, cottered crank arm to fix arm to bottom bracket axle.

Course des primes: Track race in which prizes are awarded for rider crossing finish line at completion of each or each nominated lap.

Crank set: Collective name for crank arms and bottom bracket axle, and necessary fittings.

Criterium: A road race that takes place on a short circuit, normally in a town or village, that is closed to other traffic.

Cyclo-cross: Form of cross-country racing in which competitors ride, push or carry their bicycles.

Cyclometer: Small instrument that is activated by the turning wheel and displays the distance (in kilometres or miles) covered during a ride.

Demi-fond: French term for middle-distance, motorcycle-paced racing on a banked cycle track.

Derailleur: Method of gear change whereby the chain is

SPOONING.

ON THE STILE.

Beast on a Beeston Humber

The bicycle created such an impact in the late 1800s that its praises were sung from the columns of *The Times* of London to the pages of scientific journals. It was also the subject of popular music-hall songs of the day. *Daisy*, 'on a bicycle built for two', is one example that has survived the passage of time, but there were other, equally charming songs that tie in the art of cycling with the art of wooing (or, as in this case, its pains):

I've lost my pal, that's why I've got this
    pal-lor on my brow,
I used to be a cyc-list, but I'm on the
    sick-list now.
My Sally rode a Raleigh, and we went
    out ev'ry day,
But a beast on a Beeston Humber came
    and stole my love away.
Chorus
Sally rode a Raleigh, and I journeyed
    on a Rudge,
I said I'd stick to Sally, and she said
    she'd never budge,
But Mohawks and Singers came, and

Rovers without number,
And one fine day, she rode away with
    a beast on a Beeston Humber.

However, things went better for the composer of another song of the times:

Rhoda rode a roadster on the road to
    Ryde,
I rode a roadster on the road by
    Rhoda's side,
When next I ride to Ryde with Rhoda
    she will be my bride,
Oh! Bless the day that Rhoda rode a
    roadster.

shifted from one sprocket (or chainwheel) to the next by a rear (front) derailleur mechanism.

Derny: Form of moped used for paced cycling on which speed is controlled by derny rider pedalling.

Devil (or devil-take-the-hindmost): Track race in which rider last crossing the finish line each lap is eliminated until two riders are left to contest final sprint.

Directeur sportif: French term for a racing team's manager or coach.

Dishing: Method of spoking rear wheel so that rim is off centre to compensate for extra width of a derailleur free-wheel block.

Domestique: French term for support rider in a racing team who gives up his bike or a wheel, or collects food or drink for his team leader.

Dossard: French term for a rider's race number pinned to his jersey.

Drafting: American term for *bit-and-bit*.

Draisienne: Two-wheeled machine propelled by rider striding along road while straddled across the frame, named after inventor Baron von Drais.

Drop handlebars: Curved handlebars that allow cyclist to adopt a streamlined position.

Drop-out: U-shaped metal bracket on end of front fork or rear stay into which fits the wheel hub axle.

Dynamo: Small power unit operated off tyre or hub for operating lights.

Echelon: English term for the formation adopted by racing cyclists to ride against a cross- or head-wind.

Elimination race: Same as *devil-take-the-hindmost*.

En ligne: French term for a bunched road race.

Équipe: French term for a racing team.

Ergometer: Static exercise cycle for use in gymnasium.

Étape: French term for a separate stage of a multi-day road race.

Expander bolt: Bolt that screws into tapered, cylindrical block to fix handlebar stem into front fork tube.

Extension: English term for stem into which handlebars are fixed.

Fender: American name for *mudguard*.

Fixed wheel: Method of transmission in which the pedals have to be turned continuously while bicycle is in motion.

Flint catcher: Small plastic-covered metal loop that lightly scrapes tyre to remove flints (or pieces of glass) picked up by tread.

Folding bicycle: Usually small-wheeled bicycle that has demountable frame to allow it to be placed inside a car or carried in a bag.

Fork rake: The amount by which the front fork end is offset to the line of the straight part of the fork.

Freewheel: Mechanism housed in a metal cylinder that screws on to rear wheel hub and allows the cyclist not to

pedal when bicycle is moving at speed.

Gauge: Measure of wall thickness of frame tubing or cross-section of spoke.

General classification: Overall positions in a stage race decided by accumulated time for each rider on each stage.

Generator: American term for a *dynamo*.

Giro d'Italia: Italian for the Tour of Italy, second longest stage race in professional racing.

Half-wheeling: English term for riding alongside another cyclist, but always half a wheel in front.

Handicap: Race in which the slower riders are started a certain time or distance ahead of the faster riders.

Handlebar levers: Derailleur gear levers that fix to the handlebar ends.

Headset: Bearing unit which fixes the front forks into frame head tube and allows handlebars to turn front wheel.

High pressures: English term for *wired-on tyres (clinchers)* that are pumped to a higher pressure than normal balloon-type tyres.

Honk: English term for standing on the pedals, out of the saddle, to ride more easily uphill.

Hood: Rubber covering to brake lever.

Hooks: Bottom, straight part of drop handlebars.

Hub gear: Variable gear contained within the rear wheel hub.

Independent: Former name of a racing cyclist who was permitted to receive cash prizes and was allowed to compete in professional or amateur races.

Jockey wheel: Small, pulley-shaped wheel on derailleur gear mechanism, on which runs the chain.

Keirin: Japanese term for track racing in which a set number of riders (about ten) start from a starting gate and race over a set distance.

Kermesse: Belgian term for a town or village carnival at which a cycle race takes place around a circuit measuring (probably) more than 10 km in length.

Kilo': Familiar name for the one kilometre time trial event in track racing.

King of the Mountains: Familiar name for the rider in a hilly (or mountainous) road race who accumulates the largest number of points, which are awarded at the summit of certain climbs.

Knock: English term for hunger (also see *bonk*).

Lanterne rouge: French term (literally, red light) for the last rider on general classification in a stage race.

Lug: Metal casting into which frame tubes fit to form joints.

Lugless frame: Bicycle frame in which lugs are omitted, with joints being formed by welding.

Madison: Term for two-man form of track racing, originally evolved for six-day races at Madison Square Garden in New York.

Maes bends: Handlebars with a shallow drop often used by cycle tourists.

Maillot jaune: French for *yellow jersey,* as worn by the overall race leader in an event such as the Tour de France.

Maillot vert: French for green jersey, as worn by the leader of a stage race points classifacation (points are awarded to first finishers on each stage).

Motor-paced: Form of track racing in which the competitor is paced by a motorcycle.

Moulton: Small-wheeled bicycle with sprung suspensions that was invented by former car engineer Alex Moulton.

Mudguard: (US *fender*) semi-circular strip of plastic or light alloy that prevents wet and mud from being thrown off tyre.

Musette: Usual name for light canvas shoulder bag that is used for carrying food during a race or long distance touring ride.

Neutralization: Period of race when officials declare that racing must not take place, although competitors continue to ride, without stopping.

Open race: Event in which amateurs are sanctioned to compete against professionals.

Ordinary: Official name for the high bicycle – or 'penny-farthing' – that was most popular in the mid-Victorian era.

Pace line: American term for a line of racing cyclists who take turns at setting the pace.

Pack: American term for main group of riders in a road race or long track race.

Panniers: Luggage bags that are supported by metal rack fitted above front or rear wheel.

Peloton: French term for main group of riders in road race.

Positron: Patented derailleur system in which lever clicks into position for each separate gear ratio.

Prime: Racing term (pronounced 'preem') for an intermediate cash prize (usually awarded at end of lap or top of a hill).

Puncture: English term for a flat tyre (US *a flat*).

Pursuit: Track race in which one rider (or team) starts separately from the other and each 'pursues' the other for a set distance or until one of them has been caught.

Quick-release: Mechanism used for racing hubs to allow wheel release without using a tool.

Roadster: Traditional, heavy bicycle with thick tyre treads and flat (straight) handlebars.

Roller racing: Indoor competition between cyclists riding on rollers ('home trainers') wired to distance covered indicators.

Safety bicycle: Term used for a bike with wheels small enough to allow the rider to place foot on ground while sitting on saddle.

Sag wagon: Term used for vehicle that follows last rider in a road race in order to transport any competitor that retires from race.

Sew-up: See *tubular.*

Shoeplate: See *cleat.*

Side-pull brakes: Caliper brakes that pivot on a centrally fixed bolt with the cable attached directly to one of the brake arms.

Sitting in: Racing term for a rider who rides behind others, taking shelter from the wind, without himself making the pace.

Single: See *tubular.*

Six-day: Track race contested by two-man teams in separate sessions of racing on six successive days.

Soigneur: Term used for a racing team's masseur or coach.

Spanner: Tool known as *wrench* in US.

Sprints and tubs: English term to describe lightweight sprint wheels and tubular tyres.

Stage race: Road race in which the result depends on the addition of times taken for each separate stage (normally one stage each day).

Stayer: Continental term for a rider in a motor-paced race.

Stem: Connects handlebars to headset. See *expander bolt* and *extension.*

Tandem: Bicycle that has seats and pedals for two riders, sat one behind the other.

Ten-speed: Common name for a lightweight bicycle that has derailleur gears with ten separate gear ratios.

Tied and soldered: Technical term for a wheel that has been stiffened by tying with thin wire and soldering each point where spokes cross.

Time trial: Race in which each competitor starts (and races) alone over a set distance, with winner being one who takes least time.

Track ends: Rear fork ends from which the wheel has to be removed away from the frame, not downwards or forwards as with normal ends.

Track nuts: Dome shaped nuts that screw on to conventional wheel axles to tighten wheel in frame.

Track stand: Method of standing still on a bicycle while keeping feet on pedals.

Tubular: High-pressure, ultra-lightweight tyre (tire) with inner tube sewn into the tyre which is glued onto wheel rim. Also known as *sew-up* or *single.*

Tyre saver: See *flint catcher*

Velodrome: Banked cycling track, normally with spectator accommodation.

Wheel-base: Distance between front and rear wheel hubs.

Wing nut: Track nut with levered extensions to allow removal of nut by hand.

Wired-on: High-pressure tyre (tire) that fits into rim by means of twin wires in edges of tyre cover and requires separate inflatable inner tube.

Wrench: See *spanner.*

Yellow jersey: Term used to describe race leader in a stage race (see *maillot jaune*).

Clubs & Organizations

INTERNATIONAL

Alliance Internationale de Tourisme
  (AIT),
Quai Gustave Ador 2,
1207 Geneva, Switzerland
International federation of touring clubs,
promotes all forms of touring including
cycle touring.

Union Cycliste Internationale (UCI),
8 Rue Charles Humbert,
1205 Geneva, Switzerland
International body composed of 130 member nations, controls all forms of cycle
racing.

GREAT BRITAIN

British Cycling Bureau,
Stanhope House, Stanhope Place,
London W2 2HH
Public relations office sponsored by British
bicycle industry, provides information on all
aspects of cycling including list of bike hire
locations.

British Cycling Federation (BCF),
70 Brompton Road, London SW3 1EN
Internationally recognized body for controlling cycle racing in Britain, with affiliated
clubs throughout country and useful touring
office.

British Cyclo-Cross Association (BCCA),
Secretary: R J Richards,
8 Bellam Road, Hampton Magna,
Warwick
Affiliated to BCF, controls schedule of
cyclo-cross events in Britain, provides information on cyclo-cross.

Cycle Speedway Council,
Secretary: W F Gill,
67 St Francis Way, Chadwell St Mary,
Grays, Essex RM16 4RB
Controls the domestic sport of cycle speedway, provides information of sport and list
of cinder tracks where events are held.

Cyclists' Touring Club (CTC),
Cotterell House,
69 Meadrow,
Godalming,
Surrey GU7 3HS
National organization for all cyclists
devoted to encouragement of recreational
cycling and protection of cyclists' rights in
Britain, provides members and visitors with
information on cycle touring in Britain and
all parts of the world, insurance, legal aid,
magazines and specialized shop.

English Schools Cycling Association
  (ESCA),
Secretary: G G Mayne,
8 Lady's Meadow,
Beccles, Suffolk
National body with affiliated schools cycling
clubs, organizes regional and national
events for racing and touring.

Friends of the Earth,
9 Poland Street,
London W1
National body with local branches devoted
to protecting the environment, including
improving facilities for all cyclists.

National Association of Veteran Cycle
  Clubs,
Secretary: Mrs B Ellis,
Cheylesmore,
Garnsgate Road,
Long Sutton,
Spalding, Lincolnshire
National body for exchange of information
and organizing special events for veteran
bicycles.

National Cycling Proficiency Scheme,
RoSPA, Cannon House,
The Priory,
Queensway,
Birmingham B4 6BS
Arranges training in cycling proficiency
through local road safety officers for chil-
dren aged 9-14.

Northern Ireland Cycling Federation,
Secretary: J Henry,
20 Thornleigh Gardens,
Bangor,
County Down
Governing body for cycle racing in North-
ern Ireland, with affiliated clubs throughout
province.

Road Records Association (RRA),
Secretary: W Townsend,
100 Betham Road, Greenford,
Middlesex
National body which verifies and certifies
the genuineness of all claims to best per-
formances by male cyclists over the various
recognized distance and place-to-place road
records.

Road Time Trials Council (RTTC),
Secretary: D E Roberts,
Dallacre, Mill Road, Yarwell,
Peterborough PE8 6PS
National governing body with affiliated
clubs to control organization of unpaced
cycling time trials on the public roads of
England and Wales.

Scottish Cyclists' Union (SCU),
Secretary: R K Londragan,
293 Rosemount Place,
Aberdeen AB2 4YB
Scotland's governing body with affiliated
clubs for control of cycle racing – road,
track and time trials.

Scottish Youth Hostels Association,
7 Glebe Crescent,
SK8 2JA
As YHA, but controls activities in Scotland.

The Tandem Club,
25 Hendred Way,
Abingdon,
Oxon OX14 2AN
Encourages tandem cycling; provides spare
parts service.

Veterans Time Trials Association (VTTA),
Secretary: Mrs S Hayward,
137 Glenwood Avenue,
Westcliffe-on-Sea,
Essex
Promotes and controls (in association with
RTTC) road time trials for riders over 40
years (male and female).

Women's Cycle Racing Association
  (WCRA),
Secretary: Mrs A Smith,
12 Forgefield,
Biggin Hill,
Westerham, Kent
Affiliated to the BCF, this body exists to
promote and further cause of women's cycle
racing.

'Tour de France, the Swedish way':
an award-winning press photograph
taken in 1969.

Youth Hostels Association (YHA),
Trevelyan House,
8 St Stephens Hill,
St Albans, Herts AL1 2DY
Controls chain of youth hostels in England
and Wales, provides cycling activities
through local groups and information on
youth hostels overseas.

Youth Hostel Association of Northern
    Ireland,
93 Dublin Road,
Belfast BT2 7HF
As YHA, but controls activities in Northern
Ireland.

NORTH AMERICA

American Youth Hostels Inc.,
Travel Department,
National Campus,
Delaplane,
Virginia 22025
Controls national network of low-cost hos-
tels, organizes group cycle tours and pro-
vides comprehensive details of bicycle trails
throughout US.

Bermuda Bicycle Association,
PO Box 192,
Devonshire,
Bermuda
National body for all cyclists, provides
information on touring on the island.

Bikecentennial,
PO Box 8308,
Missoula,
Montana 59807
Private organization that compiles detailed
information (maps, route data, road condi-
tions) for bicycle tourists in US, including
the TransAmerica trail.

Canadian Cycling Association,
333 River Road,
Vanier City,
Ontario K1L 8B9
Governing body for cycle racing in Canada,
with affiliated clubs in each province.

Canadian Youth Hostels Assocation,
268 First Ave,
Ottawa,
Ontario
Maintains 50 youth hostels.

Fédération Cyclotouriste Provinciale,
4305 Bossuet,
Montreal 431
Quebec
National association for cycle touring in
Canada, provides information on touring
activities.

International Bicycle Touring Society,
846 Prospect Street,
La Jolla,
California 92037

Arranges overseas trips for American
cyclists, provides information on touring.

League of American Wheelmen (LAW),
10 East Read Street,
PO Box 988, Baltimore,
Maryland 21203
National organization for all cyclists
devoted to encouragement of recreational
cycling and protection of cyclists' rights in
US, coordinates touring rallies and organized mass rides and publishes magazine.

United States Cycling Federation,
Box 669, Wall Street Station,
New York, N.Y. 10005
Internationally recognized body for control
of all forms of racing (amateur and profes-
sional) in the US. Member of US Olympic
Committee.

EUROPE

Austria
Österreichischer Automobil,
    Motorrad und Touring Club,
Schubertring 3, Vienna 1011
National body for all forms of touring
(including cycling), affiliated to AIT.

Österreichischer Radsport Kommission,
Prinz Eugenstrasse 12, Vienna 4
National body to control cycle racing, affili-
ated to UCI.

179

Belgium
Royale Ligue Vélocipédique Belge,
49 Avenue du Globe, 1190 Brussels
National body for controlling all forms of
cycling, affiliated to UCI.

Touring Club Royal de Belgique,
Rue de la Loi 44, 1040 Brussels
National body for all forms of touring,
affiliated to AIT, provides information on
cycle touring.

Bulgaria
Automobil & Touring Club,
Rue Sv. Sofia 6, Sofia
National body for all forms of touring in
Bulgaria, including cycle touring.

Fédération Bulgare de Cyclisme,
Boulevard Tolboukhine 18,
Sofia
National body for controlling all forms of
cycle racing, affiliated to UCI.

Czechoslovakia
Ustredni Automotoklub CSSR,
Opletalova 29, Prague 1
National body for touring by car and
motorcycle in Czechoslovakia, provides
information on touring.

Denmark
Danmarks Cykle Union,
Gronneraenge 21,
2920 Charlottenlund,
Copenhagen
National body for controlling cycle racing
in Denmark, affiliated to UCI.

Dansk Cyklist Forbund,
Landskronagade 32,
2100 Copenhagen
National cycle touring body that provides
information and protects cyclists' interests
in Denmark.

Finland
Suomi Touring Club,
Unioninkatu 45H,
Helsinki 17
Provides information on touring in Finland.

Touring Club of Finland,
Fabianinkatu 14,
00100 Helsinki 10
National body for all forms of touring,
affiliated to AIT.

France
Fédération Française de Cyclisme,
43 Rue de Dunkerque,
75010 Paris
National body for cycle racing in France,
affiliated to UCI.

Fédération Française de Cyclotourisme,
8 Rue Jean-Marie-Jégo,
75013 Paris
National body for cycle tourists, controls
schedule of competitive tourist events.

Touring Club de France,
65 Avenue de la Grande-Armée,
75016 Paris
National body for all forms of touring in
France, affiliated to AIT.

Germany (East)
Deutscher Radsport Verbandes,
Storkowerstrasse 118,
1055 Berlin
National body for cycle racing, affiliated to
UCI.

Germany (West)
Allgemeiner Deutscher Automobil-Club,
Königen Strasse 9-11A,
Munich 22
National body for all forms of touring in
West Germany, affiliated to AIT.

Bund Deutscher Radfahrer,
Gloeckner 6300 Strasse 2,
Giessen
National body for cycle racing, affiliated to
UCI.

Greece
Automobil & Touring Club de Grèce,
2-4 Rud Messogion,
Athens 610
National body for all forms of touring in
Greece, affiliated to AIT.

Iceland
Felag Islenzkra Bifreidaegenda,
Armula 27,
Reykjavik
National body for cycling in Iceland.

Ireland
An Oige (Irish Youth Hostel Association),
39 Mountjoy Square,
Dublin 1
As YHA, but for Irish Republic.

Irish Cycling Federation,
72 Prospect Avenue,
Glasnevin,
Dublin 9
Internationally recognized body for control-
ling cycle racing in Irish Republic.

Italy
Federazione Ciclistica Italiana,
Palazzo Delle Federazione,
Viale Tiziano 70, Rome
National body for controlling cycle racing
in Italy, affiliated to UCI.

Touring Club Italiano,
Corso Italia 10,
20122 Milan
National body for all forms of touring in
Italy, affiliated to AIT.

Luxembourg
Union Luxembourgeoise de Cyclotouristes,
39 Rue de l'Etoile,
F-57190 Florange,
France
National body for cycle tourists in Luxem-
bourg, provides information on touring and
special events.

Netherlands
Algemeene Nederlandse Wielers-Bond
    (Royal Dutch Touring Club),
Wasse-naarsweg 220,
The Hague
Dutch touring organization. Publishes maps
at 1:100,000 scale marked with network of
cycle paths.

Koninklijke Nederlandse Wieleren Unie,
15 Nieuwe Uitleg,
The Hague
National body for cycle racing in the Netherlands, affiliated to UCI.

Netherlands Cycletouring Union,
Ambachtsherenlaan 1162A,
2722-VJ-Zoetermeer
National body for cycle tourists, provides
information on touring by cycle in
Netherlands.

Stichting Fiets,
Europaplein 2,
Amsterdam
Publicity office for Dutch cycling, including
protection of cyclists' rights and cycleway
development.

Norway
Norges Cykleforbund,
Yongstorget 1, Oslo
National body for cycle racing in Norway,
affiliated to UCI.

Syklistenes Landsforening,
Storgaten 2, Oslo 1
National body for cycle tourists in Norway,
provides information on touring and events.

Poland
Polskie Towarzystwo Turystyczno-
  Krajoznawcze,
11 Senatorska St,
00-075 Warsaw
National body for all forms of touring in
Poland, affiliated to AIT.

Portugal
Automovel Club de Portugal,
Rua Rosa Araujo 24/26,
Lisbon
National
National body for all forms of touring in
Portugal, affiliated to AIT.

Romania
Assocation des Automobilistes,
Stradan Beloianis 27, Bucharest 1
National body for all forms of touring in
Romania.

Spain
Federacion Española de Ciclismo,
Alfonso XII 36,
1° Dacha, Madrid 14
National body for cycle racing in Spain,
affiliated to UCI.

Real Automobil Club de España,
General Sanjurjo 10,
Madrid 3
National body for all forms of touring in
Spain, affiliated to AIT.

Sweden
Svenska Turistföreningen,
Stureplan 2,
Stockholm 7
National body for all forms of touring in
Sweden, provides information on cycle
touring.

Switzerland
Touring Club Suisse,
Rue Peirre Fatio 9,
1211 Geneva 3

National body for all forms of touring in
Switzerland.

USSR
Fédération Cycliste USSR,
Skaternyi Pereoulok 4,
Moscow 69
National body for cycle racing throughout
USSR, affiliated to UCI.

Yugoslavia
Automoto Savez Jugoslavije,
Ruzveltova 18,
11001 Belgrade
National body for touring in Yugoslavia,
affiliated to AIT.

AUSTRALASIA

Amateur Cyclists' Association of
  Australia,
Secretary: W S Young,
34 Wardell Road,
Earlswood,
Sydney, NSW
National body for cycle racing in Australia.

Australian Cycling Council,
153 The Kingsway,
Cronulla 2230,
Sydney, NSW
National body for all cyclists in Australia,
provides information on racing and touring.

New Zealand Amateur Cycling
  Association,
PO Box 3104, Wellington
Internationally recognized body for cycle
racing in New Zealand.

ASIA

Israel
Israel Cyclists' Touring Club,
PO Box 339,
Kfar Sabe
National body for cycle tourists, provides
information on touring in Israel.

Japan
Japan Cycling Club,
Honcho 5-48-4,
Nakano-Ku,
Tokyo
National organization for all cyclists in
Japan, provides information on cycling in
Japan.

Japanese Cycling Federation,
Kishi Memorial Hall,
25 Kannami-Cho-Shipuyaku,
Tokyo
Internationally recognized body for controlling cycle racing in Japan which is affiliated
to UCI.

Touring Club of Japan,
Yayoi-Building 5F,
10-20 Jiyugaoka 2-chome Meguroku,
Tokyo 153
National body for all forms of touring in
Japan.

Philippines
Philippine Cycling Association,
Rizal Memorial Track Football Stadium,
Dakota Street,
Manila
National body for cycle racing in the
Philippines.

Turkey
Turkiye Turing ve Otomobil Kurumu,
Sisli Meydani 364,
Istanbul
National body for all forms of touring in
Turkey, affiliated to AIT.

LATIN AMERICA

Argentina
Federacion Ciclista Argentina,
Av. Pte. Figueroa,
Alcoeta 4600,
Buenos Aires
National body for cycle racing in Argen-
tina, affiliated to UCI.

Brazil
Brazilian Confederation of Sports,
Rue da Quitanda 3,
2° Andar,
Case Postale 1078,
Rio de Janeiro
National body for all Brazilian sports,
including cycle racing.

Mexico
Federacion Mexicana de Ciclismo,
Confederation Sportive Mexicaine,
Avenue Juarez Num 64-311,
Mexico City 1
National body for cycle racing, affiliated to
UCI.

Bibliography

and suggested further reading

General
The Raleigh Book of Cycling, Reginald C. Shaw (ed.), Sphere Books, London, 1978. Useful handbook for newcomers to cycling.
The Guinness Guide to Bicycling, Jean Durry (translated from French), Guinness Superlatives, London, 1977. Largely pictorial view of the sport.
Delong's Guide to Bicycles and Bicycling, Fred DeLong, Chilton Book Co, Radnor, Pa, USA, 1974. Covers most aspects of bicycling from an American viewpoint.
The New Complete Book of Bicycling, Eugene A. Sloane, Simon and Schuster, New York, 1974. Mainly technical look at American bicycling.
Cycling: fitness on wheels, John Wilcockson, The Sunday Times/World's Work, Tadworth, Surrey, England, 1978. Guide on using a bicycle for a fitness programme.
The Penguin Book of the Bicycle, Roderick Watson and Martin Gray, Penguin Books, Harmondsworth, England and New York, 1978. The bicycle in all its aspects.

History
King of the Road, Andrew Ritchie, Wildwood House, London and Ten Speed Press, Berkeley, Ca, 1975. Well researched and documented history of the bicycle.
Bicycling: a history, Frederick Alderson, David and Charles, Newton Abbot, England, 1972. General history of cycling.
The Social History of the Bicycle, Robert A. Smith, American Heritage Press, New York, 1972. The early days of bicycling.
The Story of the Bicycle, John Woodforde, Routledge & Kegan Paul, London, 1970. Largely social history of cycling.
Discovering Old Bicycles, T. E. Crowley, Shire Publications, Aylesbury, England, 1973. Brief review of the bicycle's evolution.
Cycles in Colour, Robert Wilkinson-Latham, Blandford Press, Poole, England, 1978. Historic development of the bicycle.
Winged Wheel, William Oakley, Cyclists' Touring Club, 1977. The official history of the Cyclists' Touring Club's first 100 years.

Technical and maintenance
Richard's Bicycle Book, Richard Ballantine, Pan Books, London, 1979 and Ballantine Books, New York, 1978. Emphasis on equipment and maintenance descriptions.
The Ten-Speed Bicycle, Denise M. de la Rosa and Michael J. Kolin, Rodale Books, Emmaus, Pa, USA, 1979. Complete guide to ten-speed bicycle.
Readers Digest Basic Guide: The maintenance of bicycles – and mopeds, Readers Digest Association, London, 1975. Details of bicycle parts with maintenance notes.
Bicycling Science: ergonomics and mechanics, F. R. Whitt and D. G. Wilson, MIT Press, Cambridge, Mass, USA, 1974. Technical study of bicycle mechanics.

Touring and travel
Adventure Cycling in Britain, Tim Hughes, Blandford Press, Poole, England, 1978. Comprehensive guide to cycle touring.
Bikepacking for Beginners, Robin Adshead, Oxford Illustrated Press, Oxford, England, 1978. Detailed advice on starting bicycle camping and touring.
Bike and Hike, J. Sydney Jones, Oxford Illustrated Press, 1977. Guide book for cyclists and backpackers in British Isles.
Cycle Touring in Europe, Peter Knottley, Constable, London, 1975. Description of suitable cycle touring areas in Europe.
Bicycle Touring in Europe, Karen and Gary Hawkins, Sidgwick & Jackson, London 1974. Details of favourite touring areas.
England by Bicycle, Frederick Alderson, David & Charles, Newton Abbot, England, 1974. A cycling tour around England.
The World Beneath My Wheels, Walter Stolle, Pelham Books, London, 1978. Adventures of a round-the-world cyclist.
Life and Other Punctures, Eleanor Bron, André Deutsch, London, 1979. Autobiographical account of pleasures in cycling.
North American Bicycle Atlas, American Youth Hostels publication. Maps and details of suitable bicycle trails.

Competition
Tour de France: the 75th anniversary cycle race, Robin Magowan, Stanley Paul, London, 1979. Dramatic description of 1978 Tour de France.
The Great Bike Race, Geoffrey Nicholson, Hodder and Stoughton, London, 1977. Detailed account of 1976 Tour de France.
American Bicycle Racing, James C. McCullagh (ed.), Rodale Press, Emmaus, Pa, USA, 1976. Comprehensive review of cycle racing history in North America.
Cycle Racing, John Wilcockson, EP Publishing, Wakefield, England, 1972. Basic information on types of cycle racing.
Cycle Racing: training to win, Les Woodland, Pelham Books, London, 1975. Manual for novices on cycle racing and training.
King of Sports: cycle road racing, Peter Ward, Kennedy Brothers, Keighley, Yorks, England, 1970. A training manual and text book for active road racing cyclists.
The Bicycle Racing Book, William Sanders, Domus, Northbrook, Ill, USA, 1979. Detailed introduction to American racing.
Cycling Is My Life, Tom Simpson, Stanley Paul, London, 1966. The autobiography of Britain's world professional racing champion.
Two Wheels to the Top, Reg Harris (with G. H. Bowden), W. H. Allen, London, 1976. Autobiography of Britain's multi-world sprint champion of the 1950s.
Champion on Two Wheels, Hugh Porter, Hale, London, 1975. Autobiography of four-times world pursuit champion.

Periodicals
UNITED STATES
Bicycling. Published nine times a year by Rodale Press, 33 E. Minor St, Emmaus, Pa 18049. Biggest selling US bike magazine.
Velo-news. Published 18 times a year by Barbara George, Box 1257, Brattleboro, Vt 05301. Journal of American bicycle racing.
Competitive Cycling. Monthly, published at PO Box 2066, Carson City, Nv 89701.

UNITED KINGDOM
Cycling. Published weekly by IPC Business Press, Surrey House, 1 Throwley Way, Sutton, Surrey SM1 4QQ. Emphasis on racing coverage.
Cycletouring. Published six times a year by Cyclists' Touring Club, 69 Meadrow, Godalming, Surrey GU7 3HS.
Freewheeling. Published monthly at 14 Picardy Place, Edinburgh 1.
International Cycle Sport. Published monthly by Kennedy Bros (Publishing), Howden Road, Silsden, Keighley, West Yorks.
Cycling World. Published monthly by Stone Industrial Publications, 1 Warwick Avenue, Whickham, Newcastle upon Tyne.

Index

Padlocks and chains, 67–8, 69, 85–6, *86*
Paintwork, 98
Pannier bags, 67, 140
   front, 140, 144, *144*
   rear, 140, *140*
Paris-Brest-Paris race, 34, *35*, 166
Paris-Roubaix race, *164*
Paris-Rouen race, 23–5, 34
Patterson, Sid, 169
Peace Race, East European, 168
Pedalling, 13, 100
   'ankling', *76*, 76–7
   cadence and, 75–7
   'toes down' method, 76, *76*
Pedals, 20, 21, *21*, 27, 39, 44, 48, 51, 56, *57–8*, 90
   broken, 132
   dust cap, 108, *108*
   honking on, 81, *81*
   metal platform, 58, *58*
   one-sided cage, 58, *58*
   rat-trap, 58, *58*, *108*
   repair and maintenance, 94, 107–9
   rubber platform, 57–8, *58*
   sealed bearing unit, 58
   spindle, 107, 108, *108*, 132
   toe clips or straps fitted to, 51, 58, 76, 86, *109*, 109–10
Peden, William ('Torchy'), 165
Peking rush-hour cyclists, *15*
Penny-farthing *see* Ordinary bicycle
Philip, Prince, *171*
Pollution, 14
Pope Manufacturing Co. of Hartford, 29, 32, *32*
Porter, Hugh, 162
Posters, bicycle, *31*
Pump pegs, 67
Pumps, 60, 67, *67*, *132*, 133
Punch cartoons, 82, *149*
Puncture repair outfit, 67, 90, 133, 156
Punctures, puncture repairs, 60, 128, *130–31*
   'Liberty'-type tubular tyres, 60, *60*, 128, 130
   tubular (sew-up) tyres, 128, *129*, 129–30
   wired-on tyres, *128*, 128–9

Quadricycles, 23, 148, 162

Racing, 18, 19, 23–5, 27–8, 29, 33–6, 37, 39, 47, 160–73
   cyclo-cross, 169, *169*
   how to take up, 170
   in Britain, 160–64
   in Europe, *162*, *163*, 166–8
   in North America, 165–6
   organization, 169–70
   sponsorship, 168
   techniques and training, 171–3
   see also Road racing; Track racing
Racing bicycles, 55, 59, 62, 89
   caloric consumption, 10
   fixed wheel (track), 46–7
   saddles, 65, *65*
   ten-speed, 49, 52, *53*
   wheels and tyres, 59–60
Raleigh Cycles, *31*, 33–4, 38, *161*
Rear drop-out (or fork end), *42*, 54, 55, 56, 98
Reflective over-vests and flags, 69, *69*, *79*
Reflectors, 68, *79*, 83
Repairs and maintenance, 88–133
   accessories and lighting, 133
   emergency, 132–3
   regular maintenance check, 89–96
   service and repairs, 96–131
   tools, 90, 133
Rickshaw cyclist, in Calcutta, *66*
Riding posture, 73–5, 137
Rims, 45, 49, 58, 59, 64, *64*, 94–5, 114, 116, 138
   Endrick pattern, 59
   high pressure, 51

   racing (or sprint), 51, 59–60, 133
   removing broken spoke from, *117*
   Westwood pattern, 59
Road racing, 23–5, 27–8, 29, 33–6, 37, 160–69, 171
   bunched, 163
   circuit, 165, 166
   criteriums, 165–6, 168
   hill climbs, 166, 168, 171
   kermesse, 165
   multi-day, 165
   Olympic race, 166
   place-to-place, 165
   sprint-finish, *161*
   stage (or tour), 166, 168
   time trials, 160, 161, *163*, 163–4, 166, 168, 171
   see also Racing; Track racing
Road Records Association (RRA), 161
Road Time Trials Association, 164
Roadsters, 23, 36, 48, 51, 59
Rover safety bicycle, 21, 29, 32

Saddlebag, 132–3, 140, *140*, 144
Saddle clip and seat pin, 65, *65*, 66, 74
Saddle covers, 69
Saddles, 29, 32, 46, 51–2, 65–6, 113–14, 133
   broken, 132
   Brooks professional, *112*
   cleaning, 92–3
   correct height and position, *72*, 73–4, 113
   leather, 52, 65, *65*, 93, 113, 137
   leather-covered nylon, 65
   plastic, 59, 93
   Wood's wire, 32
Safety and protective accessories, 68–9
Safety bicycles, 21, 23, 29, 30, 32, 33, 36, 39
Safety codes, 72, 83–4
Sapporo Winter Olympics, 169
Sealink International race, 163
Seat posts (or pillars), 65, 65–6, 74, 94, 97, 113, *114*
   flutes, 97, *97*
   plugging, 97, *97*
   snapped, 132
Second-hand bikes, 44–6
Security and locks, 85–6
Shaw, George Bernard, 136
Shoe plates (cleats), 58, 75–6, *76*, 139
Shoes, 76, 86
Shopper bicycles, 46, *50*
Singer's cross-frame bike, *23*
Smith, George, 32
Spanner/extractor, 90, 106, 133
Spanner(s) (US: wrench), *104*, 133, 156, 157
   adjustable, 90, 99, 106, 133
   cone, 94, 119
   C-shaped, 101, *101*
   metric, 90, 92, 109, 116, 125

   multi-purpose, 90
   peg, 101, 102
   spoke (nipple key), 94, *95*
Specialist bike shops, 40, *41*, 43, *89*
Speedometers, 68
'Spider' (on crank), 107
Splined key, 119–20
Spoke key, 118, 133, 157
Spokes, 26, 27, 34, 46, 58–9, 94, *130*
   removing and replacing, *117*, 118, *118*
   tightening, 94, *95*, 117
Sprocket remover, *121*, 122
Sprockets, 52, 78–9, *122*, 123, 125, 138, 139
   chains, gears and, 60–62
   number of teeth on, 80
   rear, 46, 48, 60, 62, 78, 122
   removing, *121*, 122
Stanley Sociable, *24*
Starley, James, 23, 27, 28, *28*, 30
Starley, John Kemp, 21, 30, 32
Stem (or extension), *64*, 64–5, *73*, 75, 94, 110, *110*, 137
   fractured, 132
   prising open, to remove handlebars, *111*
Stevens, Thomas, 32, *32*
Stoke Poges church, stained-glass bicycle at, *34*
Student cyclists, 36, *36*, *51*
'Submarine tricycle', *144*
Suriray, Jean, 25
Sutton, William, 32

Tandems, *37*, 39, 44–5
Taping handlebars, 93, 110–13, *112–13*
Ten-speed bicycles, 23, 47, 49–52, *53*, 91, 107
Terront, Charles and Jules, 28, 29, 166
Time trials, 160, 161, *163*, 163–4, 166, 168, 171
Toe clips and straps, 51, 58, 76, 86, *109*, 109–10, 139
Tool carrying bags, 67
Tools, 90, 133, 156, 157
Tour de France, 18, 34, 36, 39, *81*, 89, 133, *134–5*, 160, 166, *167*
Tour of Britain (Milk Race), 37, 163
Tour of Flanders, 162
Touring, 18, 19, 28, 33, 34, 36, 37, 136–59
   American Continental Divide Tour, 154–5, *158*
   the Americas, 156
   bags, 67, 140, 144
   Britain and Ireland, 158–9
   centre-touring, 149–50
   clothing, 144–5, 156, 157
   cycle camping, *141*, 150–51
   equipment to carry, 156, 157
   Europe, 156–8
   French Alps Tour, 146
   maps and routes, 145, 148
   South-East England Tour, 141–3
   transport of bicycles, 152–3
   where to stay, 148–50

Touring bicycles, tourers, 10, 49, 52, 55, 59, 62, 77, 137–9
Track racing, 27, 36, 47, 162, 164, 165, 169, 170, 171
   devil-take-the-hindmost, 171
   handicap, 170
   individual pursuit, 170, *170*
   Italian pursuit, 171
   kilometre time trial, 170
   Madison (or American), 172
   paced, 172
   points race, 171
   six-day, 165, 172
   scratch race, 171
   sprint, 160, 162, 170
   team pursuit, 171
   see also Racing; Road racing
Traffic, riding, in, *15*, 82–4
Trans-America trail, *139*
Tricycles, 23, *24*, 34, 47, 66, 75, 148
   'submarine', *144*
Triplets, 162
Tubing (frame), 52–4, 97–8, 132
   butted, 54, *54*
   seamed, 53, *54*
   seamless, 54, *54*
Turner, Rowley, 21, 22–3, 25–6
Tyre levers (or irons), 90, 133, 156
Tyre savers, 69
Tyres, 46, 59–60
   pneumatic, 32–3, *33*, 34
   puncture repairs, 60, *60*, 128–30
   repair and maintenance, 94
   spare inner tubes and, 133, 138, 156, 157
   tubeless tubular, 60, *60*, 128, 130
   tubular (sew-up), 51, 59, 59–60, 94, 128, *129*, 129–30
   valves, 131
   wired-on (clincher), 51, 59, *59*, 90, 94, *128*, 128–9, 133, 138

Unicycle, 50
Union Cycliste Internationale, 169–70
United States, 10, 22, 27, 29–30, 32, *32*, 37
   bikeway facilities, *9*, *11*, 17
   racing in, 165–7, *167*
United States Cycling Federation, 165
Uphill and downhill, 81–2

Valves, 42, 131
   Presta, 42, 131
   Schraeder, 131, *131*
   Woods, 67, 131, *131*
Van Neste, Rynner, 27
Velocipedes, *21*, 21–3, 25, 26–7, 160
Velodromes, 169

Watch holders, 68
Wheel-base, 55
Wheels, 45–6, 48, *50*, 51, *53*, 58–60, 61, 94, 95
   buckled, 94, 132
   'dishing' rear, 60–61
   fitting new, 98
   maintenance and repair, 117–21
   racing (sprint), 59–60
   removing, 91–2, *92*
   roadster, 59
   tourist, 59
Whitt, F. R., 10
Whitty, Calvin, 26
Wilson, Stuart, 12
Women cyclists, 27, *163*, 165, 166
World Championships, 18, 165, 166, 168–9, 172
Wreghitt, Chris, *169*
Wrenches *see* Spanners

Young, Sheila, 165
Youth hostels, 149, 153, 154, 159

Zimmerman, Arthur, 33, *160*

Acknowledgements

We wish to thank Her Majesty's Stationery Office for permission to quote from the *Highway Code* and Guinness Superlatives Ltd for permission to use information from the *Guinness Book of Records*. We are grateful also to Tim Hughes for reading the proofs, supplying the details for the suggested tour of the French Alps and providing several photographs. Thanks are also due to Stratton's Bicycle Shop, London SW18, for providing reference for several illustrations.

Artwork credits
All illustrations by Peter Campbell
Maps by Illustra Design

Picture credits
All-Sport: 167 (L)
Ambrosiana Library, Milan: 30
Barnaby's Picture Library: 75 Bill Coward, 170
Bell Street Bicycle Shop, London: 41
Bickerton Bicycle Co: 49
British Cycling Bureau: 68 (BL)
Neville Chanin: 130/1, 139, 153, 155, 158
Bruce Coleman Ltd: 15 Norman Myers, 47, 51, 66, 159, 167 (R)
Coventry Council: 28
Gerry Cranham: 45
Du Pont (UK) Ltd: 127 Judy MacCready
Mary Evans Picture Library: 7, 22, 25, 26, 31, 33, 35, 44/5
Fox Photos: 171
Freewheeling Magazine, Edinburgh, Mike Farnworth: 79
Friends of The Earth: 14
Halcyon cards: 175
Halfords Ltd: 50, 53 (L)
Tim Hughes: 2, 70/1, 136, 138, 145, 146, 150, 163
Illustrated London News: 29, 32
Keystone Press Agency Ltd: 8/9, 13, 17, 38, 83 (BR), 86, 179
Peter Knottley: 141
Mansell Collection: 24, 27, 67, 68 (TL), 160
Marshall Cavendish: 6 Robin Clifford, 83 (TL)
Popperfoto: 11, 36, 37
Presse Sports: 16, 87, 134/5, 162, 164,
Rex Features: 19
Ann Ronan Picture Library: 4, 82, 93, 149
Anita Ruddell: 89, 103
Stoke Poges Church: 34
Transport & Road Research Lab: 69
Viking Cycles Ltd: 53 (R), 91
Roger Viollet: 4/5
John Wilcockson: 81, 169
Honore Willems, Bruxelles: 161